The Ultimate PowerXL Air Fryer Grill Cookbook

The Ultimate PowerXL Air Fryer Grill Cookbook

1000 Easy and Affordable Recipes for Smart People to Master Your PowerXL Air Fryer Grill

Francis Harris

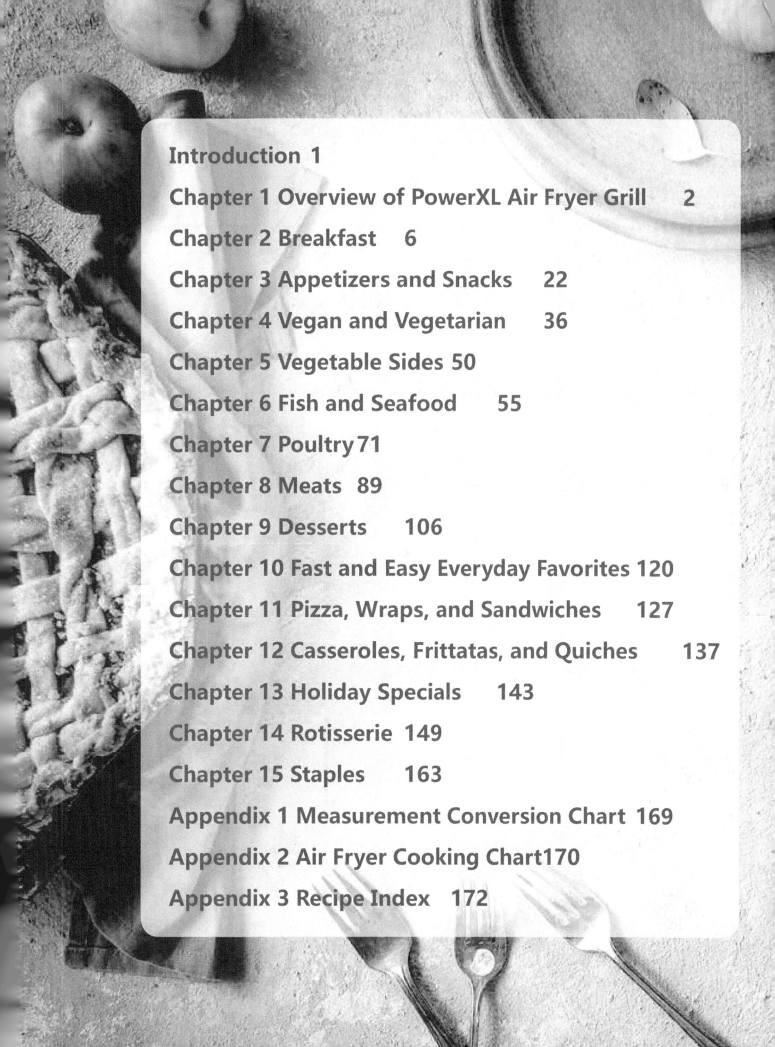

Introduction

Do you want to revolutionize your cooking experience with a multifunctional cooking appliance? Do you want to make your cooking easier? If you answered yes to any of these questions, relax and read further to know more. The PowerXL Air Fryer Grill is the perfect solution.

Over the years, PowerXL has been designing and creating quality products that cater to the needs of consumers worldwide. They have never failed to deliver. After so many years, they are still going strong. Their vision is to produce quality products that will keep up with modern trends and consumer demand, which is why we consider them a front runner in the appliance industry today.

The PowerXL Air Fryer Grill will change the way you cook in the kitchen. If you want to grill, rotisserie, roast, toast, air fry or even bake pizza, then this appliance will help you do that. It allows you to have your desired outcome without compromising on the taste and flavor of your food. Its versatility is what makes it stand out from the rest of its competitors in the market.

You can grill all your preferred meat meals with just a few minutes. It uses infrared heat to cook your food in a convenient and healthy way. Processed food is not good for the body. But with the PowerXL Air Fryer Grill, you don't have to worry about that anymore because it allows you to prepare raw meat perfectly. You can even add some vegetables and they will be cooked in no time at all. This makes it easier to stick to healthy eating habits. The more you promote healthy eating habits in the family, the more chances of living a longer and healthier life. You will also have a smaller chance of suffering from health complications.

This cookbook has all that you need to get started with the PowerXL Air Fryer Grill and make your life in the kitchen better.

Happy cooking!

Chapter 1
Overview of PowerXL
Air Fryer Grill

What is the PowerXL Air Fryer Grill?

The PowerXL Air Fryer Grill is a multifunction air fryer and grill offering eight cooking presets that let you grill and air fry at the same time, grill, broil, rotisserie, reheat, air fry, bake or toast food with less cooking oil or none at all.

It can also cook food straight from the freezer as it does not require thawing. It gives you plenty of menu possibilities with up to 70 percent fewer calories from fat than traditional frying.

The unit heats almost instantly with a smart preheat feature that starts the timer only when it reaches the desired temperature. It also shuts off automatically.

The PowerXL Air Fryer Grill has two racks which enable you to cook 4.5 times more food than traditionally smaller air fryers. Ideal for cooking meals for the whole family or when hosting a gathering, the large capacity allows the unit to accommodate a 12-inch round pizza, six toast slices or bagels, up to 10 pounds of chicken or the equivalent load of a 4.5-quart Dutch oven.

Pros of Using The Powerxl Air Fryer Grill

Multipurpose: The PowerXL Air Fryer Grill is designed with different smart cooking features. These features are as follows;

- Air Fry
- Broil
- Rotisserie
- Grill
- Reheat
- Sear
- Bake/Pizza
- Toast

Fast Cooking: It greatly decreases typically long cooking times for all dishes. Cooking time can be reduced 60% to 80% (depending on the ingredient). Faster cooking times mean you can cook real foods from scratch in the time it takes for pizza delivery or to prepare a frozen dinner.

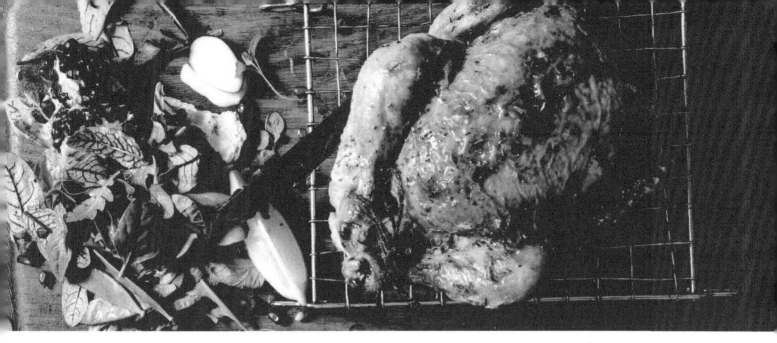

Capacious: With PowerXL Air Fryer Grill, you can cook large serving sizes because it is big and capacious. You can cook a whole duck or chicken by putting on the rotisserie rod.

Save Energy: It cooks food faster thus reducing cooking significantly. Reduced cooking time translates to energy saving. It can be the only appliance you use therefore making it economical.

Maintain Nutritional Value: As opposed to most of the existing cooking methods which drain or destroy food's nutrition, the PowerXL Air Fryer Grill preserves the nutritional value of the foods being cooked.

Components of the PowerXL Air Fryer Grill

The PowerXL Air Fryer Grill is a kitchen appliance shaped like a box and comprises of eight cooking functions. **The components are as follows:**

- The main unit is a stainless-steel construct that houses the heating element, control panel, and all the cooking accessories (trays, racks, and pans) through the three available tray ports.

- The control panel comprises of knobs and buttons to control and adjust time, temperature, and cook programs.

- The stainless-steel drip tray placed below the heating element collects fluids and oils during cooking. If the drip tray is absent while cooking, it causes smoke and damaged heating coils.

- The grill plate to grill meat, burgers, vegetables, and more.

- The tempered glass door keeps the heat in and allows for even circulation of the hot air. Open and close the door with the handle attached to avoid burns from the heated glass.

- The baking pan to bake pastries and the crisper tray to broil and make food without oil content.

- The Pizza rack to roast, toast bread & bagel, make pizza, and grill.

Cooking Functions of the PowerXL Air Fryer Grill

Air fry: It allows you to fry multiple types of food. It uses convection heat and circulates hot air around the food like a fan that cooks everything evenly. The cooking time varies with the type of food and the size of it.

Grill: This function allows you to grill your favorite meat or a steak. For grilling, the air fryer grill uses a convection heat of 350ºF to grill your food.

Bake: Using this function you can bake your favorite French fries or a muffin. For baking, the air fryer grill uses a convection heat of 360ºF to bake your food. The rule of thumb for baking is to cook at shorter times and lower temperatures.

Pizza: This function allows you to cook pizza from a frozen state in just five minutes. The air fryer grill makes the crispy pizza in about 5 minutes. It is best for cooking frozen items like fries, pizza, and shrimp tails with a variety of crust shapes and sizes.

Toast: This feature allows the user to toast bread, bagels, or pastries.

Reheat: The reheat function allows the user to quickly reheat their food without compromising the taste or healthiness of the food.

Operating Buttons

Power Button: This enables you to switch the PowerXL Air Fryer Grill on or off.

Function Button: This button contains all the different cooking functions that you will need to selectively press as per your recipe.

Timer Button: This button is used to adjust the time settings as per your recipe needs. You just need to press the timer button and adjust the timer settings by turning the control knob. You can also change the time settings at any time during the cooking cycle.

Temperature Button: This button lets you adjust the temperature settings as per your recipe needs. You just need to press the temp button and adjust the desire temperature settings by turning the control knob. You can change the temperature settings at any time during the cooking cycle.

Cleaning and Maintenance

Ensure that the PowerXL Air Fryer Grill is unplugged and allowed to cool completely before cleaning it.

Make sure that it is clean before each use. Remove any leftover food particles with a paper towel. After removing the cooking basket, clean the grilling plates and grease tray. To remove stubborn, baked-on food stains, use a metal scrubber or steel wool soap pad.

When cleaning the unit, be sure to use hot water and dishwashing liquid on a damp cloth or sponge to clean all non-stick areas inside and out. Be sure to scrub off any residue or buildup in the power cord socket area (in and around where food particles are stored).

Dry all surfaces with a clean, dry towel to remove excess moisture. Never use detergents or abrasives to clean the grill as they may damage the surface of the grill.

Once you clean it, ensure that the unit and all its parts and components dry and then store them away. Store it in a stable position.

Chapter 2 Breakfast

Western Omelet

Prep time: 5 minutes | Cook time: 18 to 21 minutes | Serves 2

¼ cup chopped bell pepper, green or red
¼ cup chopped onion
¼ cup diced ham
1 teaspoon butter
4 large eggs
2 tablespoons milk
⅛ teaspoon salt
¾ cup shredded sharp Cheddar cheese

1. Put the bell pepper, onion, ham, and butter in the baking pan and mix well.
2. Place the baking pan on the air fry position. Select Air Fry, set the temperature to 390ºF (199ºC), and set the time to 6 minutes.
3. Cook for 1 minute. Stir and continue to cook for an additional 4 to 5 minutes until the veggies are softened.
4. Meanwhile, whisk together the eggs, milk, and salt in a bowl.
5. Pour the egg mixture over the veggie mixture.
6. Reduce the grill temperature to 360ºF (182ºC) and bake for 13 to 15 minutes more, or until the top is lightly golden browned and the eggs are set.
7. Scatter the omelet with the shredded cheese. Bake for another 1 minute until the cheese has melted.
8. Let the omelet cool for 5 minutes before serving.

Bacon and Egg Stuffed Peppers

Prep time: 10 minutes | Cook time: 15 minutes | Serves 4

1 cup shredded Cheddar cheese
4 slices bacon, cooked and chopped
4 bell peppers, seeded and tops removed
4 large eggs
Sea salt, to taste
Freshly ground black pepper, to taste
Chopped fresh parsley, for garnish

1. Divide the cheese and bacon between the bell peppers. Crack one of the eggs into each bell pepper, and season with salt and pepper.
2. Place each bell pepper in the crisper tray. Place the crisper tray on the air fry position. Select Air Fry, set the temperature to 390ºF (199ºC), and set the time to 15 minutes.
3. Cook for 10 to 15 minutes, until the egg whites are cooked and the yolks are slightly runny.
4. Remove the peppers from the crisper tray, garnish with parsley, and serve.

Olives, Kale, and Pecorino Baked Eggs

Prep time: 5 minutes | Cook time: 10 to 12 minutes | Serves 2

1 cup roughly chopped kale leaves, stems and center ribs removed
¼ cup grated pecorino cheese
¼ cup olive oil
1 garlic clove, peeled
3 tablespoons whole almonds
Kosher salt and freshly ground black pepper, to taste
4 large eggs
2 tablespoons heavy cream
3 tablespoons chopped pitted mixed olives

1. Place the kale, pecorino, olive oil, garlic, almonds, salt, and pepper in a small blender and blitz until well incorporated.
2. One at a time, crack the eggs in the baking pan. Drizzle the kale pesto on top of the egg whites. Top the yolks with the cream and swirl together the yolks and the pesto.
3. Place the baking pan on the bake position. Select Bake, set the temperature to 300ºF (149ºC), and set the time to 12 minutes.
4. Cook for 10 to 12 minutes, or until the top begins to brown and the eggs are set.
5. Allow the eggs to cool for 5 minutes. Scatter the olives on top and serve warm.

Sausage Cheddar Quiche

Prep time: 5 minutes | Cook time: 25 minutes | Serves 4

12 large eggs
1 cup heavy cream
Salt and black pepper, to taste
12 ounces (340 g)
sugar-free breakfast sausage
2 cups shredded Cheddar cheese
Cooking spray

1. Coat a casserole dish with cooking spray.
2. Beat together the eggs, heavy cream, salt and pepper in a large bowl until creamy. Stir in the breakfast sausage and Cheddar cheese.
3. Pour the sausage mixture into the prepared casserole dish.
4. Place the casserole dish on the bake position. Select Bake, set the temperature to 375ºF (191ºC), and set the time to 25 minutes.
5. Cook for 25 minutes, or until the top of the quiche is golden brown and the eggs are set.
6. Remove from the grill and let sit for 5 to 10 minutes before serving.

Scrambled Eggs with Spinach

Prep time: 10 minutes | Cook time: 10 minutes | Serves 2

2 tablespoons olive oil
4 eggs, whisked
5 ounces (142 g) fresh spinach, chopped
1 medium tomato, chopped
1 teaspoon fresh

lemon juice
½ teaspoon coarse salt
½ teaspoon ground black pepper
½ cup of fresh basil, roughly chopped

1. Grease the baking pan with the oil, tilting it to spread the oil around.
2. In the pan, mix the remaining ingredients, apart from the basil leaves, whisking well until everything is completely combined.
3. Place the baking pan on the bake position. Select Bake, set the temperature to 280ºF (138ºC), and set the time to 10 minutes.
4. Top with fresh basil leaves before serving.

Tater Tot Breakfast Casserole

Prep time: 5 minutes | Cook time: 17 to 19 minutes | Serves 4

4 eggs
1 cup milk
Salt and pepper, to taste
12 ounces (340 g) ground chicken sausage

1 pound (454 g) frozen tater tots, thawed
¾ cup grated Cheddar cheese
Cooking spray

1. Whisk together the eggs and milk in a medium bowl. Season with salt and pepper to taste and stir until mixed. Set aside.
2. Place a skillet over medium-high heat and spritz with cooking spray. Place the ground sausage in the skillet and break it into smaller pieces with a spatula or spoon. Cook for 3 to 4 minutes until the sausage starts to brown, stirring occasionally. Remove from heat and set aside.
3. Coat the baking pan with cooking spray.
4. Arrange the tater tots in the baking pan.
5. Place the baking pan on the bake position. Select Bake, set the temperature to 400ºF (204ºC), and set the time to 24 minutes.
6. Cook for 15 minutes. Stir in the egg mixture and cooked sausage. Cook for another 6 minutes.
7. Scatter the cheese on top of the tater tots. Continue to cook for 2 to 3 minutes more until the cheese is bubbly and melted.
8. Let the mixture cool for 5 minutes and serve warm.

Fast Coffee Donuts

Prep time: 5 minutes | Cook time: 6 minutes | Serves 6

¼ cup sugar
½ teaspoon salt
1 cup flour
1 teaspoon baking powder

¼ cup coffee
1 tablespoon aquafaba
1 tablespoon sunflower oil

1. In a large bowl, combine the sugar, salt, flour, and baking powder.
2. Add the coffee, aquafaba, and sunflower oil and mix until a dough is formed. Leave the dough to rest in and the refrigerator.
3. Remove the dough from the fridge and divide up, kneading each section into a doughnut.
4. Put the doughnuts in the crisper tray. Place the crisper tray on the air fry position. Select Air Fry, set the temperature to 400ºF (204ºC), and set the time to 6 minutes.
5. Serve immediately.

Banana Bread

Prep time: 10 minutes | Cook time: 22 minutes | Makes 3 loaves

3 ripe bananas, mashed
1 cup sugar
1 large egg
4 tablespoons (½ stick) unsalted butter,

melted
1½ cups all-purpose flour
1 teaspoon baking soda
1 teaspoon salt

1. Coat the insides of 3 mini loaf pans with cooking spray.
2. In a large mixing bowl, mix the bananas and sugar.
3. In a separate large mixing bowl, combine the egg, butter, flour, baking soda, and salt and mix well.
4. Add the banana mixture to the egg and flour mixture. Mix well.
5. Divide the batter evenly among the prepared pans.
6. Place the loaf pans on the bake position. Select Bake, set the temperature to 310ºF (154ºC), and set the time to 22 minutes.
7. Insert a toothpick into the center of each loaf; if it comes out clean, they are done.
8. When the loaves are cooked through, remove the pans from the grill. Turn out the loaves onto a wire rack to cool.
9. Serve warm.

Crustless Broccoli Quiche

Prep time: 5 minutes | Cook time: 10 minutes | Serves 4

1 cup broccoli florets
¾ cup chopped roasted red peppers
1¼ cups grated Fontina cheese
6 eggs
¾ cup heavy cream
½ teaspoon salt
Freshly ground black pepper, to taste
Cooking spray

1. Spritz the baking pan with cooking spray.
2. Add the broccoli florets and roasted red peppers to the pan and scatter the grated Fontina cheese on top.
3. In a bowl, beat together the eggs and heavy cream. Sprinkle with salt and pepper. Pour the egg mixture over the top of the cheese. Wrap the pan in foil.
4. Place the baking pan on the air fry position. Select Air Fry, set the temperature to 325ºF (163ºC), and set the time to 10 minutes.
5. Cook for 8 minutes. Remove the foil and continue to cook another 2 minutes until the quiche is golden brown.
6. Rest for 5 minutes before cutting into wedges and serve warm.

Chicken Breakfast Sausages

Prep time: 15 minutes | Cook time: 8 to 12 minutes | Makes 8 patties

1 Granny Smith apple, peeled and finely chopped
2 tablespoons apple juice
2 garlic cloves, minced
1 egg white
¹⁄₃ cup minced onion
3 tablespoons ground almonds
⅛ teaspoon freshly ground black pepper
1 pound (454 g) ground chicken breast

1. Combine all the ingredients except the chicken in a medium mixing bowl and stir well.
2. Add the chicken breast to the apple mixture and mix with your hands until well incorporated.
3. Divide the mixture into 8 equal portions and shape into patties. Arrange the patties in the crisper tray.
4. Place the crisper tray on the air fry position. Select Air Fry, set the temperature to 330ºF (166ºC), and set the time to 12 minutes.
5. Cook for 8 to 12 minutes, or until a meat thermometer inserted in the center of the chicken reaches at least 165ºF (74ºC).
6. Let cool for 5 minutes and serve warm.

Ham and Corn Muffins

Prep time: 10 minutes | Cook time: 6 minutes | Makes 8 muffins

¾ cup yellow cornmeal
¼ cup flour
1½ teaspoons baking powder
¼ teaspoon salt
1 egg, beaten
2 tablespoons canola oil
½ cup milk
½ cup shredded sharp Cheddar cheese
½ cup diced ham

1. In a medium bowl, stir together the cornmeal, flour, baking powder, and salt.
2. Add the egg, oil, and milk to dry ingredients and mix well.
3. Stir in shredded cheese and diced ham.
4. Divide batter among 8 parchment paper-lined muffin cups.
5. Put 4 filled muffin cups in the pan.
6. Place the baking pan on the bake position. Select Bake, set the temperature to 390ºF (199ºC), and set the time to 5 minutes.
7. Reduce temperature to 330ºF (166ºC) and bake for 1 minute or until a toothpick inserted in center of the muffin comes out clean.
8. Repeat steps 6 and 7 to bake remaining muffins.
9. Serve warm.

Mixed Berry Dutch Baby Pancake

Prep time: 10 minutes | Cook time: 12 to 16 minutes | Serves 4

1 tablespoon unsalted butter, at room temperature
1 egg
2 egg whites
½ cup 2% milk
½ cup whole-wheat pastry flour
1 teaspoon pure vanilla extract
1 cup sliced fresh strawberries
½ cup fresh raspberries
½ cup fresh blueberries

1. Grease the baking pan with the butter.
2. Using a hand mixer, beat together the egg, egg whites, milk, pastry flour, and vanilla in a medium mixing bowl until well incorporated.
3. Pour the batter into the pan.
4. Place the baking pan on the bake position. Select Bake, set the temperature to 330ºF (166ºC), and set the time to 16 minutes.
5. Cook for 12 to 16 minutes, or until the pancake puffs up in the center and the edges are golden brown.
6. Allow the pancake to cool for 5 minutes and serve topped with the berries.

Mushroom and Yellow Squash Toast

Prep time: 10 minutes | Cook time: 10 minutes | Serves 4

1 tablespoon olive oil
1 red bell pepper, cut into strips
2 green onions, sliced
1 cup sliced button or cremini mushrooms
1 small yellow squash, sliced
2 tablespoons softened butter
4 slices bread
½ cup soft goat cheese

1. Brush the crisper tray with the olive oil.
2. Put the red pepper, green onions, mushrooms, and squash inside the crisper tray and give them a stir.
3. Place the crisper tray on the air fry position. Select Air Fry, set the temperature to 350ºF (177ºC), and set the time to 7 minutes.
4. Cook for 7 minutes or the vegetables are tender, shaking the crisper tray once throughout the cooking time.
5. Remove the vegetables and set them aside.
6. Spread the butter on the slices of bread and transfer to the crisper tray, butter-side up. Air fry for 3 minutes.
7. Remove the toast from the grill and top with goat cheese and vegetables. Serve warm.

Cornflakes Toast Sticks

Prep time: 10 minutes | Cook time: 6 minutes | Serves 4

2 eggs
½ cup milk
⅛ teaspoon salt
½ teaspoon pure vanilla extract
¾ cup crushed cornflakes
6 slices sandwich bread, each slice cut into 4 strips
Maple syrup, for dipping
Cooking spray

1. In a small bowl, beat together the eggs, milk, salt, and vanilla.
2. Put crushed cornflakes on a plate or in a shallow dish.
3. Dip bread strips in egg mixture, shake off excess, and roll in cornflake crumbs.
4. Spray both sides of bread strips with oil.
5. Put bread strips in crisper tray in a single layer. Place the crisper tray on the air fry position. Select Air Fry, set the temperature to 390ºF (199ºC), and set the time to 6 minutes.
6. Cook for 6 minutes or until golden brown.
7. Repeat steps 5 and 6 to air fry remaining French toast sticks.
8. Serve with maple syrup.

Pumpkin Egg Bake

Prep time: 10 minutes | Cook time: 10 minutes | Serves 2

2 eggs
½ cup milk
2 cups flour
2 tablespoons cider vinegar
2 teaspoons baking powder
1 tablespoon sugar
1 cup pumpkin purée
1 teaspoon cinnamon powder
1 teaspoon baking soda
1 tablespoon olive oil

1. Crack the eggs into a bowl and beat with a whisk. Combine with the milk, flour, cider vinegar, baking powder, sugar, pumpkin purée, cinnamon powder, and baking soda, mixing well.
2. Grease the baking pan with oil. Add the mixture to the pan.
3. Place the baking pan on the bake position. Select Bake, set the temperature to 300ºF (149ºC), and set the time to 10 minutes.
4. Serve warm.

Maple Walnut Pancake

Prep time: 10 minutes | Cook time: 20 minutes | Serves 4

3 tablespoons melted butter, divided
1 cup flour
2 tablespoons sugar
1½ teaspoons baking powder
¼ teaspoon salt
1 egg, beaten
¾ cup milk
1 teaspoon pure vanilla extract
½ cup roughly chopped walnuts
Maple syrup or fresh sliced fruit, for serving

1. Grease the baking pan with 1 tablespoon of melted butter.
2. Mix together the flour, sugar, baking powder, and salt in a medium bowl. Add the beaten egg, milk, the remaining 2 tablespoons of melted butter, and vanilla and stir until the batter is sticky but slightly lumpy.
3. Slowly pour the batter into the greased baking pan and scatter with the walnuts.
4. Place the baking pan on the bake position. Select Bake, set the temperature to 330ºF (166ºC), and set the time to 20 minutes.
5. Cook for 20 minutes until golden brown and cooked through.
6. Let the pancake rest for 5 minutes and serve topped with the maple syrup or fresh fruit, if desired.

Avocado Quesadillas

Prep time: 10 minutes | Cook time: 11 minutes | Serves 4

4 eggs
2 tablespoons skim milk
Salt and ground black pepper, to taste
Cooking spray
4 flour tortillas
4 tablespoons salsa
2 ounces (57 g) Cheddar cheese, grated
½ small avocado, peeled and thinly sliced

1. Beat together the eggs, milk, salt, and pepper.
2. Spray the baking pan lightly with cooking spray and add egg mixture.
3. Place the baking pan on the bake position. Select Bake, set the temperature to 270ºF (132ºC), and set the time to 8 minutes.
4. Cook for 8 minutes, stirring every 1 to 2 minutes, until eggs are scrambled to the liking. Remove and set aside.
5. Spray one side of each tortilla with cooking spray. Flip over.
6. Divide eggs, salsa, cheese, and avocado among the tortillas, covering only half of each tortilla.
7. Fold each tortilla in half and press down lightly. Increase the temperature of the grill to 390ºF (199ºC).
8. Put 2 tortillas in crisper tray and air fry for 3 minutes or until cheese melts and outside feels slightly crispy. Repeat with remaining two tortillas.
9. Cut each cooked tortilla into halves. Serve warm.

Spinach and Cheese Omelet

Prep time: 10 minutes | Cook time: 10 minutes | Serves 1

1 teaspoon olive oil
3 eggs
Salt and ground black pepper, to taste
1 tablespoon ricotta
cheese
¼ cup chopped spinach
1 tablespoon chopped parsley

1. Grease the baking pan with olive oil.
2. In a bowl, beat the eggs with a fork and sprinkle salt and pepper.
3. Add the ricotta, spinach, and parsley and then transfer to the baking pan.
4. Place the baking pan on the bake position. Select Bake, set the temperature to 330ºF (166ºC), and set the time to 10 minutes.
5. Cook for 10 minutes or until the egg is set.
6. Serve warm.

Mushroom and Onion Frittata

Prep time: 10 minutes | Cook time: 10 minutes | Serves 4

4 large eggs
¼ cup whole milk
Sea salt, to taste
Freshly ground black pepper, to taste
½ bell pepper, seeded
and diced
½ onion, chopped
4 cremini mushrooms, sliced
½ cup shredded Cheddar cheese

1. In a medium bowl, whisk together the eggs and milk. Season with the salt and pepper. Add the bell pepper, onion, mushrooms, and cheese. Mix until well combined.
2. Pour the egg mixture into the baking pan, spreading evenly.
3. Place the baking pan on the bake position. Select Bake, set the temperature to 400ºF (204ºC), and set the time to 10 minutes.
4. Cook for 10 minutes, or until lightly golden.

PB&J

Prep time: 5 minutes | Cook time: 6 minutes | Serves 4

½ cup cornflakes, crushed
¼ cup shredded coconut
8 slices oat nut bread or any whole-grain, oversize bread
6 tablespoons peanut
butter
2 medium bananas, cut into ½-inch-thick slices
6 tablespoons pineapple preserves
1 egg, beaten
Cooking spray

1. In a shallow dish, mix the cornflake crumbs and coconut.
2. For each sandwich, spread one bread slice with 1½ tablespoons of peanut butter. Top with banana slices. Spread another bread slice with 1½ tablespoons of preserves. Combine to make a sandwich.
3. Using a pastry brush, brush top of sandwich lightly with beaten egg. Sprinkle with about 1½ tablespoons of crumb coating, pressing it in to make it stick. Spray with cooking spray.
4. Turn sandwich over and repeat to coat and spray the other side. Place the sandwiches in the crisper tray. Place the crisper tray on the air fry position. Select Air Fry, set the temperature to 360ºF (182ºC), and set the time to 6 minutes.
5. Cook for 6 minutes or until coating is golden brown and crispy.
6. Cut the cooked sandwiches in half and serve warm.

Veggie Frittata

Prep time: 10 minutes | Cook time: 8 to 12 minutes | Serves 4

½ cup chopped red bell pepper
⅓ cup grated carrot
⅓ cup minced onion
1 teaspoon olive oil
1 egg
6 egg whites
⅓ cup 2% milk
1 tablespoon shredded Parmesan cheese

1. Mix together the red bell pepper, carrot, onion, and olive oil in the baking pan and stir to combine.
2. Place the baking pan on the bake position. Select Bake, set the temperature to 350ºF (177ºC), and set the time to 6 minutes.
3. Cook for 4 to 6 minutes, or until the veggies are soft. Stir once during cooking.
4. Meantime, whisk together the egg, egg whites, and milk in a medium bowl until creamy.
5. When the veggies are done, pour the egg mixture over the top. Scatter with the Parmesan cheese.
6. Bake for an additional 4 to 6 minutes, or until the eggs are set and the top is golden around the edges.
7. Allow the frittata to cool for 5 minutes before slicing and serving.

Hash Brown Casserole

Prep time: 15 minutes | Cook time: 30 minutes | Serves 4

3½ cups frozen hash browns, thawed
1 teaspoon salt
1 teaspoon freshly ground black pepper
3 tablespoons butter, melted
1 (10.5-ounce / 298-
g) can cream of chicken soup
½ cup sour cream
1 cup minced onion
½ cup shredded sharp Cheddar cheese
Cooking spray

1. Put the hash browns in a large bowl and season with salt and black pepper. Add the melted butter, cream of chicken soup, and sour cream and stir until well incorporated. Mix in the minced onion and cheese and stir well.
2. Place the baking pan on the bake position. Select Bake, set the temperature to 325ºF (163ºC), and set the time to 30 minutes.
3. Spray the baking pan with cooking spray.
4. Spread the hash brown mixture evenly into the baking pan.
5. Cook for 30 minutes until browned.
6. Cool for 5 minutes before serving.

Ritzy Vegetable Omelet

Prep time: 10 minutes | Cook time: 13 minutes | Serves 2

2 teaspoons canola oil
4 eggs, whisked
3 tablespoons plain milk
1 teaspoon melted butter
1 red bell pepper, seeded and chopped
1 green bell pepper, seeded and chopped
1 white onion, finely chopped
½ cup baby spinach leaves, roughly chopped
½ cup Halloumi cheese, shaved
Kosher salt and freshly ground black pepper, to taste

1. Grease the baking pan with canola oil.
2. Put the remaining ingredients in the baking pan and stir well.
3. Place the baking pan on the bake position. Select Bake, set the temperature to 350ºF (177ºC), and set the time to 13 minutes.
4. Serve warm.

Bacon and Egg Bread Cups

Prep time: 10 minutes | Cook time: 8 to 12 minutes | Serves 4

4 (3-by-4-inch) crusty rolls
4 thin slices Gouda or Swiss cheese mini wedges
5 eggs
2 tablespoons heavy cream
3 strips precooked bacon, chopped
½ teaspoon dried thyme
Pinch salt
Freshly ground black pepper, to taste

1. On a clean work surface, cut the tops off the rolls. Using your fingers, remove the insides of the rolls to make bread cups, leaving a ½-inch shell. Place a slice of cheese onto each roll bottom.
2. Whisk together the eggs and heavy cream in a medium bowl until well combined. Fold in the bacon, thyme, salt, and pepper and stir well.
3. Scrape the egg mixture into the prepared bread cups.
4. Place the bread cups directly in the pan.
5. Place the baking pan on the bake position. Select Bake, set the temperature to 330ºF (166ºC), and set the time to 12 minutes.
6. Cook for 8 to 12 minutes, or until the eggs are cooked to your preference.
7. Serve warm.

Grit Fritters with Ham

Prep time: 15 minutes | Cook time: 20 minutes | Serves 6 to 8

4 cups water
1 cup quick-cooking grits
¼ teaspoon salt
2 tablespoons butter
2 cups grated Cheddar cheese, divided
1 cup finely diced ham
1 tablespoon chopped

chives
Salt and freshly ground black pepper, to taste
1 egg, beaten
2 cups panko bread crumbs
Cooking spray

1. Bring the water to a boil in a saucepan. Whisk in the grits and ¼ teaspoon of salt, and cook for 7 minutes until the grits are soft. Remove the pan from the heat and stir in the butter and 1 cup of the grated Cheddar cheese. Transfer the grits to a bowl and let them cool for 10 to 15 minutes.
2. Stir the ham, chives and the rest of the cheese into the grits and season with salt and pepper to taste. Add the beaten egg and refrigerate the mixture for 30 minutes.
3. Put the panko bread crumbs in a shallow dish. Measure out ¼-cup portions of the grits mixture and shape them into patties. Coat all sides of the patties with the panko bread crumbs, patting them with the hands so the crumbs adhere to the patties. You should have about 16 patties. Spritz both sides of the patties with cooking spray.
4. Place the fritters in the crisper tray.
5. Place the crisper tray on the air fry position. Select Air Fry, set the temperature to 400ºF (204ºC), and set the time to 12 minutes.
6. Cook for 8 minutes. Using a flat spatula, flip the fritters over and cook for another 4 minutes.
7. Serve hot.

Potato Rolls

Prep time: 15 minutes | Cook time: 20 minutes | Serves 5

5 large potatoes, boiled and mashed
Salt and ground black pepper, to taste
½ teaspoon mustard seeds
1 tablespoon olive oil
2 small onions, chopped

2 sprigs curry leaves
½ teaspoon turmeric powder
2 green chilis, seeded and chopped
1 bunch coriander, chopped
8 slices bread, brown sides discarded

1. Put the mashed potatoes in a bowl and sprinkle on salt and pepper. Set to one side.
2. Fry the mustard seeds in olive oil over a medium-low heat in a skillet, stirring continuously, until they sputter.
3. Add the onions and cook until they turn translucent. Add the curry leaves and turmeric powder and stir. Cook for a further 2 minutes until fragrant.
4. Remove the skillet from the heat and combine with the potatoes. Mix in the green chilies and coriander.
5. Wet the bread slightly and drain of any excess liquid.
6. Spoon a small amount of the potato mixture into the center of the bread and enclose the bread around the filling, sealing it entirely. Continue until the rest of the bread and filling is used up. Brush each bread roll with some oil and transfer to the crisper tray.
7. Place the crisper tray on the air fry position. Select Air Fry, set the temperature to 400ºF (204ºC), and set the time to 15 minutes.
8. Cook for 15 minutes, gently shaking the crisper tray at the halfway point to ensure each roll is cooked evenly.
9. Serve immediately.

Cheesy Breakfast Casserole

Prep time: 10 minutes | Cook time: 14 minutes | Serves 4

6 slices bacon
6 eggs
Salt and pepper, to taste
Cooking spray

½ cup chopped green bell pepper
½ cup chopped onion
¾ cup shredded Cheddar cheese

1. Place the bacon in a skillet over medium-high heat and cook each side for about 4 minutes until evenly crisp. Remove from the heat to a paper towel-lined plate to drain. Crumble it into small pieces and set aside.
2. Whisk the eggs with the salt and pepper in a medium bowl.
3. Spritz the baking pan with cooking spray.
4. Place the whisked eggs, crumbled bacon, green bell pepper, and onion in the prepared pan.
5. Place the baking pan on the bake position. Select Bake, set the temperature to 400ºF (204ºC), and set the time to 8 minutes.
6. Cook for 6 minutes. Scatter the Cheddar cheese all over and cook for 2 minutes more.
7. Allow to sit for 5 minutes and serve on plates.

Spinach, Leek and Cheese Frittata

Prep time: 10 minutes | Cook time: 20 to 23 minutes | Serves 2

4 large eggs
4 ounces (113 g) baby bella mushrooms, chopped
1 cup (1 ounce / 28-g) baby spinach, chopped
½ cup (2 ounces / 57-g) shredded Cheddar cheese
$^1/_3$ cup (from 1 large) chopped leek, white part only
¼ cup halved grape tomatoes
1 tablespoon 2% milk
¼ teaspoon dried oregano
¼ teaspoon garlic powder
½ teaspoon kosher salt
Freshly ground black pepper, to taste
Cooking spray

1. Lightly spritz the baking pan with cooking spray.
2. Whisk the eggs in a large bowl until frothy. Add the mushrooms, baby spinach, cheese, leek, tomatoes, milk, oregano, garlic powder, salt, and pepper and stir until well blended. Pour the mixture into the prepared baking pan.
3. Place the baking pan on the bake position. Select Bake, set the temperature to 300ºF (149ºC), and set the time to 23 minutes.
4. Cook for 20 to 23 minutes, or until the center is puffed up and the top is golden brown.
5. Let the frittata cool for 5 minutes before slicing to serve.

Posh Orange Rolls

Prep time: 15 minutes | Cook time: 8 minutes | Makes 8 rolls

3 ounces (85 g) low-fat cream cheese
1 tablespoon low-fat sour cream or plain yogurt
2 teaspoons sugar
¼ teaspoon pure vanilla extract
¼ teaspoon orange extract
1 can (8 count)
Orange Glaze:
½ cup powdered sugar
1 tablespoon orange juice
organic crescent roll dough
¼ cup chopped walnuts
¼ cup dried cranberries
¼ cup shredded, sweetened coconut
Butter-flavored cooking spray

¼ teaspoon orange extract
Dash of salt

1. Cut a circular piece of parchment paper slightly smaller than the bottom of the crisper tray. Set aside.

2. In a small bowl, combine the cream cheese, sour cream or yogurt, sugar, and vanilla and orange extracts. Stir until smooth.
3. Separate crescent roll dough into 8 triangles and divide cream cheese mixture among them. Starting at wide end, spread cheese mixture to within 1 inch of point.
4. Sprinkle nuts and cranberries evenly over cheese mixture.
5. Starting at wide end, roll up triangles, then sprinkle with coconut, pressing in lightly to make it stick. Spray tops of rolls with butter-flavored cooking spray.
6. Put parchment paper in crisper tray, and place 4 rolls on top, spaced evenly.
7. Place the crisper tray on the air fry position. Select Air Fry, set the temperature to 300ºF (149ºC), and set the time to 8 minutes.
8. Cook for 8 minutes, until rolls are golden brown and cooked through.
9. Repeat steps 7 and 8 to air fry remaining 4 rolls. You should be able to use the same piece of parchment paper twice.
10. In a small bowl, stir together ingredients for glaze and drizzle over warm rolls. Serve warm.

Honey-Lime Glazed Grilled Fruit Salad

Prep time: 10 minutes | Cook time: 4 minutes | Serves 4

½ pound (227 g) strawberries, washed, hulled and halved
1 (9-ounce / 255-g) can pineapple chunks, drained, juice reserved
2 peaches, pitted and sliced
6 tablespoons honey, divided
1 tablespoon freshly squeezed lime juice

1. Combine the strawberries, pineapple, and peaches in a large bowl with 3 tablespoons of honey. Toss to coat evenly.
2. Place the fruit on the grill plate. Gently press the fruit down to maximize grill marks. Place the grill plate on the grill position. Select Grill, set the temperature to 450ºF (232ºC), and set the time to 4 minutes.
3. Meanwhile, in a small bowl, combine the remaining 3 tablespoons of honey, lime juice, and 1 tablespoon of reserved pineapple juice.
4. When cooking is complete, place the fruit in a large bowl and toss with the honey mixture. Serve immediately.

Soufflé

Prep time: 10 minutes | Cook time: 22 minutes | Serves 4

⅓ cup butter, melted
¼ cup flour
1 cup milk
1 ounce (28 g) sugar
4 egg yolks
1 teaspoon vanilla

extract
6 egg whites
1 teaspoon cream of tartar
Cooking spray

1. In a bowl, mix the butter and flour until a smooth consistency is achieved.
2. Pour the milk into a saucepan over medium-low heat. Add the sugar and allow to dissolve before raising the heat to boil the milk.
3. Pour in the flour and butter mixture and stir rigorously for 7 minutes to eliminate any lumps. Make sure the mixture thickens. Take off the heat and allow to cool for 15 minutes.
4. Spritz 6 soufflé dishes with cooking spray.
5. Put the egg yolks and vanilla extract in a separate bowl and beat them together with a fork. Pour in the milk and combine well to incorporate everything.
6. In a smaller bowl mix the egg whites and cream of tartar with a fork. Fold into the egg yolks-milk mixture before adding in the flour mixture. Transfer equal amounts to the 6 soufflé dishes.
7. Put the dishes in the pan.
8. Place the baking pan on the bake position. Select Bake, set the temperature to 320ºF (160ºC), and set the time to 15 minutes.
9. Serve warm.

Apple and Walnut Muffins

Prep time: 15 minutes | Cook time: 10 minutes | Makes 8 muffins

1 cup flour
⅓ cup sugar
1 teaspoon baking powder
¼ teaspoon baking soda
¼ teaspoon salt
1 teaspoon cinnamon
¼ teaspoon ginger
¼ teaspoon nutmeg
1 egg
2 tablespoons

pancake syrup, plus 2 teaspoons
2 tablespoons melted butter, plus 2 teaspoons
¾ cup unsweetened applesauce
½ teaspoon vanilla extract
¼ cup chopped walnuts
¼ cup diced apple

1. In a large bowl, stir together the flour, sugar, baking powder, baking soda, salt, cinnamon, ginger, and nutmeg.
2. In a small bowl, beat egg until frothy. Add syrup, butter, applesauce, and vanilla and mix well.
3. Pour egg mixture into dry ingredients and stir just until moistened.
4. Gently stir in nuts and diced apple.
5. Divide batter among 8 parchment paper-lined muffin cups.
6. Put 4 muffin cups in the baking pan.
7. Place the baking pan on the bake position. Select Bake, set the temperature to 330ºF (166ºC), and set the time to 10 minutes.
8. Repeat with remaining 4 muffins or until toothpick inserted in center comes out clean.
9. Serve warm.

Buttermilk Biscuits

Prep time: 5 minutes | Cook time: 5 minutes | Makes 12 biscuits

2 cups all-purpose flour, plus more for dusting the work surface
1 tablespoon baking powder
¼ teaspoon baking soda

2 teaspoons sugar
1 teaspoon salt
6 tablespoons cold unsalted butter, cut into 1-tablespoon slices
¾ cup buttermilk

1. Spray the crisper tray with olive oil.
2. In a large mixing bowl, combine the flour, baking powder, baking soda, sugar, and salt and mix well.
3. Using a fork, cut in the butter until the mixture resembles coarse meal.
4. Add the buttermilk and mix until smooth.
5. Dust more flour on a clean work surface. Turn the dough out onto the work surface and roll it out until it is about ½ inch thick.
6. Using a 2-inch biscuit cutter, cut out the biscuits. Put the uncooked biscuits in the greased crisper tray in a single layer. Place the crisper tray on the bake position. Select Bake, set the temperature to 360ºF (182ºC), and set the time to 5 minutes.
7. Transfer the cooked biscuits from the grill to a platter.
8. Cut the remaining biscuits. Bake the remaining biscuits.
9. Serve warm.

Cashew Granola

Prep time: 5 minutes | Cook time: 12 minutes | Serves 6

3 cups old-fashioned rolled oats
2 cups raw cashews or mixed raw nuts (such as pecans, walnuts, almonds)
1 cup unsweetened coconut chips
½ cup honey
¼ cup vegetable oil,

extra-virgin olive oil, or walnut oil
⅓ cup packed light brown sugar
¼ teaspoon kosher salt or ⅛ teaspoon fine salt
1 cup dried cranberries (optional)

1. Place the oats, nuts, coconut, honey, oil, brown sugar, and salt in a large bowl and mix until well combined. Spread the mixture in an even layer in the baking pan.
2. Place the pan on the bake position. Select Bake, set temperature to 325ºF (163ºC), and set time to 12 minutes.
3. After 5 to 6 minutes, remove the pan and stir the granola, return the pan to the grill, and continue cooking.
4. When cooking is complete, remove the pan. Let the granola cool to room temperature, then stir in the cranberries, if using. If not serving right away, store in an airtight container at room temperature.

Corned Beef Hash

Prep time: 10 minutes | Cook time: 12 minutes | Serves 4

2 medium Yukon Gold potatoes, peeled, cut into ¼-inch cubes (about 3 cups)
1 medium onion, chopped (about 1 cup)
⅓ cup diced red bell pepper
3 tablespoons vegetable oil
½ teaspoon dried

thyme
½ teaspoon kosher salt or ¼ teaspoon fine salt, divided
½ teaspoon freshly ground black pepper, divided
¾ pound (340 g) corned beef, cut into ¼-inch pieces
4 large eggs

1. In a large bowl, mix the potatoes, onion, red pepper, oil, thyme, ¼ teaspoon of salt, and ¼ teaspoon of pepper. Spread the vegetables in the baking pan in an even layer.
2. Place the pan on the roast position. Select Roast, set temperature to 375ºF (191ºC), and set time to 25 minutes.

3. After 15 minutes, remove the pan from the grill and add the corned beef. Stir the mixture to incorporate the corned beef. Return the pan to the grill and continue cooking for 5 minutes.
4. After 5 minutes (20 minutes total), remove the pan from the grill. Using a large spoon, create 4 circles in the hash to hold the eggs. Gently crack an egg into each circle; season eggs with remaining ¼ teaspoon of salt and ¼ teaspoon of pepper. Return the baking pan to the grill. Continue cooking for 3 to 8 minutes, depending on how you like your eggs (3 to 4 minutes for runny yolks; 8 minutes for firm yolks).
5. When cooking is complete, remove the pan from the grill. Serve immediately.

Spinach and Egg Florentine

Prep time: 10 minutes | Cook time: 12 minutes | Serves 4

3 cups frozen spinach, thawed and drained
¼ teaspoon kosher salt or ⅛ teaspoon fine salt
4 ounces (113 g) ricotta cheese
2 tablespoons heavy (whipping) cream
2 garlic cloves, minced
⅛ teaspoon freshly

ground white or black pepper
2 teaspoons unsalted butter, melted
3 tablespoons grated Parmesan or similar cheese
½ cup panko bread crumbs
4 large eggs

1. In a medium bowl, stir together the spinach, salt, ricotta, cream, garlic, and pepper.
2. In a small bowl, stir together the butter, cheese, and panko. Set aside.
3. Scoop the spinach mixture into four even circles in the baking pan.
4. Place the pan on the roast position. Select Roast, set temperature to 375ºF (191ºC), and set time to 15 minutes.
5. After 8 minutes, remove the pan. The spinach should be bubbling. With the back of a large spoon, make indentations in the spinach for the eggs. Crack the eggs into the indentations and sprinkle the panko mixture over the surface of the eggs.
6. Return the pan to the grill and continue cooking. After 5 minutes, check the eggs. If the eggs are done to your liking, remove the pan. If not, continue cooking.
7. When cooking is complete, remove the pan from the grill. Serve the eggs with toasted English muffins, if desired.

Banana and Oat Bread Pudding

Prep time: 10 minutes | Cook time: 16 to 20 minutes | Serves 4

2 medium ripe bananas, mashed
½ cup low-fat milk
2 tablespoons maple syrup
2 tablespoons peanut butter
1 teaspoon vanilla extract
1 teaspoon ground cinnamon
2 slices whole-grain bread, cut into bite-sized cubes
¼ cup quick oats
Cooking spray

1. Spritz the baking pan lightly with cooking spray.
2. Mix the bananas, milk, maple syrup, peanut butter, vanilla, and cinnamon in a large mixing bowl and stir until well incorporated.
3. Add the bread cubes to the banana mixture and stir until thoroughly coated. Fold in the oats and stir to combine.
4. Transfer the mixture to the baking pan. Wrap the baking pan in aluminum foil.
5. Place the baking pan on the air fry position. Select Air Fry, set the temperature to 350ºF (177ºC), and set the time to 20 minutes.
6. Cook for 10 to 12 minutes until heated through. Remove the foil and cook for an additional 6 to 8 minutes, or until the pudding has set.
7. Let the pudding cool for 5 minutes before serving.

Apple Turnovers

Prep time: 15 minutes | Cook time: 20 minutes | Serves 4

1 cup diced apple (about 1 medium apple)
1 tablespoon brown sugar
¼ teaspoon cinnamon
⅛ teaspoon allspice
1 teaspoon freshly squeezed lemon juice
1 teaspoon all-purpose flour, plus more for dusting
½ package (1 sheet) frozen puff pastry, thawed
1 large egg, beaten
2 teaspoons granulated sugar

1. In a medium bowl, stir together the apple, brown sugar, cinnamon, allspice, lemon juice, and flour.
2. Lightly flour a cutting board. Unfold the puff pastry sheet onto the board. Using a rolling pin, gently roll the dough to smooth out the folds, seal any tears, and form it into a square. Cut the dough into four squares.
3. Scoop a quarter of the apple mixture into the center of each puff pastry square and spread it evenly in a triangle shape over half the pastry, leaving a border of about ½ inch around the edges of the pastry. Fold the pastry diagonally over the filling to form triangles. With a fork, crimp the edges to seal them. Place the turnovers in the baking pan, spacing them evenly.
4. Cut two or three small slits in the top of each turnover. Brush with the egg. Sprinkle evenly with the granulated sugar.
5. Place the pan on the bake position. Select Bake, set temperature to 350ºF (177ºC), and set time to 20 minutes.
6. After 10 to 12 minutes, remove the pan from the grill. Check the pastries; if they are browning unevenly, rotate the pan. Return the pan to the grill and continue cooking.
7. When cooking is complete, remove the pan from the grill. The turnovers should be golden brown and the filling bubbling. Let cool for about 10 minutes before serving (the filling will be very hot).

Asparagus and Cheese Strata

Prep time: 10 minutes | Cook time: 14 to 19 minutes | Serves 4

6 asparagus spears, cut into 2-inch pieces
1 tablespoon water
2 slices whole-wheat bread, cut into ½-inch cubes
4 eggs
3 tablespoons whole milk
2 tablespoons chopped flat-leaf parsley
½ cup grated Havarti or Swiss cheese
Pinch salt
Freshly ground black pepper, to taste
Cooking spray

1. Add the asparagus spears and 1 tablespoon of water in the baking pan.
2. Place the baking pan on the bake position. Select Bake, set the temperature to 330ºF (166ºC), and set the time to 19 minutes.
3. Cook for 3 to 5 minutes until crisp-tender. Remove the asparagus from the pan and drain on paper towels. Spritz the pan with cooking spray.
4. Place the bread and asparagus in the pan.
5. Whisk together the eggs and milk in a medium mixing bowl until creamy. Fold in the parsley, cheese, salt, and pepper and stir to combine. Pour this mixture into the baking pan.
6. Bake for 11 to 14 minutes, or until the eggs are set and the top is lightly browned.
7. Let cool for 5 minutes before slicing and serving.

Coconut Brown Rice Porridge with Dates

Prep time: 5 minutes | Cook time: 23 minutes | Serves 1 or 2

½ cup cooked brown rice
1 cup canned coconut milk
¼ cup unsweetened shredded coconut
¼ cup packed dark brown sugar
4 large Medjool dates,

pitted and roughly chopped
½ teaspoon kosher salt
¼ teaspoon ground cardamom
Heavy cream, for serving (optional)

1. Place all the ingredients except the heavy cream in the baking pan and stir until blended.
2. Place the baking pan on the bake position. Select Bake, set the temperature to 375ºF (191ºC), and set the time to 23 minutes.
3. Cook for 23 minutes until the porridge is thick and creamy. Stir the porridge halfway through the cooking time.
4. Remove from the grill and ladle the porridge into bowls.
5. Serve hot with a drizzle of the cream, if desired.

Crouton Casserole

Prep time: 10 minutes | Cook time: 12 minutes | Serves 6

3 large eggs
1 cup whole milk
¼ teaspoon kosher salt or ⅛ teaspoon fine salt
1 tablespoon pure maple syrup
1 teaspoon vanilla

¼ teaspoon cinnamon
3 cups (1-inch) stale bread cubes (3 to 4 slices)
1 tablespoon unsalted butter, at room temperature

1. In a medium bowl, whisk the eggs until the yolks and whites are completely mixed. Add the milk, salt, maple syrup, vanilla, and cinnamon and whisk to combine. Add the bread cubes and gently stir to coat with the egg mixture. Let sit for 2 to 3 minutes so the bread absorbs some of the custard, then gently stir again.
2. Grease the bottom of the baking pan with the butter. Pour the bread mixture into the pan, spreading it out evenly.

3. Place the pan on the roast position. Select Roast, set temperature to 350ºF (177ºC), and set time to 12 minutes.
4. After about 10 minutes, remove the pan and check the casserole. The top should be browned and the middle of the casserole just set. If more time is needed, return the pan to the grill and continue cooking.
5. When cooking is complete, serve warm with additional butter and maple syrup, if desired.

Chocolate Banana Bread with White Chocolate

Prep time: 10 minutes | Cook time: 30 minutes | Serves 4

¼ cup cocoa powder
6 tablespoons plus 2 teaspoons all-purpose flour, divided
½ teaspoon kosher salt
¼ teaspoon baking soda
1½ ripe bananas
1 large egg, whisked
¼ cup vegetable oil

½ cup sugar
3 tablespoons buttermilk or plain yogurt (not Greek)
½ teaspoon vanilla extract
6 tablespoons chopped white chocolate
6 tablespoons chopped walnuts

1. Mix together the cocoa powder, 6 tablespoons of the flour, salt, and baking soda in a medium bowl.
2. Mash the bananas with a fork in another medium bowl until smooth. Fold in the egg, oil, sugar, buttermilk, and vanilla, and whisk until thoroughly combined. Add the wet mixture to the dry mixture and stir until well incorporated.
3. Combine the white chocolate, walnuts, and the remaining 2 tablespoons of flour in a third bowl and toss to coat. Add this mixture to the batter and stir until well incorporated. Pour the batter into the baking pan and smooth the top with a spatula.
4. Place the baking pan on the bake position. Select Bake, set the temperature to 310ºF (154ºC), and set the time to 30 minutes.
5. Check the bread for doneness: If a toothpick inserted into the center of the bread comes out clean, it's done.
6. Remove from the grill and allow to cool on a wire rack for 10 minutes before serving.

Fried Potatoes with Peppers and Onions

Prep time: 10 minutes | Cook time: 35 minutes | Serves 4

1 pound (454 g) red potatoes, cut into ½-inch dices
1 large red bell pepper, cut into ½-inch dices
1 large green bell pepper, cut into ½-inch dices
1 medium onion, cut into ½-inch dices

1½ tablespoons extra-virgin olive oil
1¼ teaspoons kosher salt
¾ teaspoon sweet paprika
¾ teaspoon garlic powder
Freshly ground black pepper, to taste

1. Mix together the potatoes, bell peppers, onion, oil, salt, paprika, garlic powder, and black pepper in a large mixing and toss to coat.
2. Transfer the potato mixture to the crisper tray.
3. Place the crisper tray on the air fry position. Select Air Fry, set the temperature to 350ºF (177ºC), and set the time to 35 minutes.
4. Cook for 35 minutes, or until the potatoes are nicely browned. Shake the crisper tray three times during cooking.
5. Remove from the crisper tray to a plate and serve warm.

Nut and Seed Muffins

Prep time: 15 minutes | Cook time: 10 minutes | Makes 8 muffins

½ cup whole-wheat flour, plus 2 tablespoons
¼ cup oat bran
2 tablespoons flaxseed meal
¼ cup brown sugar
½ teaspoon baking soda
½ teaspoon baking powder
¼ teaspoon salt
½ teaspoon cinnamon
½ cup buttermilk

2 tablespoons melted butter
1 egg
½ teaspoon pure vanilla extract
½ cup grated carrots
¼ cup chopped pecans
¼ cup chopped walnuts
1 tablespoon pumpkin seeds
1 tablespoon sunflower seeds
Cooking spray

Special Equipment:
16 foil muffin cups, paper liners removed

1. In a large bowl, stir together the flour, bran, flaxseed meal, sugar, baking soda, baking powder, salt, and cinnamon.

2. In a medium bowl, beat together the buttermilk, butter, egg, and vanilla. Pour into flour mixture and stir just until dry ingredients moisten. Do not beat.
3. Gently stir in carrots, nuts, and seeds.
4. Double up the foil cups so you have 8 total and spritz with cooking spray.
5. Put 4 foil cups in the pan and divide half the batter among them.
6. Place the baking pan on the bake position. Select Bake, set the temperature to 330ºF (166ºC), and set the time to 10 minutes.
7. Cook for 10 minutes, or until a toothpick inserted in center comes out clean.
8. Repeat step 7 to bake remaining 4 muffins.
9. Serve warm.

Tomato-Corn Frittata with Avocado Dressing

Prep time: 10 minutes | Cook time: 20 minutes | Serves 2 or 3

½ cup cherry tomatoes, halved
Kosher salt and freshly ground black pepper, to taste
6 large eggs, lightly beaten
Avocado Dressing:
1 ripe avocado, pitted and peeled
2 tablespoons fresh lime juice
¼ cup olive oil

½ cup corn kernels, thawed if frozen
¼ cup milk
1 tablespoon finely chopped fresh dill
½ cup shredded Monterey Jack cheese

1 scallion, finely chopped
8 fresh basil leaves, finely chopped

1. Put the tomato halves in a colander and lightly season with salt. Set aside for 10 minutes to drain well. Pour the tomatoes into a large bowl and fold in the eggs, corn, milk, and dill. Sprinkle with salt and pepper and stir until mixed.
2. Pour the egg mixture into the baking pan.
3. Place the baking pan on the bake position. Select Bake, set the temperature to 300ºF (149ºC), and set the time to 15 minutes.
4. Scatter the cheese on top. Increase the grill temperature to 315ºF (157ºC) and continue to bake for another 5 minutes, or until the frittata is puffy and set.
5. Meanwhile, make the avocado dressing: Mash the avocado with the lime juice in a medium bowl until smooth. Mix in the olive oil, scallion, and basil and stir until well incorporated.
6. Let the frittata cool for 5 minutes and serve alongside the avocado dressing.

Cinnamon Rolls

Prep time: 10 minutes | Cook time: 25 minutes | Makes 18 rolls

2 teaspoons cinnamon
1/3 cup light brown sugar
1 (9-by-9-inch) frozen puff pastry sheet, thawed
All-purpose flour, for dusting
6 teaspoons (2 tablespoons) unsalted butter, melted, divided

1. In a small bowl, mix together the cinnamon and brown sugar.
2. Unfold the puff pastry on a lightly floured surface. Using a rolling pin, press the folds together and roll the dough out in one direction so that it measures about 9 by 11 inches. Cut it in half to form two squat rectangles of about 5½ by 9 inches.
3. Brush 2 teaspoons of butter over each pastry half, and then sprinkle with 2 generous tablespoons of the cinnamon sugar. Pat it down lightly with the palm of your hand to help it adhere to the butter.
4. Starting with the 9-inch side of one rectangle and using your hands, carefully roll the dough into a cylinder. Repeat with the other rectangle. To make slicing easier, refrigerate the rolls for 10 to 20 minutes.
5. Using a sharp knife, slice each roll into nine 1-inch pieces. Transfer the rolls to the center of the baking pan. They should be very close to each other, but not quite touching. For neater rolls, turn the outside rolls so that the seam is to the inside. Drizzle the remaining 2 teaspoons of butter over the rolls and sprinkle with the remaining cinnamon sugar.
6. Place the pan on the bake position. Select Bake, set temperature to 350ºF (177ºC), and set time to 25 minutes.
7. When cooking is complete, remove the pan and check the rolls. They should be puffed up and golden brown. If the rolls in the center are not quite done, return the pan to the grill for another 3 to 5 minutes. If the outside rolls are dark golden brown before the inside rolls are done, you can remove those with a small spatula before returning the pan to the grill.
8. Let the rolls cool for a couple of minutes, then transfer them to a rack to cool completely.

Mushroom and Artichoke Frittata

Prep time: 10 minutes | Cook time: 15 minutes | Serves 6

2 tablespoons unsalted butter, melted
¼ cup chopped onion
1 cup coarsely chopped artichoke hearts (drained if canned; thawed if frozen)
8 eggs
½ teaspoon kosher salt or ¼ teaspoon
fine salt
¼ cup whole milk
¾ cup shredded Mozzarella cheese, divided
½ cup Roasted Mushrooms
¼ cup grated Parmesan cheese
¼ teaspoon freshly ground black pepper

1. Brush the baking pan with the butter. Add the onion and artichoke hearts and toss to coat with the butter.
2. Place the pan on the roast position. Select Roast, set temperature to 375ºF (191ºC), and set time to 12 minutes.
3. While the vegetables cook, whisk the eggs with the salt in a medium bowl. Let sit for a minute or two, then add the milk and whisk again. The eggs should be thoroughly mixed with no streaks of white remaining, but not foamy. Stir in ½ cup of Mozzarella cheese.
4. After the vegetables have cooked for 5 minutes, remove the pan. Spread the mushrooms over the vegetables. Pour the egg mixture over the vegetables. Stir gently just to distribute the vegetables evenly. Return the pan to the grill and resume cooking for 5 to 7 minutes, or until the edges are set. The center will still be quite liquid. (If the frittata begins to form large bubbles on the bottom, use a silicone spatula to break the bubbles and let the air out so the frittata flattens out again.)
5. Place the pan on the broil position. Select Broil, set temperature to 400ºF (204ºC), and set time to 3 minutes.
6. After 1 minute, remove the pan and sprinkle the remaining ¼ cup of Mozzarella and the Parmesan cheese over the frittata. Return the pan to the grill and continue cooking for the remaining 2 minutes.
7. When cooking is complete, the cheese should be melted, with the top completely set but not browned. Sprinkle the black pepper over the frittata.

Egg and Avocado Burrito

Prep time: 10 minutes | Cook time: 3 to 5 minutes | Serves 4

4 low-sodium whole-wheat flour tortillas
Filling:

1 hard-boiled egg, chopped
2 hard-boiled egg whites, chopped
1 ripe avocado, peeled, pitted, and chopped
1 red bell pepper, chopped

1 (1.2-ounce / 34-g) slice low-sodium, low-fat American cheese, torn into pieces
3 tablespoons low-sodium salsa, plus additional for serving (optional)

Special Equipment:
4 toothpicks (optional), soaked in water for at least 30 minutes

1. Make the filling: Combine the egg, egg whites, avocado, red bell pepper, cheese, and salsa in a medium bowl and stir until blended.
2. Assemble the burritos: Arrange the tortillas on a clean work surface and place ¼ of the prepared filling in the middle of each tortilla, leaving about 1½-inch on each end unfilled. Fold in the opposite sides of each tortilla and roll up. Secure with toothpicks through the center, if needed.
3. Transfer the burritos to the crisper tray.
4. Place the crisper tray on the air fry position. Select Air Fry, set the temperature to 390ºF (199ºC), and set the time to 5 minutes.
5. Cook for 3 to 5 minutes, or until the burritos are crisp and golden brown.
6. Allow to cool for 5 minutes and serve with salsa, if desired.

Lemon Blueberry Cake

Prep time: 8 minutes | Cook time: 10 minutes | Serves 8

1½ cups Bisquick or similar baking mix
¼ cup granulated sugar (use ⅓ cup for a sweeter cake)
¾ cup whole milk
2 large eggs
1 teaspoon vanilla extract
½ teaspoon lemon

zest (optional)
Cooking oil spray
2 cups blueberries
1 tablespoon butter, melted (optional)
½ cup syrup (optional)
2 tablespoons confectioners' sugar (optional)

1. In a medium bowl, whisk together the baking mix and sugar. In a small bowl, whisk together the milk, eggs, vanilla, and lemon zest (if using). Add the wet ingredients to the dry ingredients and stir just until combined (the mixture will be a little bit lumpy).
2. Spray the baking pan with cooking oil spray, then place a square of parchment paper in the pan. Spray the parchment with cooking oil spray. Pour the batter into the pan and spread it out evenly. (It's okay if it doesn't go all the way into the corners; it will spread.) Sprinkle the blueberries evenly over the top.
3. Place the pan on the bake position. Select Bake, set temperature to 375ºF (191ºC), and set time to 10 minutes.
4. When cooking is complete, the pan cake should be pulling away from the edges of the pan and the top should be just starting to turn golden brown.
5. If serving as pancakes, let the cake cool for a minute, then cut into 16 squares and serve with butter and syrup.
6. If serving as "muffins," brush the top of the cake with the melted butter. Let the cake cool for 3 to 4 minutes, then dust with the confectioners' sugar. Slice and serve.

Chapter 3 Appetizers and Snacks

Sesame Nut Mix

Prep time: 10 minutes | Cook time: 2 minutes | Makes 4 cups

1 tablespoon buttery spread, melted
2 teaspoons honey
¼ teaspoon cayenne pepper
2 teaspoons sesame seeds
¼ teaspoon kosher salt
¼ teaspoon freshly ground black pepper
1 cup cashews
1 cup almonds
1 cup mini pretzels
1 cup rice squares cereal
Cooking spray

1. In a large bowl, combine the buttery spread, honey, cayenne pepper, sesame seeds, kosher salt, and black pepper, then add the cashews, almonds, pretzels, and rice squares, tossing to coat.
2. Spray the baking pan with cooking spray, then pour the mixture into the pan.
3. Place the baking pan on the bake position. Select Bake, set the temperature to 360ºF (182ºC), and set the time to 2 minutes.
4. Remove the sesame mix from the grill and allow to cool in the pan on a wire rack for 5 minutes before serving.

Cajun Zucchini Chips

Prep time: 5 minutes | Cook time: 15 to 16 minutes | Serves 4

2 large zucchini, cut into ⅛-inch-thick slices
2 teaspoons Cajun seasoning
Cooking spray

1. Spray the crisper tray lightly with cooking spray.
2. Put the zucchini slices in a medium bowl and spray them generously with cooking spray.
3. Sprinkle the Cajun seasoning over the zucchini and stir to make sure they are evenly coated with oil and seasoning.
4. Place the slices in a single layer in the crisper tray, making sure not to overcrowd. You will need to cook these in several batches.
5. Place the crisper tray on the air fry position. Select Air Fry, set the temperature to 370ºF (188ºC), and set the time to 16 minutes.
6. Cook for 8 minutes. Flip the slices over and cook for an additional 7 to 8 minutes, or until they are as crisp and brown as you prefer.
7. Serve immediately.

Honey Glazed Carrots

Prep time: 10 minutes | Cook time: 10 minutes | Serves 4

6 medium carrots, peeled and cut lengthwise
1 tablespoon canola oil
2 tablespoons unsalted
butter, melted
¼ cup brown sugar, melted
¼ cup honey
⅛ teaspoon sea salt

1. In a large bowl, toss the carrots and oil until well coated.
2. Place carrots on the center of the grill plate.
3. Place the grill plate on the grill position. Select Grill, set the temperature to 450ºF (232ºC), and set the time to 10 minutes.
4. Meanwhile, in a small bowl, whisk together the butter, brown sugar, honey, and salt.
5. After 5 minutes, baste the carrots with the glaze. Using tongs, turn the carrots and baste the other side. Cook for another 5 minutes.
6. When cooking is complete, serve immediately.

Fried Green Olives

Prep time: 5 minutes | Cook time: 8 minutes | Serves 4

1 (5½-ounce / 156-g) jar pitted green olives
½ cup all-purpose flour
Salt and pepper, to
taste
½ cup bread crumbs
1 egg
Cooking spray

1. Remove the olives from the jar and dry thoroughly with paper towels.
2. In a small bowl, combine the flour with salt and pepper to taste. Place the bread crumbs in another small bowl. In a third small bowl, beat the egg.
3. Spritz the crisper tray with cooking spray.
4. Dip the olives in the flour, then the egg, and then the bread crumbs.
5. Place the breaded olives in the crisper tray. It is okay to stack them. Spray the olives with cooking spray.
6. Place the crisper tray on the air fry position. Select Air Fry, set the temperature to 400ºF (204ºC), and set the time to 8 minutes.
7. Cook for 6 minutes. Flip the olives and cook for an additional 2 minutes, or until brown and crisp.
8. Cool before serving.

Summer Squash with Red Onion

Prep time: 15 minutes | Cook time: 15 minutes | Serves 4

½ cup vegetable oil, plus 3 tablespoons
¼ cup white wine vinegar
1 garlic clove, grated
2 summer squash, sliced lengthwise about ¼-inch thick
1 red onion, peeled

and cut into wedges
Sea salt, to taste
Freshly ground black pepper, to taste
1 (8-ounce / 227-g) package crumbled feta cheese
Red pepper flakes, as needed

1. In a small bowl, whisk together ½ cup oil, vinegar, and garlic, and set aside.
2. In a large bowl, toss the squash and onion with remaining 3 tablespoons of oil until evenly coated. Season with the salt and pepper.
3. Arrange the squash and onions on the grill plate.
4. Place the grill plate on the grill position. Select Grill, set the temperature to 450ºF (232ºC), and set the time to 15 minutes.
5. After 6 minutes, flip the squash. Cook for 6 to 9 minutes more.
6. When vegetables are cooked to desired doneness, remove them from the grill. Arrange the vegetables on a large platter and top with the feta cheese. Drizzle the dressing over the top, and sprinkle with the red pepper flakes. Let stand for 15 minutes before serving.

Kale Chips

Prep time: 5 minutes | Cook time: 8 to 12 minutes | Serves 4

5 cups kale, large stems removed and chopped
2 teaspoons canola oil
¼ teaspoon smoked

paprika
¼ teaspoon kosher salt
Cooking spray

1. In a large bowl, toss the kale, canola oil, smoked paprika, and kosher salt.
2. Spray the crisper tray with cooking spray, then place half the kale in the crisper tray.
3. Place the crisper tray on the air fry position. Select Air Fry, set the temperature to 390ºF (199ºC), and set the time to 6 minutes.
4. Cook for 2 to 3 minutes. Shake the crisper tray and cook for 2 to 3 more minutes, or until crispy. Repeat this process with the remaining kale.
5. Remove the kale and allow to cool on a wire rack for 3 to 5 minutes before serving.

Lemon Green Beans

Prep time: 5 minutes | Cook time: 10 minutes | Serves 4

1 pound (454 g) haricots verts or green beans, trimmed
2 tablespoons vegetable oil
Juice of 1 lemon

Pinch red pepper flakes
Flaky sea salt, to taste
Freshly ground black pepper, to taste

1. In a medium bowl, toss the green beans in oil until evenly coated.
2. Place the green beans on the grill plate.
3. Place the grill plate on the grill position. Select Grill, set the temperature to 450ºF (232ºC), and set the time to 10 minutes.
4. Cook for 8 to 10 minutes, tossing frequently until blistered on all sides.
5. When cooking is complete, place the green beans on a large serving platter. Squeeze lemon juice over the green beans, top with red pepper flakes, and season with sea salt and black pepper.

Mozzarella Steak Fries

Prep time: 5 minutes | Cook time: 20 minutes | Serves 5

1 (28-ounce / 794-g) bag frozen steak fries
Cooking spray
Salt and pepper, to taste

½ cup beef gravy
1 cup shredded Mozzarella cheese
2 scallions, green parts only, chopped

1. Place the frozen steak fries in the crisper tray.
2. Place the crisper tray on the air fry position. Select Air Fry, set the temperature to 400ºF (204ºC), and set the time to 20 minutes.
3. Cook for 10 minutes. Shake the crisper tray and spritz the fries with cooking spray. Sprinkle with salt and pepper. Cook for an additional 8 minutes.
4. Pour the beef gravy into a medium, microwave-safe bowl. Microwave for 30 seconds, or until the gravy is warm.
5. Sprinkle the fries with the cheese. Cook for an additional 2 minutes, until the cheese is melted.
6. Transfer the fries to a serving dish. Drizzle the fries with gravy and sprinkle the scallions on top for a green garnish. Serve.

Brussels Sprouts with Bacon

Prep time: 10 minutes | Cook time: 12 minutes | Serves 4

1 pound (454 g) Brussels sprouts, trimmed and halved
2 tablespoons extra-virgin olive oil
1 teaspoon sea salt
½ teaspoon freshly ground black pepper
6 slices bacon, chopped

1. In a large bowl, toss the Brussels sprouts with the olive oil, salt, pepper, and bacon.
2. Add the Brussels sprouts to the crisper tray.
3. Place the crisper tray on the air fry position. Select Air Fry, set the temperature to 390ºF (199ºC), and set the time to 12 minutes.
4. After 6 minutes, shake the crisper tray of Brussels sprouts. Place the crisper tray back in the grill to resume cooking.
5. After 6 minutes, check for desired crispness. Continue cooking up to 2 more minutes, if necessary.

Italian Artichoke Hearts

Prep time: 5 minutes | Cook time: 8 minutes | Serves 14

14 whole artichoke hearts, packed in water
1 egg
½ cup all-purpose flour
$\frac{1}{3}$ cup panko bread crumbs
1 teaspoon Italian seasoning
Cooking spray

1. Squeeze excess water from the artichoke hearts and place them on paper towels to dry.
2. In a small bowl, beat the egg. In another small bowl, place the flour. In a third small bowl, combine the bread crumbs and Italian seasoning, and stir.
3. Spritz the crisper tray with cooking spray.
4. Dip the artichoke hearts in the flour, then the egg, and then the bread crumb mixture.
5. Place the breaded artichoke hearts in the crisper tray. Spray them with cooking spray.
6. Place the crisper tray on the air fry position. Select Air Fry, set the temperature to 380ºF (193ºC), and set the time to 8 minutes.
7. Cook for 8 minutes, or until the artichoke hearts have browned and are crisp, flipping once halfway through.
8. Let cool for 5 minutes before serving.

Grilled Shishito Peppers

Prep time: 5 minutes | Cook time: 10 minutes | Serves 4

3 cups whole shishito peppers
2 tablespoons
vegetable oil
Flaky sea salt, for garnish

1. In a medium bowl, toss the peppers in the oil until evenly coated.
2. Place the peppers on the grill plate. Gently press the peppers down to maximize grill marks.
3. Place the grill plate on the grill position. Select Grill, set the temperature to 450ºF (232ºC), and set the time to 10 minutes.
4. Cook for 8 to 10 minutes, until they are blistered on all sides.
5. When cooking is complete, place the peppers in a serving dish and top with the flaky sea salt. Serve immediately.

Heirloom Tomato BLTs

Prep time: 10 minutes | Cook time: 10 minutes | Serves 4

8 slices white bread
8 tablespoons mayonnaise
2 heirloom tomatoes, sliced ¼-inch thick
2 tablespoons canola oil
Sea salt, to taste
Freshly ground black pepper, to taste
8 slices bacon, cooked
8 leaves iceberg lettuce

1. Spread a thin layer of mayonnaise on one side of each piece of bread.
2. Place the bread, mayonnaise-side down, on the grill plate.
3. Place the grill plate on the grill position. Select Grill, set the temperature to 450ºF (232ºC), and set the time to 10 minutes.
4. Meanwhile, remove the watery pulp and seeds from the tomato slices. Brush both sides of the tomatoes with the oil and season with salt and pepper.
5. After 2 to 3 minutes, remove the bread and place the tomatoes on the grill. Continue grilling for the remaining 6 to 8 minutes.
6. To assemble, spread a thin layer of mayonnaise on the non-grilled sides of the bread. Layer the tomatoes, bacon, and lettuce on the bread, and top with the remaining slices of bread. Slice each sandwich in half and serve.

Rosemary Cashews

Prep time: 5 minutes | Cook time: 3 minutes | Makes 2 cups

2 sprigs of fresh rosemary (1 chopped and 1 whole)
1 teaspoon olive oil
1 teaspoon kosher salt
½ teaspoon honey
2 cups roasted and unsalted whole cashews
Cooking spray

1. In a medium bowl, whisk together the chopped rosemary, olive oil, kosher salt, and honey. Set aside.
2. Spray the crisper tray with cooking spray, then place the cashews and the whole rosemary sprig in the crisper tray.
3. Place the crisper tray on the bake position. Select Bake, set the temperature to 300ºF (149ºC), and set the time to 3 minutes.
4. Remove the cashews and rosemary from the grill, then discard the rosemary and add the cashews to the olive oil mixture, tossing to coat.
5. Allow to cool for 15 minutes before serving.

Crab Toasts

Prep time: 10 minutes | Cook time: 5 minutes | Makes 15 to 18 toasts

1 (6-ounce / 170-g) can flaked crab meat, well drained
3 tablespoons light mayonnaise
¼ cup shredded Parmesan cheese
¼ cup shredded Cheddar cheese
1 teaspoon Worcestershire sauce
½ teaspoon lemon juice
1 loaf artisan bread, French bread, or baguette, cut into ⅜-inch-thick slices

1. In a large bowl, stir together all the ingredients except the bread slices.
2. On a clean work surface, lay the bread slices. Spread ½ tablespoon of crab mixture onto each slice of bread.
3. Arrange the bread slices in the crisper tray in a single layer. You'll need to work in batches to avoid overcrowding.
4. Place the crisper tray on the bake position. Select Bake, set the temperature to 360ºF (182ºC), and set the time to 5 minutes.
5. Cook for 5 minutes until the tops are lightly browned.
6. Transfer to a plate and repeat with the remaining bread slices.
7. Serve warm.

Spiced Red Potatoes

Prep time: 10 minutes | Cook time: 20 minutes | Serves 4

2 pounds (907 g) baby red potatoes, quartered
2 tablespoons extra-virgin olive oil
¼ cup dried onion flakes
1 teaspoon dried rosemary
½ teaspoon onion powder
½ teaspoon garlic powder
¼ teaspoon celery powder
¼ teaspoon freshly ground black pepper
½ teaspoon dried parsley
½ teaspoon sea salt

1. Place all the ingredients in a large bowl and toss until evenly coated.
2. Add the potatoes to the crisper tray.
3. Place the crisper tray on the air fry position. Select Air Fry, set the temperature to 390ºF (199ºC), and set the time to 20 minutes.
4. After 10 minutes, shake the crisper tray well. Place the crisper tray back in the grill to resume cooking.
5. After 10 minutes, check for desired crispness. Continue cooking up to 5 minutes more, if necessary.

Balsamic Broccoli

Prep time: 10 minutes | Cook time: 10 minutes | Serves 4

4 tablespoons soy sauce
4 tablespoons balsamic vinegar
2 tablespoons canola oil
2 teaspoons maple syrup
2 heads broccoli, trimmed into florets
Red pepper flakes, for garnish
Sesame seeds, for garnish

1. In a large bowl, whisk together the soy sauce, balsamic vinegar, oil, and maple syrup. Add the broccoli and toss to coat evenly.
2. Place the broccoli on the grill plate.
3. Place the grill plate on the grill position. Select Grill, set the temperature to 450ºF (232ºC), and set the time to 10 minutes.
4. Cook for 8 to 10 minutes, until charred on all sides.
5. When cooking is complete, place the broccoli on a large serving platter. Garnish with red pepper flakes and sesame seeds. Serve immediately.

Garlic Artichokes

Prep time: 10 minutes | Cook time: 10 minutes | Serves 4

Juice of ½ lemon
½ cup canola oil
3 garlic cloves, chopped
Sea salt, to taste
Freshly ground black pepper, to taste
2 large artichokes, trimmed and halved

1. In a medium bowl, combine the lemon juice, oil, and garlic. Season with salt and pepper, then brush the artichoke halves with the lemon-garlic mixture.
2. Place the artichokes on the grill plate, cut side down. Gently press them down to maximize grill marks.
3. Place the grill plate on the grill position. Select Grill, set the temperature to 450ºF (232ºC), and set the time to 10 minutes.
4. Cook for 8 to 10 minutes, occasionally basting generously with the lemon-garlic mixture throughout cooking, until blistered on all sides.

Bruschetta with Tomato and Basil

Prep time: 5 minutes | Cook time: 6 minutes | Serves 6

4 tomatoes, diced
¹⁄₃ cup shredded fresh basil
¼ cup shredded Parmesan cheese
1 tablespoon balsamic vinegar
1 tablespoon minced garlic
1 teaspoon olive oil
1 teaspoon salt
1 teaspoon freshly ground black pepper
1 loaf French bread, cut into 1-inch-thick slices
Cooking spray

1. Mix together the tomatoes and basil in a medium bowl. Add the cheese, vinegar, garlic, olive oil, salt, and pepper and stir until well incorporated. Set aside.
2. Spritz the crisper tray with cooking spray. Working in batches, lay the bread slices in the crisper tray in a single layer. Spray the slices with cooking spray.
3. Place the crisper tray on the bake position. Select Bake, set the temperature to 250ºF (121ºC), and set the time to 3 minutes.
4. Cook for 3 minutes until golden brown.
5. Remove from the crisper tray to a plate. Repeat with the remaining bread slices.
6. Top each slice with a generous spoonful of the tomato mixture and serve.

French Fries

Prep time: 15 minutes | Cook time: 25 minutes | Serves 4

1 pound (454 g) russet or Idaho potatoes, cut in 2-inch strips
3 tablespoons canola oil

1. Place the potatoes in a large bowl and cover them with cold water. Let soak for 30 minutes. Drain well, then pat with a paper towel until very dry.
2. In the large bowl, toss the potatoes with the oil.
3. Add the potatoes to the crisper tray.
4. Place the crisper tray on the air fry position. Select Air Fry, set the temperature to 390ºF (199ºC), and set the time to 20 minutes.
5. After 10 minutes, shake the crisper tray well. Place the crisper tray back in the grill to resume cooking.
6. After 10 minutes, check for desired crispness. Continue cooking up to 5 minutes more, if necessary.
7. When cooking is complete, serve immediately with your favorite dipping sauce.

Apple Roll-Ups

Prep time: 5 minutes | Cook time: 4 to 5 minutes | Makes 8 roll-ups

8 slices whole wheat sandwich bread
4 ounces (113 g) Colby Jack cheese, grated
½ small apple, chopped
2 tablespoons butter, melted

1. Remove the crusts from the bread and flatten the slices with a rolling pin. Don't be gentle. Press hard so that bread will be very thin.
2. Top bread slices with cheese and chopped apple, dividing the ingredients evenly.
3. Roll up each slice tightly and secure each with one or two toothpicks.
4. Brush outside of rolls with melted butter.
5. Place in the crisper tray.
6. Place the crisper tray on the air fry position. Select Air Fry, set the temperature to 390ºF (199ºC), and set the time to 5 minutes.
7. Cook for 4 to 5 minutes, or until outside is crisp and nicely browned.
8. Serve hot.

Pears in Prosciutto

Prep time: 12 minutes | Cook time: 6 minutes | Serves 8

2 large ripe Anjou pears
4 thin slices Parma prosciutto (about 2 ounces / 57 g)
2 teaspoons aged balsamic vinegar

1. Peel the pears. Slice into 6 or 8 wedges (depending on the size of the pears) and cut out the core from each wedge.
2. Cut the prosciutto into long strips (one strip per pear wedge). Wrap each pear wedge with a strip of prosciutto. Place the wrapped pears in the baking pan.
3. Place the pan on the broil position. Select Broil, set temperature to 450ºF (232ºC), and set time to 6 minutes.
4. After 2 or 3 minutes, check the pears. The pears should be turned over if the prosciutto is beginning to crisp up and brown. Return the pan to the grill and continue cooking.
5. When cooking is complete, remove the pan from the grill. Serve the pears warm or at room temperature with a drizzle of the balsamic vinegar.

Cuban Sandwiches

Prep time: 20 minutes | Cook time: 8 minutes | Makes 4 sandwiches

8 slices ciabatta bread, about ¼-inch thick
Cooking spray
1 tablespoon brown mustard
Toppings:
6 to 8 ounces (170 to 227 g) thinly sliced leftover roast pork
4 ounces (113 g) thinly sliced deli turkey
1/3 cup bread and butter pickle slices
2 to 3 ounces (57 to 85 g) Pepper Jack cheese slices

1. On a clean work surface, spray one side of each slice of bread with cooking spray. Spread the other side of each slice of bread evenly with brown mustard.
2. Top 4 of the bread slices with the roast pork, turkey, pickle slices, cheese, and finish with remaining bread slices. Transfer to the crisper tray.
3. Place the crisper tray on the air fry position. Select Air Fry, set the temperature to 390ºF (199ºC), and set the time to 8 minutes.
4. Cook for 8 minutes until golden brown.
5. Cool for 5 minutes and serve warm.

Herbed Pita Chips

Prep time: 5 minutes | Cook time: 5 to 6 minutes | Serves 4

¼ teaspoon dried basil
¼ teaspoon marjoram
¼ teaspoon ground oregano
¼ teaspoon garlic powder
¼ teaspoon ground thyme
¼ teaspoon salt
2 whole 6-inch pitas, whole grain or white
Cooking spray

1. Mix all the seasonings together.
2. Cut each pita half into 4 wedges. Break apart wedges at the fold.
3. Mist one side of pita wedges with oil. Sprinkle with half of seasoning mix.
4. Turn pita wedges over, mist the other side with oil, and sprinkle with remaining seasonings.
5. Place pita wedges in crisper tray.
6. Place the crisper tray on the bake position. Select Bake, set the temperature to 330ºF (166ºC), and set the time to 6 minutes.
7. Cook for 2 minutes. Shake the crisper tray and cook for 2 minutes longer. Shake again, and if needed, cook for 1 or 2 more minutes, or until crisp. Watch carefully because at this point they will cook very quickly.
8. Serve hot.

Caramelized Peaches

Prep time: 10 minutes | Cook time: 10 to 13 minutes | Serves 4

2 tablespoons sugar
¼ teaspoon ground cinnamon
4 peaches, cut into wedges
Cooking spray

1. Lightly spray the crisper tray with cooking spray.
2. Toss the peaches with the sugar and cinnamon in a medium bowl until evenly coated.
3. Arrange the peaches in the crisper tray in a single layer. Lightly mist the peaches with cooking spray. You may need to work in batches to avoid overcrowding.
4. Place the crisper tray on the air fry position. Select Air Fry, set the temperature to 350ºF (177ºC), and set the time to 13 minutes.
5. Cook for 5 minutes. Flip the peaches and cook for another 5 to 8 minutes, or until the peaches are caramelized.
6. Repeat with the remaining peaches.
7. Let the peaches cool for 5 minutes and serve warm.

Roasted Mixed Nuts

Prep time: 5 minutes | Cook time: 20 minutes | Serves 6

2 cups mixed nuts (walnuts, pecans, and almonds)
2 tablespoons egg white

2 tablespoons sugar
1 teaspoon paprika
1 teaspoon ground cinnamon
Cooking spray

1. Spray the crisper tray with cooking spray.
2. Stir together the mixed nuts, egg white, sugar, paprika, and cinnamon in a small bowl until the nuts are fully coated.
3. Put the nuts in the crisper tray.
4. Place the crisper tray on the roast position. Select Roast, set the temperature to 300°F (149°C), and set the time to 20 minutes.
5. Shake the crisper tray halfway through the cooking time for even cooking.
6. Transfer the nuts to a bowl and serve warm.

Chile Rellenos Nachos

Prep time: 10 minutes | Cook time: 10 minutes | Serves 6

8 ounces (227 g) tortilla chips
3 cups shredded Monterey Jack cheese
2 (7-ounce / 198-g) cans chopped green chiles, drained
1 (8-ounce / 227-g) can tomato sauce

¼ teaspoon granulated garlic
¼ teaspoon dried oregano
¼ teaspoon freshly ground black pepper
Pinch cinnamon
Pinch cayenne pepper

1. Arrange the tortilla chips close together in a single layer in the baking pan. Sprinkle half of the cheese over the chips. Arrange the green chiles over the cheese as evenly as possible, then cover with the remaining cheese.
2. Place the pan on the roast position. Select Roast, set temperature to 375°F (191°C), and set time to 10 minutes.
3. After 5 minutes, rotate the pan 180 degrees and continue cooking.
4. While the nachos are cooking, stir together the tomato sauce, garlic, oregano, pepper, cinnamon, and cayenne in a small bowl.
5. When cooking is complete, the cheese will be melted and starting to crisp around the edges of the pan. Remove the pan from the grill. Drizzle a couple of tablespoons of the sauce over the nachos and serve the rest of the sauce for dipping (you can warm it up, if you like).

Prosciutto-Wrapped Asparagus

Prep time: 5 minutes | Cook time: 16 to 24 minutes | Serves 6

12 asparagus spears, woody ends trimmed
24 pieces thinly sliced

prosciutto
Cooking spray

1. Wrap each asparagus spear with 2 slices of prosciutto, then repeat this process with the remaining asparagus and prosciutto.
2. Spray the crisper tray with cooking spray, then place 2 to 3 bundles in the crisper tray.
3. Place the crisper tray on the air fry position. Select Air Fry, set the temperature to 360°F (182°C), and set the time to 4 minutes.
4. Repeat this process with the remaining asparagus bundles.
5. Remove the bundles and allow to cool on a wire rack for 5 minutes before serving.

Sausage and Mushroom Empanadas

Prep time: 5 minutes | Cook time: 12 minutes | Serves 4

½ pound (227 g) Kielbasa smoked sausage, chopped
4 chopped canned mushrooms
2 tablespoons chopped onion
½ teaspoon ground cumin

¼ teaspoon paprika
Salt and black pepper, to taste
½ package puff pastry dough, at room temperature
1 egg, beaten
Cooking spray

1. Spritz the crisper tray with cooking spray.
2. Combine the sausage, mushrooms, onion, cumin, paprika, salt, and pepper in a bowl and stir to mix well.
3. Make the empanadas: Place the puff pastry dough on a lightly floured surface. Cut circles into the dough with a glass. Place 1 tablespoon of the sausage mixture into the center of each pastry circle. Fold each in half and pinch the edges to seal. Using a fork, crimp the edges. Brush them with the beaten egg and mist with cooking spray.
4. Place the empanadas in the crisper tray.
5. Place the crisper tray on the air fry position. Select Air Fry, set the temperature to 360°F (182°C), and set the time to 12 minutes.
6. Cook for 12 minutes until golden brown. Flip the empanadas halfway through the cooking time.
7. Allow them to cool for 5 minutes and serve hot.

Deluxe Cheese Sandwiches

Prep time: 10 minutes | Cook time: 5 to 6 minutes | Serves 4 to 8

8 ounces (227 g) Brie
8 slices oat nut bread
1 large ripe pear, cored and cut into

½-inch-thick slices
2 tablespoons butter, melted

1. Make the sandwiches: Spread each of 4 slices of bread with ¼ of the Brie. Top the Brie with the pear slices and remaining 4 bread slices.
2. Brush the melted butter lightly on both sides of each sandwich.
3. Arrange the sandwiches in the baking pan. You may need to work in batches to avoid overcrowding.
4. Place the baking pan on the bake position. Select Bake, set the temperature to 360ºF (182ºC), and set the time to 6 minutes. .
5. Cook for 5 to 6 minutes until the cheese is melted. Repeat with the remaining sandwiches.
6. Serve warm.

Mini Tuna Melts

Prep time: 12 minutes | Cook time: 6 minutes | Serves 6

2 (5- to 6-ounce / 142- to 170-g) cans oil-packed tuna, drained
1 small stalk celery, chopped
1 large scallion, chopped
¹⁄₃ cup mayonnaise, or more to taste
1 tablespoon capers, drained

¼ teaspoon celery salt (optional)
1 tablespoon chopped fresh dill (optional)
12 slices cocktail rye bread
2 tablespoons butter, melted
6 slices sharp Cheddar or Swiss-style cheese (about 3 ounces / 85 g)

1. In a medium bowl, mix together the tuna, celery, scallion, mayonnaise, capers, celery salt, and dill (if using).
2. Brush one side of the bread slices with the butter. Arrange the bread slices in the baking pan, buttered-sides down. Scoop a heaping tablespoon of the tuna mixture on each slice of bread, spreading it out evenly to the edges.
3. Cut the cheese slices to fit the dimensions of the bread and place a cheese slice on each piece.

4. Place the pan on the roast position. Select Roast, set temperature to 375ºF (191ºC), and set time to 6 minutes.
5. After 4 minutes, remove the pan from the grill and check the tuna melts. They usually take at least 5 minutes, but depending on the cheese you're using and the temperature of the tuna salad, it can take anywhere from 4 to 6 minutes. The tuna melts are done when the cheese has melted and the tuna is heated through. If needed, continue cooking.
6. When cooking is complete, remove the pan from the grill. Use a spatula to transfer the tuna melts to a cutting board and slice each one in half diagonally (this will make them easier to eat). Serve warm.

Cheese and Ham Stuffed Mushrooms

Prep time: 15 minutes | Cook time: 12 minutes | Serves 8

4 ounces (113 g) Mozzarella cheese, cut into pieces
½ cup diced ham
2 green onions, chopped
2 tablespoons bread crumbs
½ teaspoon garlic powder

¼ teaspoon ground oregano
¼ teaspoon ground black pepper
1 to 2 teaspoons olive oil
16 fresh Baby Bella mushrooms, stemmed removed

1. Process the cheese, ham, green onions, bread crumbs, garlic powder, oregano, and pepper in a food processor until finely chopped.
2. With the food processor running, slowly drizzle in 1 to 2 teaspoons olive oil until a thick paste has formed. Transfer the mixture to a bowl.
3. Evenly divide the mixture into the mushroom caps and lightly press down the mixture.
4. Lay the mushrooms in the crisper tray in a single layer. You'll need to work in batches to avoid overcrowding.
5. Place the crisper tray on the roast position. Select Roast, set the temperature to 390ºF (199ºC), and set the time to 12 minutes.
6. Cook for 12 minutes until the mushrooms are lightly browned and tender.
7. Remove from the crisper tray to a plate and repeat with the remaining mushrooms.
8. Let the mushrooms cool for 5 minutes and serve warm.

Lemon-Pepper Chicken Wings

Prep time: 5 minutes | Cook time: 24 minutes | Serves 10

2 pounds (907 g) chicken wing flats and drumettes (about 16 to 20 pieces)	fine salt
	1½ teaspoons baking powder
1½ teaspoons kosher salt or ¾ teaspoon	4½ teaspoons salt-free lemon pepper seasoning

1. Place the wings in a large bowl.
2. In a small bowl, stir together the salt, baking powder, and seasoning mix. Sprinkle the mixture over the wings and toss thoroughly to coat the wings. (This works best with your hands.) If you have time, let the wings sit for 20 to 30 minutes. Place the wings in the baking pan, making sure they don't crowd each other too much.
3. Place the pan on the air fry position. Select Air Fry, set temperature to 375°F (191°C), and set time to 24 minutes.
4. After 12 minutes, remove the pan from the grill. Using tongs, turn the wings over. Rotate the pan 180 degrees and return the pan to the grill to continue cooking.
5. When cooking is complete, the wings should be dark golden brown and a bit charred in places. Remove the pan from the grill and let cool for before serving.

Sweet-and-Spicy Walnuts

Prep time: 5 minutes | Cook time: 15 minutes | Makes 4 cups

1 pound (454 g) walnut halves and pieces	pepper, or to taste
	3 tablespoons vegetable oil or walnut oil
½ cup granulated sugar	½ teaspoon fine salt, or to taste
1 teaspoon cayenne	

1. Place the nuts in a large bowl and cover with boiling water. Let them steep for a minute or two.
2. While the nuts are steeping, mix the sugar and cayenne together in a small bowl (1 teaspoon of cayenne produces nuts that are spicy but not too hot; use more or less to your taste).
3. Drain the nuts and return them to the bowl. Add the sugar mixture and oil. Stir until the sugar melts and the nuts are coated evenly. Spread the nuts in a single layer in the baking pan.

4. Place the pan on the roast position. Select Roast, set temperature to 325°F (163°C), and set time to 15 minutes.
5. After 7 or 8 minutes, remove the pan from the grill. Stir the nuts; they should be browning and fragrant. Return the pan to the grill and continue cooking, but check the nuts frequently. They can go from brown to burned pretty quickly.
6. When cooking is complete, the nuts should be dark golden brown. Remove the pan from the grill. Sprinkle the nuts with the salt and let cool. They can be frozen in an airtight container for up to 1 month.

Buttermilk Chicken Wings

Prep time: 1 hour 20 minutes | Cook time: 17 to 19 minutes | Serves 4

2 pounds (907 g) chicken wings
Marinade:

1 cup buttermilk	½ teaspoon black pepper
½ teaspoon salt	

Coating:

1 cup flour	seasoning
1 cup panko bread crumbs	2 teaspoons salt
2 tablespoons poultry	Cooking spray

1. Whisk together all the ingredients for the marinade in a large bowl.
2. Add the chicken wings to the marinade and toss well. Transfer to the refrigerator to marinate for at least an hour.
3. Spritz the crisper tray with cooking spray.
4. Thoroughly combine all the ingredients for the coating in a shallow bowl.
5. Remove the chicken wings from the marinade and shake off any excess. Roll them in the coating mixture.
6. Place the chicken wings in the crisper tray in a single layer. Mist the wings with cooking spray. You'll need to work in batches to avoid overcrowding.
7. Place the crisper tray on the air fry position. Select Air Fry, set the temperature to 360°F (182°C), and set the time to 19 minutes.
8. Cook for 17 to 19 minutes, or until the wings are crisp and golden brown on the outside. Flip the wings halfway through the cooking time.
9. Remove from the crisper tray to a plate and repeat with the remaining wings.
10. Serve hot.

Turkey Bacon-Wrapped Dates

Prep time: 10 minutes | Cook time: 5 to 7 minutes | Makes 16 appetizers

16 whole dates, pitted
16 whole almonds
6 to 8 strips turkey bacon, cut in half

Special Equipment:
16 toothpicks, soaked in water for at least 30 minutes

1. On a flat work surface, stuff each pitted date with a whole almond.
2. Wrap half slice of bacon around each date and secure it with a toothpick.
3. Place the bacon-wrapped dates in the crisper tray.
4. Place the crisper tray on the air fry position. Select Air Fry, set the temperature to 390°F (199°C), and set the time to 7 minutes.
5. Cook for 5 to 7 minutes, or until the bacon is cooked to your desired crispiness.
6. Transfer the dates to a paper towel-lined plate to drain. Serve hot.

Mushroom and Spinach Calzones

Prep time: 15 minutes | Cook time: 26 to 27 minutes | Serves 4

2 tablespoons olive oil
1 onion, chopped
2 garlic cloves, minced
¼ cup chopped mushrooms
1 pound (454 g) spinach, chopped
1 tablespoon Italian seasoning
½ teaspoon oregano
Salt and black pepper, to taste
1½ cups marinara sauce
1 cup ricotta cheese, crumbled
1 (13-ounce / 369-g) pizza crust
Cooking spray

Make the Filling:
1. Heat the olive oil in a pan over medium heat until shimmering.
2. Add the onion, garlic, and mushrooms and sauté for 4 minutes, or until softened.
3. Stir in the spinach and sauté for 2 to 3 minutes, or until the spinach is wilted. Sprinkle with the Italian seasoning, oregano, salt, and pepper and mix well.
4. Add the marinara sauce and cook for about 5 minutes, stirring occasionally, or until the sauce is thickened.
5. Remove the pan from the heat and stir in the ricotta cheese. Set aside.

Make the Calzones:
6. Spritz the crisper tray with cooking spray.

7. Roll the pizza crust out with a rolling pin on a lightly floured work surface, then cut it into 4 rectangles.
8. Spoon ¼ of the filling into each rectangle and fold in half. Crimp the edges with a fork to seal. Mist them with cooking spray.
9. Place the calzones in the crisper tray.
10. Place the crisper tray on the air fry position. Select Air Fry, set the temperature to 375°F (191°C), and set the time to 15 minutes.
11. Cook for 15 minutes, flipping once, or until the calzones are golden brown and crisp.
12. Transfer the calzones to a paper towel-lined plate and serve.

Dill Pickles

Prep time: 10 minutes | Cook time: 10 minutes | Serves 4

20 dill pickle slices
¼ cup all-purpose flour
⅛ teaspoon baking powder
3 tablespoons beer or seltzer water
⅛ teaspoon sea salt
2 tablespoons water, plus more if needed
2 tablespoons
cornstarch
1½ cups panko bread crumbs
1 teaspoon paprika
1 teaspoon garlic powder
¼ teaspoon cayenne pepper
2 tablespoons canola oil, divided

1. Pat the pickle slices dry, and place them on a dry plate in the freezer.
2. In a medium bowl, stir together the flour, baking powder, beer, salt, and water. The batter should be the consistency of cake batter. If it is too thick, add more water, 1 teaspoon at a time.
3. Place the cornstarch in a small shallow bowl.
4. In a separate large shallow bowl, combine the bread crumbs, paprika, garlic powder, and cayenne pepper.
5. Remove the pickles from the freezer. Dredge each one in cornstarch. Tap off any excess, then coat in the batter. Lastly, coat evenly with the bread crumb mixture.
6. Place the breaded pickles in the crisper tray, stacking them if necessary, and gently brush them with 1 tablespoon of oil.
7. Place the crisper tray on the air fry position. Select Air Fry, set the temperature to 360°F (182°C), and set the time to 10 minutes.
8. After 5 minutes, shake the crisper tray and gently brush the pickles with the remaining 1 tablespoon of oil. Place the crisper tray back in the grill to resume cooking.
9. When cooking is complete, serve immediately.

Cod Fingers

Prep time: 5 minutes | Cook time: 12 minutes | Serves 4

2 eggs
2 tablespoons milk
2 cups flour
1 cup cornmeal
1 teaspoon seafood seasoning

Salt and black pepper, to taste
1 cup bread crumbs
1 pound (454 g) cod fillets, cut into 1-inch strips

1. Beat the eggs with the milk in a shallow bowl. In another shallow bowl, combine the flour, cornmeal, seafood seasoning, salt, and pepper. On a plate, place the bread crumbs.
2. Dredge the cod strips, one at a time, in the flour mixture, then in the egg mixture, finally in the bread crumb to coat evenly.
3. Arrange the cod strips in the crisper tray.
4. Place the crisper tray on the air fry position. Select Air Fry, set the temperature to 400ºF (204ºC), and set the time to 12 minutes.
5. Transfer the cod strips to a paper towel-lined plate and serve warm.

Muffuletta Sliders with Olives

Prep time: 10 minutes | Cook time: 5 to 7 minutes | Makes 8 sliders

¼ pound (113 g) thinly sliced deli ham
¼ pound (113 g) thinly sliced pastrami
4 ounces (113 g) low-fat Mozzarella cheese,
Olive Mix:
½ cup sliced green olives with pimentos
¼ cup sliced black olives
¼ cup chopped kalamata olives

grated
8 slider buns, split in half
Cooking spray
1 tablespoon sesame seeds

1 teaspoon red wine vinegar
¼ teaspoon basil
⅛ teaspoon garlic powder

1. Combine all the ingredients for the olive mix in a small bowl and stir well.
2. Stir together the ham, pastrami, and cheese in a medium bowl and divide the mixture into 8 equal portions.
3. Assemble the sliders: Top each bottom bun with 1 portion of meat and cheese, 2 tablespoons of olive mix, finished by the remaining buns. Lightly spritz the tops with cooking spray. Scatter the sesame seeds on top.
4. Working in batches, arrange the sliders in the crisper tray.

5. Place the crisper tray on the bake position. Select Bake, set the temperature to 360ºF (182ºC), and set the time to 7 minutes.
6. Cook for 5 t0 7 minutes until the cheese melts.
7. Transfer to a large plate and repeat with the remaining sliders.
8. Serve immediately.

Sausage Rolls

Prep time: 15 minutes | Cook time: 15 minutes | Serves 12

1 pound (454 g) bulk breakfast sausage
½ cup finely chopped onion (about ½ medium onion)
1 garlic clove, minced or pressed
½ teaspoon dried sage (optional)
¼ teaspoon cayenne pepper

½ teaspoon dried mustard
1 large egg, beaten lightly
½ cup fresh bread crumbs
2 sheets (1 package) frozen puff pastry, thawed
All-purpose flour, for dusting

1. In a medium bowl, break up the sausage. Add the onion, garlic, sage (if using), cayenne, mustard, egg, and bread crumbs. Mix to combine. Divide the sausage mixture in half and tightly wrap each half in plastic wrap. Refrigerate for 5 to 10 minutes.
2. Lay out one of the pastry sheets on a lightly floured cutting board. Using a rolling pin, lightly roll out the pastry to smooth out the dough. Take out one of the sausage packages and form the sausage into a long roll (it's easiest to do this while the sausage is in the plastic wrap). Remove the plastic wrap and place the sausage on top of the puff pastry about 1 inch from one of the long edges. Roll the pastry around the sausage and pinch the edges of the dough together to seal. Repeat with the other pastry sheet and sausage. Slice the logs into lengths about 1½ inches long. (If you have the time, freeze the logs for 10 minutes or so before slicing; it's much easier to slice.) Place the sausage rolls in the baking pan, cut-side down.
3. Place the pan on the roast position. Select Roast, set temperature to 350ºF (177ºC), and set time to 15 minutes.
4. After 7 or 8 minutes, rotate the pan 180 degrees and continue cooking.
5. When cooking is complete, the rolls will be golden brown and sizzling. Remove the pan from the grill and let cool for 5 minutes or so. If you like, serve them with honey mustard for dipping.

Bacon-Wrapped Dates

Prep time: 10 minutes | Cook time: 10 to 14 minutes | Serves 6

12 dates, pitted
6 slices high-quality

bacon, cut in half
Cooking spray

1. Wrap each date with half a bacon slice and secure with a toothpick.
2. Spray the crisper tray with cooking spray, then place 6 bacon-wrapped dates in the crisper tray.
3. Place the crisper tray on the bake position. Select Bake, set the temperature to 360ºF (182ºC), and set the time to 7 minutes.
4. Cook for 5 to 7 minutes or until the bacon is crispy. Repeat this process with the remaining dates.
5. Remove the dates and allow to cool on a wire rack for 5 minutes before serving.

Super Cheesy Pimento Stuffed Mushrooms

Prep time: 15 minutes | Cook time: 12 minutes | Serves 12

24 medium raw white button or cremini mushrooms (about 1½ inches in diameter)
4 ounces (113 g) shredded extra-sharp Cheddar cheese
2 tablespoons grated onion
1 ounce (28 g) chopped jarred pimientos or roasted red pepper (about ¼

cup)
⅛ teaspoon smoked paprika
⅛ teaspoon hot sauce
2 ounces (57 g) cream cheese, at room temperature
2 tablespoons butter, melted, divided
2 tablespoons grated Parmesan cheese
⅓ cup panko bread crumbs

1. Wash the mushrooms and drain. Gently pull out the stems and discard (or save for another use; they make great vegetable stock). If your mushrooms are on the small side, or you feel like some extra work, you can use a small spoon or melon baller to remove some of the gills to form a larger cavity. Set aside.
2. In a medium bowl, combine the Cheddar cheese, onion, pimientos, paprika, hot sauce, and cream cheese. The mixture should be smooth with no large streaks of cream cheese visible.
3. Brush the baking pan with 1 tablespoon of melted butter. Arrange the mushrooms evenly over the pan, hollow-side up.

4. Place the cheese mixture into a large heavy plastic bag and cut off the end. Fill the mushrooms with the cheese mixture.
5. In a small bowl, stir together the Parmesan, panko, and remaining 1 tablespoon of melted butter. Sprinkle a little of the panko mixture over each mushroom (or carefully dip the filled tops of the mushrooms into the mixture to coat).
6. Place the pan on the roast position. Select Roast, set temperature to 350ºF (177ºC), and set time to 18 minutes.
7. After about 9 minutes, rotate the pan 180 degrees and continue cooking.
8. When cooking is complete, let the stuffed mushrooms cool slightly before serving.

Jalapeño Poppers

Prep time: 10 minutes | Cook time: 15 minutes | Serves 8

12 large jalapeño peppers (about 3 inches long)
6 ounces (170 g) cream cheese, at room temperature
1 teaspoon chili powder
4 ounces (113 g)

shredded Cheddar cheese
2 slices cooked bacon, chopped fine
¼ cup panko bread crumbs
1 tablespoon butter, melted

1. If the jalapeños have stems, cut them off flush with the tops of the chiles. Slice the jalapeños in half lengthwise and scoop out the seeds. For milder poppers, remove the white membranes (the ribs). (You should probably wear latex gloves when you do this, to avoid possible burns. I often forget, and I often regret it.)
2. In a medium bowl, mix the cream cheese, chili powder, and Cheddar cheese. Spoon the cheese mixture into the jalapeño halves and place them in the baking pan. If the jalapeños roll or tip, use a vegetable peeler to scrape away a thin layer of skin on the base so they're more stable.
3. In a small bowl, stir together the bacon, panko, and butter. Top each of the jalapeño halves with the panko mixture.
4. Place the pan on the roast position. Select Roast, set temperature to 375ºF (191ºC), and set time to 15 minutes.
5. After 7 or 8 minutes, rotate the pan 180 degrees and continue cooking until the peppers have softened somewhat, the filling is bubbling, and the panko is browned.
6. When cooking is complete, remove the pan from the grill. Let the poppers cool for a few minutes before serving.

Zucchini and Potato Tots

Prep time: 5 minutes | Cook time: 20 minutes | Serves 4

1 large zucchini, grated
1 medium baked potato, skin removed and mashed
¼ cup shredded Cheddar cheese
1 large egg, beaten
½ teaspoon kosher salt
Cooking spray

1. Wrap the grated zucchini in a paper towel and squeeze out any excess liquid, then combine the zucchini, baked potato, shredded Cheddar cheese, egg, and kosher salt in a large bowl.
2. Spray the baking pan with cooking spray, then place individual tablespoons of the zucchini mixture in the pan.
3. Place the baking pan on the air fry position. Select Air Fry, set the temperature to 390ºF (199ºC), and set the time to 10 minutes.
4. Repeat this process with the remaining mixture.
5. Remove the tots and allow to cool on a wire rack for 5 minutes before serving.

Oyster Cracker and Cereal Snack Mix

Prep time: 10 minutes | Cook time: 6 minutes | Makes 6 cups

2 cups oyster crackers
2 cups Chex-style cereal (rice, corn, or wheat, or a combination)
1 cup sesame sticks
8 tablespoons unsalted butter, melted
²/₃ cup finely grated Parmesan cheese
1½ teaspoon granulated garlic
½ teaspoon kosher salt or ¼ teaspoon fine salt

1. Place the oyster crackers in a large bowl. Add the cereal and sesame sticks. Drizzle with the butter and sprinkle on the cheese, garlic, and salt. Toss to coat. Place the mix in the baking pan in an even layer.
2. Place the pan on the roast position. Select Roast, set temperature to 350ºF (177ºC), and set time to 6 minutes.
3. About halfway through cooking, remove the pan and stir the mixture. Return the pan to the grill and continue cooking.
4. When cooking is complete, the mix should be lightly browned and fragrant. Let cool. The mixture can be stored at room temperature in an airtight container for 3 to 4 days.

Baked Mini Potatoes

Prep time: 15 minutes | Cook time: 20 minutes | Serves 6

12 small red or yellow potatoes, about 2 inches in diameter, depending on size
1 teaspoon kosher salt or ½ teaspoon fine salt, divided
1 tablespoon extra-virgin olive oil
¼ cup grated sharp Cheddar cheese
¼ cup sour cream
2 tablespoons chopped chives
2 tablespoons grated Parmesan cheese

1. Place the potatoes in a large bowl. Sprinkle with the kosher salt and drizzle with the olive oil. Toss to coat. Place the potatoes in the baking pan. Wipe out the bowl and set aside.
2. Place the pan on the roast position. Select Roast, set temperature to 375ºF (191ºC), and set time to 15 minutes.
3. After 10 minutes, rotate the pan 180 degrees and continue cooking.
4. When cooking is complete, check the potatoes. A sharp knife should pierce the flesh easily; if not, cook for a few more minutes. Remove the pan and let the potatoes cool until you can handle them. Halve the potatoes lengthwise. If needed, cut a small slice from the uncut side for stability. Using a small melon baller or spoon, scoop the flesh into the bowl, leaving a thin shell of skin. Place the potato halves in the baking pan.
5. Mash the scooped-out potatoes until smooth. Add the remaining ½ teaspoon of salt, Cheddar cheese, sour cream, and chives and mix until well combined. Taste and adjust the salt, if needed. Spoon the filling into a pastry bag or heavy plastic bag with one corner snipped off. Pipe the filling into the potato shells, mounding up slightly. Sprinkle with the Parmesan cheese.
6. Place the pan on the roast position. Select Roast, set temperature to 375ºF (191ºC), and set time to 5 minutes.
7. When cooking is complete, the tops should be browning slightly. If necessary, cook for a couple of minutes longer. Remove the pan from the grill and let the potatoes cool slightly before serving.

Chapter 4 Vegan and Vegetarian

Black Bean-Tomato Chili

Prep time: 15 minutes | Cook time: 23 minutes | Serves 6

1 tablespoon olive oil
1 medium onion, diced
3 garlic cloves, minced
1 cup vegetable broth
3 cans black beans, drained and rinsed
2 cans diced tomatoes
2 chipotle peppers, chopped
2 teaspoons cumin
2 teaspoons chili powder
1 teaspoon dried oregano
½ teaspoon salt

1. Over a medium heat, fry the garlic and onions in the olive oil for 3 minutes.
2. Add the remaining ingredients, stirring constantly and scraping the bottom to prevent sticking.
3. Take the baking pan and place the mixture inside. Put a sheet of aluminum foil on top.
4. Place the baking pan on the bake position. Select Bake, set the temperature to 400ºF (204ºC), and set the time to 20 minutes.
5. When ready, plate up and serve immediately.

Cheesy Creamed Spinach

Prep time: 10 minutes | Cook time: 15 minutes | Serves 4

Vegetable oil spray
1 (10-ounce / 283-g) package frozen spinach, thawed and squeezed dry
½ cup chopped onion
2 cloves garlic, minced
4 ounces (113 g) cream cheese, diced
½ teaspoon ground nutmeg
1 teaspoon kosher salt
1 teaspoon black pepper
½ cup grated Parmesan cheese

1. Spray the baking pan with vegetable oil spray.
2. In a medium bowl, combine the spinach, onion, garlic, cream cheese, nutmeg, salt, and pepper. Transfer to the prepared pan.
3. Place the baking pan on the bake position. Select Bake, set the temperature to 350ºF (177ºC), and set the time to 15 minutes.
4. Cook for 10 minutes. Open and stir to thoroughly combine the cream cheese and spinach.
5. Sprinkle the Parmesan cheese on top. Cook for 5 minutes, or until the cheese has melted and browned.
6. Serve hot.

Hearty Roasted Veggie Salad

Prep time: 5 minutes | Cook time: 20 minutes | Serves 2

1 potato, chopped
1 carrot, sliced diagonally
1 cup cherry tomatoes
½ small beetroot, sliced
¼ onion, sliced
½ teaspoon turmeric
½ teaspoon cumin
¼ teaspoon sea salt
2 tablespoons olive oil, divided
A handful of arugula
A handful of baby spinach
Juice of 1 lemon
3 tablespoons canned chickpeas, for serving
Parmesan shavings, for serving

1. Combine the potato, carrot, cherry tomatoes, beetroot, onion, turmeric, cumin, salt, and 1 tablespoon of olive oil in a large bowl and toss until well coated.
2. Arrange the veggies in the crisper tray.
3. Place the crisper tray on the roast position. Select Roast, set the temperature to 370ºF (188ºC), and set the time to 20 minutes.
4. Cook for 20 minutes, shaking the crisper tray halfway through.
5. Let the veggies cool for 5 to 10 minutes in the crisper tray.
6. Put the arugula, baby spinach, lemon juice, and remaining 1 tablespoon of olive oil in a salad bowl and stir to combine. Mix in the roasted veggies and toss well.
7. Scatter the chickpeas and Parmesan shavings on top and serve immediately.

Honey-Glazed Baby Carrots

Prep time: 5 minutes | Cook time: 12 minutes | Serves 4

1 pound (454 g) baby carrots
2 tablespoons olive oil
1 tablespoon honey
1 teaspoon dried dill
Salt and black pepper, to taste

1. Place the carrots in a large bowl. Add the olive oil, honey, dill, salt, and pepper and toss to coat well.
2. Arrange the carrots in the crisper tray.
3. Place the crisper tray on the roast position. Select Roast, set the temperature to 350ºF (177ºC), and set the time to 12 minutes.
4. Cook for 12 minutes, until crisp-tender. Shake the crisper tray once during cooking.
5. Serve warm.

Baked Italian Herb Tofu

Prep time: 5 minutes | Cook time: 10 minutes | Serves 2

1 tablespoon soy sauce
1 tablespoon water
1/3 teaspoon garlic powder
1/3 teaspoon onion powder
1/3 teaspoon dried oregano
1/3 teaspoon dried basil
Black pepper, to taste
6 ounces (170 g) extra firm tofu, pressed and cubed

1. In a large mixing bowl, whisk together the soy sauce, water, garlic powder, onion powder, oregano, basil, and black pepper. Add the tofu cubes, stirring to coat, and let them marinate for 10 minutes.
2. Arrange the tofu in the baking pan.
3. Place the baking pan on the bake position. Select Bake, set the temperature to 390°F (199°C), and set the time to 10 minutes.
4. Cook for 10 minutes until crisp. Flip the tofu halfway through the cooking time.
5. Remove from the crisper tray to a plate and serve.

Sesame Maitake Mushrooms

Prep time: 5 minutes | Cook time: 15 minutes | Serves 2

1 tablespoon soy sauce
2 teaspoons toasted sesame oil
3 teaspoons vegetable oil, divided
1 garlic clove, minced
7 ounces (198 g) maitake (hen of the woods) mushrooms
1/2 teaspoon flaky sea salt
1/2 teaspoon sesame seeds
1/2 teaspoon finely chopped fresh thyme leaves

1. Whisk together the soy sauce, sesame oil, 1 teaspoon of vegetable oil, and garlic in a small bowl.
2. Arrange the mushrooms in the crisper tray in a single layer. Drizzle the soy sauce mixture over the mushrooms.
3. Place the crisper tray on the roast position. Select Roast, set the temperature to 300°F (149°C), and set the time to 15 minutes.
4. Cook for 10 minutes. Flip the mushrooms and sprinkle the sea salt, sesame seeds, and thyme leaves on top. Drizzle the remaining 2 teaspoons of vegetable oil all over. Cook for an additional 5 minutes.
5. Remove the mushrooms from the crisper tray to a plate and serve hot.

Rosemary Roasted Squash with Cheese

Prep time: 5 minutes | Cook time: 20 minutes | Serves 2

1 pound (454 g) butternut squash, cut into wedges
2 tablespoons olive oil
1 tablespoon dried rosemary
Salt, to salt
1 cup crumbled goat cheese
1 tablespoon maple syrup

1. Toss the squash wedges with the olive oil, rosemary, and salt in a large bowl until well coated.
2. Transfer the squash wedges to the crisper tray, spreading them out in as even a layer as possible.
3. Place the crisper tray on the roast position. Select Roast, set the temperature to 350°F (177°C), and set the time to 20 minutes.
4. Cook for 10 minutes. Flip the squash and cook for another 10 minutes until golden brown.
5. Sprinkle the goat cheese on top and serve drizzled with the maple syrup.

Asian-Inspired Broccoli

Prep time: 5 minutes | Cook time: 10 minutes | Serves 2

12 ounces (340 g) broccoli florets
2 tablespoons Asian hot chili oil
1 teaspoon ground Sichuan peppercorns (or black pepper)
2 garlic cloves, finely chopped
1 (2-inch) piece fresh ginger, peeled and finely chopped
Kosher salt and freshly ground black pepper

1. Toss the broccoli florets with the chili oil, Sichuan peppercorns, garlic, ginger, salt, and pepper in a mixing bowl until thoroughly coated.
2. Transfer the broccoli florets to the crisper tray.
3. Place the crisper tray on the roast position. Select Roast, set the temperature to 375°F (191°C), and set the time to 10 minutes.
4. Cook for 10 minutes, shaking the crisper tray halfway through, or until the broccoli florets are lightly browned and tender.
5. Remove the broccoli from the crisper tray and serve on a plate.

Cashew Stuffed Mushrooms

Prep time: 10 minutes | Cook time: 15 minutes | Serves 6

1 cup basil
½ cup cashew, soaked overnight
½ cup nutritional yeast
1 tablespoon lemon juice
2 cloves garlic
1 tablespoon olive oil
Salt, to taste
1 pound (454 g) baby bella mushroom, stems removed

1. Prepare the pesto. In a food processor, blend the basil, cashew nuts, nutritional yeast, lemon juice, garlic and olive oil to combine well. Sprinkle with salt, as desired.
2. Turn the mushrooms cap-side down and spread the pesto on the underside of each cap.
3. Transfer to the crisper tray.
4. Place the crisper tray on the air fry position. Select Air Fry, set the temperature to 400°F (204°C), and set the time to 15 minutes.
5. Serve warm.

Rice and Olives Stuffed Peppers

Prep time: 5 minutes | Cook time: 16 to 17 minutes | Serves 4

4 red bell peppers, tops sliced off
2 cups cooked rice
1 cup crumbled feta cheese
1 onion, chopped
¼ cup sliced kalamata olives
¾ cup tomato sauce
1 tablespoon Greek seasoning
Salt and black pepper, to taste
2 tablespoons chopped fresh dill, for serving

1. Microwave the red bell peppers for 1 to 2 minutes until tender.
2. When ready, transfer the red bell peppers to a plate to cool.
3. Mix together the cooked rice, feta cheese, onion, kalamata olives, tomato sauce, Greek seasoning, salt, and pepper in a medium bowl and stir until well combined.
4. Divide the rice mixture among the red bell peppers and transfer to the greased baking pan.
5. Place the baking pan on the bake position. Select Bake, set the temperature to 360°F (182°C), and set the time to 15 minutes.
6. Cook for 15 minutes, or until the rice is heated through and the vegetables are soft.
7. Remove from the crisper tray and serve with the dill sprinkled on top.

Ratatouille

Prep time: 15 minutes | Cook time: 16 minutes | Serves 2

2 Roma tomatoes, thinly sliced
1 zucchini, thinly sliced
2 yellow bell peppers, sliced
2 garlic cloves, minced
2 tablespoons olive oil
2 tablespoons herbes de Provence
1 tablespoon vinegar
Salt and black pepper, to taste

1. Place the tomatoes, zucchini, bell peppers, garlic, olive oil, herbes de Provence, and vinegar in a large bowl and toss until the vegetables are evenly coated. Sprinkle with salt and pepper and toss again. Pour the vegetable mixture into the pan.
2. Place the baking pan on the roast position. Select Roast, set the temperature to 390°F (199°C), and set the time to 16 minutes.
3. Cook for 8 minutes. Stir and continue cooking for 8 minutes until tender.
4. Let the vegetable mixture stand for 5 minutes before removing and serving.

Mozzarella Eggplant Stacks

Prep time: 10 minutes | Cook time: 14 minutes | Serves 4

1 eggplant, sliced ¼-inch thick
2 tablespoons canola oil
2 beefsteak or heirloom tomatoes, sliced ¼-inch thick
12 large basil leaves
½ pound (227 g) buffalo Mozzarella, sliced ¼-inch thick
Sea salt, to taste

1. In a large bowl, toss the eggplant and oil until evenly coated.
2. Place the eggplant on the grill plate.
3. Place the grill plate on the grill position. Select Grill, set the temperature to 450°F (232°C), and set the time to 14 minutes.
4. After 8 to 12 minutes, top the eggplant with one slice each of tomato and Mozzarella. Cook for 2 minutes, until the cheese melts.
5. When cooking is complete, remove the eggplant stacks from the grill. Place 2 or 3 basil leaves on top of half of the stacks. Place the remaining eggplant stacks on top of those with basil so that there are four stacks total. Season with salt, garnish with the remaining basil, and serve.

Cauliflower Rice with Turmeric Tofu

Prep time: 10 minutes | Cook time: 22 minutes | Serves 4

½ block tofu, crumbled
1 cup diced carrot
½ cup diced onions
Cauliflower:
3 cups cauliflower rice
½ cup chopped broccoli
½ cup frozen peas
2 tablespoons soy sauce
1 tablespoon minced

2 tablespoons soy sauce
1 teaspoon turmeric

ginger
2 garlic cloves, minced
1 tablespoon rice vinegar
1½ teaspoons toasted sesame oil

1. Mix together the tofu, carrot, onions, soy sauce, and turmeric in the baking pan and stir until well incorporated.
2. Place the baking pan on the roast position. Select Roast, set the temperature to 370ºF (188ºC), and set the time to 22 minutes.
3. Meanwhile, in a large bowl, combine all the ingredients for the cauliflower and toss well.
4. After 10 minutes, remove the pan and add the cauliflower mixture to the tofu and stir to combine.
5. Return the pan to the grill and continue cooking for 12 minutes, or until the vegetables are cooked to your preference.
6. Cool for 5 minutes before serving.

Balsamic Mushroom Sliders with Pesto

Prep time: 10 minutes | Cook time: 8 minutes | Serves 4

8 small portobello mushrooms, trimmed with gills removed
2 tablespoons canola oil
2 tablespoons

balsamic vinegar
8 slider buns
1 tomato, sliced
½ cup pesto
½ cup micro greens

1. Brush the mushrooms with the oil and balsamic vinegar.
2. Place the mushrooms, gill-side down, on the grill plate.
3. Place the grill plate on the grill position. Select Grill, set the temperature to 400ºF (204ºC), and set the time to 8 minutes.
4. Cook for 8 minutes until the mushrooms are tender.
5. When cooking is complete, remove the mushrooms from the grill, and layer on the buns with tomato, pesto, and micro greens.

Broccoli and Arugula Salad

Prep time: 10 minutes | Cook time: 12 minutes | Serves 4

2 heads broccoli, trimmed into florets
½ red onion, sliced
1 tablespoon canola oil
2 tablespoons extra-virgin olive oil
1 tablespoon freshly squeezed lemon juice
1 teaspoon honey
1 teaspoon Dijon

mustard
1 garlic clove, minced
Pinch red pepper flakes
¼ teaspoon fine sea salt
Freshly ground black pepper, to taste
4 cups arugula, torn
2 tablespoons grated Parmesan cheese

1. In a large bowl, combine the broccoli, sliced onions, and canola oil and toss until coated.
2. Place the vegetables on the grill plate.
3. Place the grill plate on the grill position. Select Grill, set the temperature to 450ºF (232ºC), and set the time to 12 minutes.
4. Cook for 8 to 12 minutes, until charred on all sides.
5. Meanwhile, in a medium bowl, whisk together the olive oil, lemon juice, honey, mustard, garlic, red pepper flakes, salt, and pepper.
6. When cooking is complete, combine the roasted vegetables and arugula in a large serving bowl. Drizzle with the vinaigrette, and sprinkle with the Parmesan cheese.

Potatoes with Zucchinis

Prep time: 10 minutes | Cook time: 45 minutes | Serves 4

2 potatoes, peeled and cubed
4 carrots, cut into chunks
1 head broccoli, cut into florets
4 zucchinis, sliced

thickly
Salt and ground black pepper, to taste
¼ cup olive oil
1 tablespoon dry onion powder

1. In the baking pan, add all the ingredients and combine well.
2. Place the baking pan on the bake position. Select Bake, set the temperature to 400ºF (204ºC), and set the time to 45 minutes.
3. Cook for 45 minutes, ensuring the vegetables are soft and the sides have browned before serving.

Vegetarian Meatballs

Prep time: 15 minutes | Cook time: 18 minutes | Serves 3

½ cup grated carrots
½ cup sweet onions
2 tablespoons olive oil
1 cup rolled oats
½ cup roasted cashews
2 cups cooked chickpeas

Juice of 1 lemon
2 tablespoons soy sauce
1 tablespoon flax meal
1 teaspoon garlic powder
1 teaspoon cumin
½ teaspoon turmeric

1. Mix together the carrots, onions, and olive oil in the pan and stir to combine.
2. Place the baking pan on the roast position. Select Roast, set the temperature to 350ºF (177ºC), and set the time to 6 minutes.
3. Meanwhile, put the oats and cashews in a food processor or blender and pulse until coarsely ground. Transfer the mixture to a large bowl. Add the chickpeas, lemon juice, and soy sauce to the food processor and pulse until smooth. Transfer the chickpea mixture to the bowl of oat and cashew mixture.
4. Remove the carrots and onions from the pan to the bowl of chickpea mixture. Add the flax meal, garlic powder, cumin, and turmeric and stir to incorporate.
5. Scoop tablespoon-sized portions of the veggie mixture and roll them into balls with your hands. Transfer the balls to the crisper tray in a single layer.
6. Increase the temperature to 370ºF (188ºC) and bake for 12 minutes until golden through. Flip the balls halfway through the cooking time.
7. Serve warm.

Zucchini and Summer Squash Salad

Prep time: 10 minutes | Cook time: 20 minutes | Serves 4

1 zucchini, sliced lengthwise about ¼-inch thick
1 summer squash, sliced lengthwise about ¼-inch thick
½ red onion, sliced
4 tablespoons canola oil, divided
2 portobello

mushroom caps, trimmed with gills removed
2 ears corn, shucked
2 teaspoons freshly squeezed lemon juice
Sea salt, to taste
Freshly ground black pepper, to taste

1. In a large bowl, toss the zucchini, squash, and onion with 2 tablespoons of oil until evenly coated.
2. Arrange the zucchini, squash, and onions on the grill plate.
3. Place the grill plate on the grill position. Select Grill, set the temperature to 450ºF (232ºC), and set the time to 15 minutes.
4. After 6 minutes, flip the squash. Cook for 6 to 9 minutes more.
5. Meanwhile, brush the mushrooms and corn with the remaining 2 tablespoons of oil.
6. When cooking is complete, remove the zucchini, squash, and onions and swap in the mushrooms and corn. Grill for another 10 minutes.
7. When cooking is complete, remove the mushrooms and corn, and let cool.
8. Cut the kernels from the cobs. Roughly chop all the vegetables into bite-size pieces.
9. Place the vegetables in a serving bowl and drizzle with lemon juice. Season with salt and pepper, and toss until evenly mixed.

Vegetable and Cheese Stuffed Tomatoes

Prep time: 10 minutes | Cook time: 16 to 20 minutes | Serves 4

4 medium beefsteak tomatoes, rinsed
½ cup grated carrot
1 medium onion, chopped
1 garlic clove, minced

2 teaspoons olive oil
2 cups fresh baby spinach
¼ cup crumbled low-sodium feta cheese
½ teaspoon dried basil

1. On your cutting board, cut a thin slice off the top of each tomato. Scoop out a ¼- to ½-inch-thick tomato pulp and place the tomatoes upside down on paper towels to drain. Set aside.
2. Stir together the carrot, onion, garlic, and olive oil in the baking pan.
3. Place the baking pan on the bake position. Select Bake, set the temperature to 350ºF (177ºC), and set the time to 20 minutes.
4. Cook for 4 to 6 minutes, or until the carrot is crisp-tender.
5. Remove the pan from the grill and stir in the spinach, feta cheese, and basil.
6. Spoon ¼ of the vegetable mixture into each tomato and transfer the stuffed tomatoes to the pan.
7. Continue to cook for 12 to 14 minutes, or until the filling is hot and the tomatoes are lightly caramelized.
8. Let the tomatoes cool for 5 minutes and serve.

Black Bean and Corn Stuffed Peppers

Prep time: 15 minutes | Cook time: 32 minutes | Serves 6

6 red or green bell peppers, seeded, ribs removed, and top ½-inch cut off and reserved	enchilada sauce ½ teaspoon chili powder ¼ teaspoon ground cumin
4 garlic cloves, minced 1 small white onion, diced	½ cup canned black beans, rinsed and drained
2 (8½-ounce / 241-g) bags instant rice, cooked in microwave	½ cup frozen corn ½ cup vegetable stock 1 (8-ounce / 227-g) bag shredded Colby Jack cheese, divided
1 (10-ounce / 284-g) can red or green	

1. Chop the ½-inch portions of reserved bell pepper and place in a large mixing bowl. Add the garlic, onion, cooked instant rice, enchilada sauce, chili powder, cumin, black beans, corn, vegetable stock, and half the cheese. Mix to combine.
2. Spoon the mixture into the peppers, filling them up as full as possible. If necessary, lightly press the mixture down into the peppers to fit more in.
3. Place the peppers, upright, in the pan.
4. Place the baking pan on the roast position. Select Roast, set the temperature to 350ºF (177ºC), and set the time to 32 minutes.
5. After 30 minutes, sprinkle the remaining cheese over the top of the peppers. Cook for the remaining 2 minutes.
6. When cooking is complete, serve immediately.

Potato Corn Chowder

Prep time: 15 minutes | Cook time: 50 minutes | Serves 4

4 ears corn, shucked 2 tablespoons canola oil 1½ teaspoons sea salt, plus additional to season the corn ½ teaspoon freshly ground black pepper, plus additional to season the corn 3 tablespoons unsalted	butter 1 small onion, finely chopped 2½ cups vegetable broth 1½ cups milk 4 cups diced potatoes 2 cups half-and-half 1½ teaspoons chopped fresh thyme

1. Brush each ear of corn with ½ tablespoon of oil. Season the corn with salt and pepper to taste.
2. Place the corn on the grill plate.
3. Place the grill plate on the grill position. Select Grill, set the temperature to 450ºF (232ºC), and set the time to 12 minutes.
4. After 6 minutes, flip the corn. Continue cooking for the remaining 6 minutes.
5. When cooking is complete, remove the corn and let cool. Cut the kernels from the cobs.
6. In a food processor, purée 1 cup of corn kernels until smooth.
7. In a large pan over medium-high heat, melt the butter. Add the onion and sauté until soft, 5 to 7 minutes. Add the broth, milk, and potatoes. Bring to a simmer and cook until the potatoes are just tender, 10 to 12 minutes. Stir in the salt and pepper.
8. Stir in the puréed corn, remaining corn kernels, and half-and-half. Bring to a simmer and cook, stirring occasionally, until the potatoes are cooked through, for 15 to 20 minutes.
9. Using a potato masher or immersion blender, slightly mash some of the potatoes. Stir in the thyme, and additional salt and pepper to taste.

Kidney Beans Oatmeal in Peppers

Prep time: 15 minutes | Cook time: 6 minutes | Serves 2 to 4

2 large bell peppers, halved lengthwise, deseeded 2 tablespoons cooked kidney beans 2 tablespoons cooked chickpeas 2 cups cooked oatmeal	1 teaspoon ground cumin ½ teaspoon paprika ½ teaspoon salt or to taste ¼ teaspoon black pepper powder ¼ cup yogurt

1. Put the bell peppers, cut-side down, in the crisper tray.
2. Place the crisper tray on the air fry position. Select Air Fry, set the temperature to 355ºF (179ºC), and set the time to 6 minutes.
3. Cook for 2 minutes. Take the peppers out of the grill and let cool.
4. In a bowl, combine the rest of the ingredients.
5. Divide the mixture evenly and use each portion to stuff a pepper.
6. Return the stuffed peppers to the crisper tray. Continue to cook for 4 minutes.
7. Serve hot.

Cauliflower Roast

Prep time: 15 minutes | Cook time: 20 minutes | Serves 4

Cauliflower:

5 cups cauliflower florets	cumin
3 tablespoons vegetable oil	½ teaspoon ground coriander
½ teaspoon ground	½ teaspoon kosher salt

Sauce:

½ cup Greek yogurt or sour cream	chopped
¼ cup chopped fresh cilantro	4 cloves garlic, peeled
	½ teaspoon kosher salt
1 jalapeño, coarsely	2 tablespoons water

1. In a large bowl, combine the cauliflower, oil, cumin, coriander, and salt. Toss to coat.
2. Put the cauliflower in the crisper tray.
3. Place the crisper tray on the roast position. Select Roast, set the temperature to 400ºF (204ºC), and set the time to 20 minutes.
4. Cook for 20 minutes, stirring halfway through the roasting time.
5. Meanwhile, in a blender, combine the yogurt, cilantro, jalapeño, garlic, and salt. Blend, adding the water as needed to keep the blades moving and to thin the sauce.
6. At the end of roasting time, transfer the cauliflower to a large serving bowl. Pour the sauce over and toss gently to coat. Serve immediately.

Honey-Glazed Roasted Veggies

Prep time: 15 minutes | Cook time: 20 minutes | Makes 3 cups

Glaze:

2 tablespoons raw honey	⅛ teaspoon dried sage
2 teaspoons minced garlic	⅛ teaspoon dried rosemary
¼ teaspoon dried marjoram	⅛ teaspoon dried thyme
¼ teaspoon dried basil	½ teaspoon salt
¼ teaspoon dried oregano	¼ teaspoon ground black pepper

Veggies:

3 to 4 medium red potatoes, cut into 1- to 2-inch pieces	into ¼-inch rounds
	1 (10.5-ounce / 298-g) package cherry tomatoes, halved
1 small zucchini, cut into 1- to 2-inch pieces	1 cup sliced mushrooms
1 small carrot, sliced	3 tablespoons olive oil

1. Combine the honey, garlic, marjoram, basil, oregano, sage, rosemary, thyme, salt, and pepper in a small bowl and stir to mix well. Set aside.
2. Place the red potatoes, zucchini, carrot, cherry tomatoes, and mushroom in a large bowl. Drizzle with the olive oil and toss to coat.
3. Pour the veggies into the crisper tray.
4. Place the crisper tray on the roast position. Select Roast, set the temperature to 380ºF (193ºC), and set the time to 15 minutes.
5. Cook for 15 minutes, shaking the crisper tray halfway through.
6. When ready, transfer the roasted veggies to the large bowl. Pour the honey mixture over the veggies, tossing to coat.
7. Spread out the veggies in the baking pan and place in the grill.
8. Increase the temperature to 390ºF (199ºC) and roast for an additional 5 minutes, or until the veggies are tender and glazed. Serve warm.

Mascarpone Mushrooms

Prep time: 10 minutes | Cook time: 15 minutes | Serves 4

Vegetable oil spray	thyme
4 cups sliced mushrooms	1 teaspoon kosher salt
1 medium yellow onion, chopped	1 teaspoon black pepper
2 cloves garlic, minced	½ teaspoon red pepper flakes
¼ cup heavy whipping cream or half-and-half	4 cups cooked konjac noodles, for serving
8 ounces (227 g) mascarpone cheese	½ cup grated Parmesan cheese
1 teaspoon dried	

1. Spray the baking pan with vegetable oil spray.
2. In a medium bowl, combine the mushrooms, onion, garlic, cream, mascarpone, thyme, salt, black pepper, and red pepper flakes. Stir to combine. Transfer the mixture to the prepared pan.
3. Place the baking pan on the bake position. Select Bake, set the temperature to 350ºF (177ºC), and set the time to 15 minutes.
4. Cook for 15 minutes, stirring halfway through the baking time.
5. Divide the pasta among four shallow bowls. Spoon the mushroom mixture evenly over the pasta. Sprinkle with Parmesan cheese and serve.

Cauliflower Steaks with Ranch Dressing

Prep time: 10 minutes | Cook time: 15 minutes | Serves 2

1 head cauliflower, stemmed and leaves removed
¼ cup canola oil
½ teaspoon garlic powder
½ teaspoon paprika
Sea salt, to taste
Freshly ground black pepper, to taste
1 cup shredded Cheddar cheese
Ranch dressing, for garnish
4 slices bacon, cooked and crumbled
2 tablespoons chopped fresh chives

1. Cut the cauliflower from top to bottom into two 2-inch "steaks"; reserve the remaining cauliflower to cook separately.
2. In a small bowl, whisk together the oil, garlic powder, and paprika. Season with salt and pepper. Brush each steak with the oil mixture on both sides.
3. Place the steaks on the grill plate.
4. Place the grill plate on the grill position. Select Grill, set the temperature to 450ºF (232ºC), and set the time to 15 minutes.
5. After 10 minutes, flip the steaks and top each with ½ cup of cheese. Continue to cook until the cheese is melted, about 5 minutes.
6. When cooking is complete, place the cauliflower steaks on a plate and drizzle with the ranch dressing. Top with the bacon and chives.

Chermoula Beet Roast

Prep time: 15 minutes | Cook time: 25 minutes | Serves 4

Chermoula:
1 cup packed fresh cilantro leaves
½ cup packed fresh parsley leaves
6 cloves garlic, peeled
2 teaspoons smoked paprika
2 teaspoons ground cumin
1 teaspoon ground coriander
½ to 1 teaspoon cayenne pepper
Pinch of crushed saffron (optional)
½ cup extra-virgin olive oil
Kosher salt, to taste
Beets:
3 medium beets, trimmed, peeled, and cut into 1-inch chunks
2 tablespoons chopped
fresh cilantro
2 tablespoons chopped fresh parsley

1. In a food processor, combine the cilantro, parsley, garlic, paprika, cumin, coriander, and cayenne. Pulse until coarsely chopped. Add the saffron, if using, and process until combined. With the food processor running, slowly add the olive oil in a steady stream; process until the sauce is uniform. Season with salt.
2. In a large bowl, drizzle the beets with ½ cup of the chermoula to coat. Arrange the beets in the crisper tray.
3. Place the crisper tray on the roast position. Select Roast, set the temperature to 375ºF (191ºC), and set the time to 25 minutes.
4. Cook for 25 minutes, or until the beets are tender.
5. Transfer the beets to a serving platter. Sprinkle with the chopped cilantro and parsley and serve.

Stuffed Squash with Tomatoes and Poblano

Prep time: 5 minutes | Cook time: 30 minutes | Serves 4

1 pound (454 g) butternut squash, ends trimmed
2 teaspoons olive oil, divided
6 grape tomatoes, halved
1 poblano pepper, cut into strips
Salt and black pepper, to taste
¼ cup grated Mozzarella cheese

1. Using a large knife, cut the squash in half lengthwise on a flat work surface. This recipe just needs half of the squash. Scoop out the flesh to make room for the stuffing. Coat the squash half with 1 teaspoon of olive oil.
2. Put the squash half in the crisper tray.
3. Place the crisper tray on the roast position. Select Roast, set the temperature to 350ºF (177ºC), and set the time to 15 minutes.
4. Meanwhile, thoroughly combine the tomatoes, poblano pepper, remaining 1 teaspoon of olive oil, salt, and pepper in a bowl.
5. Remove the crisper tray and spoon the tomato mixture into the squash. Return to the grill and roast for 12 minutes until the tomatoes are soft.
6. Scatter the Mozzarella cheese on top and continue roasting for about 3 minutes, or until the cheese is melted.
7. Cool for 5 minutes before serving.

Spinach and Zucchini Rolls

Prep time: 15 minutes | Cook time: 18 minutes | Serves 6

3 large zucchinis
2½ teaspoons kosher salt or 1¼ teaspoons fine salt, divided
1½ cups cooked chopped spinach
1½ cups whole milk ricotta cheese
½ cup freshly grated Parmesan cheese
1½ cups shredded Mozzarella, divided
1 large egg, lightly beaten
1 teaspoon Italian seasoning or ½ teaspoon each dried basil and oregano
Freshly ground black pepper
Cooking oil spray
1½ cups Marinara Sauce or store-bought variety

1. Cut off the ends of the zucchini and peel several strips off one side to make a flat base. Use a large Y-shaped peeler or sharp cheese plane to cut long slices about ⅛-inch thick. When you get to a point where you can't get any more slices, set that zucchini aside and start on the next. You need 8 good slices per squash, for a total of 24 slices (a few extra never hurts). Save the rest of the zucchini pieces for another recipe, such as the Ratatouille Casserole.
2. Salt one side of the zucchini slices with 1 teaspoon of kosher salt. Place the slices salted-side down on a rack placed over a baking sheet. Salt the other sides with another teaspoon of kosher salt. Let the slices sit for 10 minutes, or until they start to exude water (you'll see it beading up on the surface of the slices and dripping onto the baking sheet).
3. While the zucchini sits, in a medium bowl, combine the spinach, ricotta, Parmesan cheese, ¾ cup of Mozzarella, egg, Italian seasoning, remaining ½ teaspoon of kosher salt, and pepper.
4. Spray the baking pan with cooking oil spray.
5. Rinse the zucchini slices off and blot them dry with a paper towel. Spread about 2 tablespoons of the ricotta mixture evenly along each zucchini slice. Roll up the slice and place each seam-side down on the prepared baking pan. Place the rolls so they touch, working from the center of the pan out toward the edges. Repeat with remaining zucchini slices and filling. Top the rolls with the marinara sauce and sprinkle with the remaining ¾ cup of Mozzarella.
6. Place the pan on the roast position. Select Roast, set temperature to 375ºF (191ºC), and set time to 18 minutes.
7. After about 15 minutes, check the rolls. They are done when the cheese is melted and beginning to brown, and the filling is bubbling. If necessary, continue cooking for another 3 to 4 minutes.
8. When cooking is complete, remove the pan from the grill. Serve.

Roasted Asparagus with Eggs

Prep time: 10 minutes | Cook time: 12 minutes | Serves 4

2 pounds (907 g) asparagus, trimmed
3 tablespoons extra-virgin olive oil, divided
1 teaspoon kosher salt or ½ teaspoon fine
salt, divided
1 pint cherry tomatoes
4 large eggs
¼ teaspoon freshly ground black pepper

1. Place the asparagus in the baking pan. Drizzle with 2 tablespoons of olive oil and use tongs (or your hands) to toss the asparagus to coat it with the oil. Sprinkle with ½ teaspoon of kosher salt.
2. Place the pan on the roast position. Select Roast, set temperature to 375ºF (191ºC), and set time to 12 minutes.
3. While the asparagus is cooking, place the tomatoes in a medium bowl and drizzle with the remaining 1 tablespoon of olive oil. Toss to coat.
4. After 6 minutes, remove the pan from the grill. Using tongs, toss the asparagus; it should be starting to get crisp at the tips. Spread the asparagus evenly in the center of the pan. Add the tomatoes around the perimeter of the pan. Return the pan to the grill and continue cooking.
5. After 2 minutes, remove the pan from the grill.
6. Carefully crack the eggs over the asparagus, being careful to space them out so they aren't touching. Sprinkle the eggs with the remaining ½ teaspoon of kosher salt and the pepper. Return the pan to the grill and continue cooking. Cook for another 3 to 7 minutes, depending on how you like your eggs.
7. When cooking is complete, use a large spatula to transfer an egg with the asparagus underneath to plates. Spoon the tomatoes onto the plates.

Asparagus, Pea, and Tortellini Primavera

Prep time: 10 minutes | Cook time: 16 minutes | Serves 4

½ pound (227 g) asparagus, trimmed and cut into 1-inch pieces
8 ounces (227 g) sugar snap peas, trimmed
1 tablespoon extra-virgin olive oil
2 teaspoons kosher salt or 1 teaspoon fine salt, divided
1½ cups water
1 (20-ounce / 567-g) package frozen cheese tortellini
1 cup heavy (whipping) cream
2 garlic cloves, minced
1 cup cherry tomatoes, halved
½ cup grated Parmesan cheese
¼ cup chopped fresh parsley or basil

1. Place the asparagus and peas in a large bowl. Add the olive oil and ½ teaspoon of kosher salt. Toss to coat. Place the vegetables in the baking pan.
2. Place the pan on the bake position. Select Bake, set temperature to 450ºF (232ºC), and set time to 4 minutes.
3. While the vegetables are cooking, dissolve 1 teaspoon of kosher salt in the water. When cooking is complete, remove the pan from the grill and place the tortellini into the pan with the vegetables. Pour the salted water over the tortellini. Return the pan to the grill.
4. Place the pan on the bake position. Select Bake, set temperature to 450ºF (232ºC), and set time to 7 minutes.
5. While the pasta cooks, place the heavy cream in a small bowl. Stir in the garlic and remaining ½ teaspoon of kosher salt.
6. When cooking is complete, remove the pan from the grill and blot off any remaining water with a paper towel. Gently stir the ingredients. Pour the cream over everything and scatter the tomatoes on top.
7. Place the pan on the roast position. Select Roast, set temperature to 375ºF (191ºC), and set time to 5 minutes.
8. After 4 minutes, remove the pan from the grill. The tortellini should be tender and the vegetables just barely crisp; if not, cook for 1 minute more.
9. Remove the pan from the grill. Stir in the Parmesan cheese until it's melted (you might find it easier to transfer the mixture to a bowl to do this). Top with the parsley, and serve.

Lush Ratatouille Casserole

Prep time: 10 minutes | Cook time: 12 minutes | Serves 6

1 small eggplant, peeled and sliced ½-inch thick
1 medium zucchini, sliced ½-inch thick
2 teaspoons kosher salt or 1 teaspoon fine salt, divided
4 tablespoons extra-virgin olive oil, divided
1 small onion, chopped (about 1 cup)
3 garlic cloves, minced or pressed
1 small green bell pepper, cut into ½-inch
chunks (about 1 cup)
1 small red bell pepper, cut into ½-inch chunks (about 1 cup)
½ teaspoon dried oregano
¼ teaspoon freshly ground black pepper
1 pint cherry tomatoes
2 tablespoons minced fresh basil
1 cup panko bread crumbs
½ cup grated Parmesan cheese (optional)

1. Salt one side of the eggplant and zucchini slices with ¾ teaspoon of salt. Place the slices salted-side down on a rack placed over a baking sheet. Salt the other sides with another ¾ teaspoon of salt. Let the slices sit for 10 minutes, or until they start to exude water (it will bead up on the surface of the slices and drip down into the baking sheet). Rinse the slices off and blot them dry with a paper towel. Cut the zucchini slices into quarters and the eggplant slices into eighths.
2. Place the zucchini and eggplant in a large bowl and add 2 tablespoons of olive oil, the onion, garlic, bell peppers, oregano, and black pepper. Toss to coat the vegetables with the oil. Place the vegetables in the baking pan.
3. Place the pan on the roast position. Select Roast, set temperature to 375ºF (191ºC), and set time to 12 minutes.
4. While the vegetables are cooking, place the tomatoes and basil into the bowl. Add 1 tablespoon of olive oil and the remaining ½ teaspoon of salt.
5. In a small bowl, mix the panko, remaining 1 tablespoon of olive oil, and Parmesan cheese (if using).
6. After 6 minutes, remove the pan from the grill. Add the tomato mixture to the vegetables in the baking pan and stir to combine. Top with the panko mixture. Return the pan to the grill and continue cooking.
7. When cooking is complete, the vegetables should be tender and the topping golden brown. Remove the pan from the grill and serve.

Mushroom and Bean Enchiladas

Prep time: 10 minutes | Cook time: 17 minutes | Serves 4

8 (6-inch) corn tortillas
Cooking oil spray or vegetable oil, for brushing
1 (15-ounce / 425-g) can black beans, drained
¾ cups frozen corn, thawed
1 teaspoon chili powder
2 tablespoons salsa
1½ cups red enchilada sauce
1 recipe Roasted Mushrooms
8 ounces (227 g) shredded Monterey Jack cheese

1. Spray the tortillas on both sides with cooking oil spray or brush lightly with the oil. Arrange them in the baking pan, overlapping as little as possible.
2. Place the pan on the roast position. Select Roast, set temperature to 325ºF (163ºC), and set time to 5 minutes.
3. While the tortillas warm, place the beans in a medium bowl. Add the corn, chili powder, and salsa and stir to combine. Transfer the mixture to a large sheet of aluminum foil. Fold the foil over the mixture and seal the edges to create a packet. Set aside.
4. After 5 minutes, remove the pan from the grill. Stack the tortillas on a plate and cover with foil.
5. Pour about half of the enchilada sauce on one end of the baking pan. Place a tortilla in the sauce, turning it over to coat it thoroughly. Spoon a couple of tablespoons of mushrooms down the middle of the tortilla and top with a couple tablespoons of cheese. Roll up the tortilla and place it seam-side down on one edge of the pan. Repeat with the remaining tortillas, adding more sauce to the pan as necessary, forming a row of enchiladas from one side of the pan to the other. (Leave room along one side for the beans.) You may not use all the mushrooms, and you should have about ⅓ cup of cheese remaining.
6. Spoon most of the remaining sauce over the enchiladas. You don't want them drowning, but they should be nicely coated. Sprinkle the remaining cheese over the enchiladas.
7. Place the packet of beans and corn next to the row of enchiladas.
8. Place the pan on the roast position. Select Roast, set temperature to 350ºF (177ºC), and set time to 12 minutes.
9. When cooking is complete, the cheese will be melted and the sauce will be bubbling. Remove the pan from the grill. Open the beans and corn and stir gently. Adjust the seasoning, adding salt or more salsa as desired.

Broccoli and Cheese Calzones

Prep time: 10 minutes | Cook time: 24 minutes | Serves 4

1 head broccoli, trimmed into florets
2 tablespoons extra-virgin olive oil
1 store-bought pizza dough (about 16 ounces / 454 g)
2 to 3 tablespoons all-purpose flour, plus more for dusting
1 egg, beaten
2 cups shredded Mozzarella cheese
1 cup ricotta cheese
½ cup grated Parmesan cheese
1 garlic clove, grated
Grated zest of 1 lemon
½ teaspoon red pepper flakes
Cooking oil spray

1. In a large bowl, toss the broccoli and olive oil until evenly coated.
2. Add the broccoli to the crisper tray. Place the crisper tray on the air fry position. Select Air Fry, set the temperature to 390ºF (199ºC), and set the time to 12 minutes.
3. While the broccoli is cooking, divide the pizza dough into four equal pieces. Dust a clean work surface with the flour. Place the dough on the floured surface and roll each piece into an 8-inch round of even thickness. Dust your rolling pin and work surface with additional flour, as needed, to ensure the dough does not stick. Brush a thin coating of egg wash around the edges of each round.
4. After 6 minutes, shake the crisper tray. Place the crisper tray back in the grill to resume cooking.
5. Meanwhile, in a medium bowl, combine the Mozzarella, ricotta, Parmesan cheese, garlic, lemon zest, and red pepper flakes.
6. After cooking is complete, add the broccoli to the cheese mixture. Spoon one-quarter of the mixture onto one side of each dough. Fold the other half over the filling, and press firmly to seal the edges together. Brush each calzone all over with the remaining egg wash.
7. Coat the crisper tray with cooking spray and place the calzones in the crisper tray. Air fry for 10 to 12 minutes, until golden brown.

Cheese Pepper in Roasted Portobellos

Prep time: 15 minutes | Cook time: 15 minutes | Serves 4

8 portobello mushroom caps, each about 3 inches across
4 tablespoons sherry vinegar or white wine vinegar
1 tablespoon fresh thyme leaves or 1 teaspoon dried
6 garlic cloves, minced or pressed, divided
1 teaspoon Dijon mustard
1 teaspoon kosher salt or ½ teaspoon fine salt, divided
¼ cup plus 3¼ teaspoons extra-virgin olive oil, divided
1 small green bell pepper, thinly sliced
1 small red or yellow bell pepper, thinly sliced
1 small onion, thinly sliced
¼ teaspoon red pepper flakes
Several grinds freshly ground black pepper
4 ounces (113 g) shredded Fontina cheese or other mild melting cheese

1. Rinse off any dirt from the mushroom caps and pat dry.
2. In a small bowl, whisk together the vinegar, thyme, 4 minced garlic cloves, mustard, and ½ teaspoon of kosher salt. Slowly pour in ¼ cup of olive oil, whisking constantly, until an emulsion forms. Alternatively, place the ingredients in a small jar with a tight-fitting lid and shake. Measure out 2 tablespoons and set aside.
3. Place the mushrooms in a resealable plastic bag and add the marinade. Seal the bag, squeezing out as much air as possible. Massage the mushrooms to coat them in the marinade. If you have the time, let marinate about 20 minutes at room temperature, turning the bag over after 10 minutes.
4. In a medium bowl, place the bell peppers, onion, remaining 2 minced garlic cloves, red pepper flakes, remaining ½ teaspoon of salt, and black pepper. Drizzle the remaining 3¼ teaspoons of olive oil over the vegetables and toss to coat.
5. Remove the mushrooms from the marinade and place them gill-side down on one end of the baking pan. Place the bell pepper mixture on the other side of the pan.
6. Place the pan on the roast position. Select Roast, set temperature to 375ºF (191ºC), and set time to 12 minutes.
7. After 7 minutes, remove the pan from the grill. Stir the peppers and turn the mushrooms over. Return the pan to the grill and continue cooking.
8. When cooking is complete, the peppers are tender and browned in places, and the mushrooms have shrunk somewhat. Remove the pan from the grill. Transfer the pepper mixture to a cutting board and coarsely chop.
9. Brush the mushrooms on both sides with the reserved 2 tablespoons marinade. Fill the caps with the pepper mixture. Sprinkle the cheese over the stuffing.
10. Place the pan on the broil position. Select Broil, set temperature to 450ºF (232ºC), and set time to 3 minutes.
11. The mushrooms are done when the cheese is melted and bubbling. Remove the pan and garnish with fresh thyme or parsley, if desired.

Thai Vegetable Mix

Prep time: 10 minutes | Cook time: 8 minutes | Serves 4

1 small head Napa cabbage, shredded, divided
8 ounces (227 g) snow peas
1 medium carrot, cut into thin coins
1 red or green bell pepper, sliced into thin strips
1 tablespoon vegetable oil
1 tablespoon sesame oil
2 tablespoons soy sauce
2 tablespoons freshly squeezed lime juice
2 tablespoons brown sugar
2 teaspoons red or green Thai curry paste
1 cup frozen mango slices, thawed
1 serrano chile, seeded and minced
½ cup chopped roasted peanuts or cashews

1. Place half the Napa cabbage in a large bowl. Add the snow peas, carrot, and bell pepper. Drizzle with the vegetable oil and toss to coat. Place in the baking pan in an even layer.
2. Place the pan on the roast position. Select Roast, set temperature to 375ºF (191ºC), and set time to 8 minutes.
3. While the vegetables cook, in a small bowl, whisk together the sesame oil, soy sauce, lime juice, brown sugar, and curry paste.
4. When cooking is complete, the vegetables should be crisp-tender. If necessary, continue cooking for a minute or two longer. Remove the pan from the grill and place the vegetables back in the bowl. Add the mango slices, chile, and the remaining Napa cabbage. Add the dressing and toss to coat.
5. Serve topped with the nuts.

Chickpea and Rice Stuffed Peppers

Prep time: 10 minutes | Cook time: 18 minutes | Serves 4

4 medium red, green, or yellow bell peppers
4 tablespoons extra-virgin olive oil, divided
½ teaspoon kosher salt or ¼ teaspoon fine salt, divided
1 (15-ounce / 425-g) can chickpeas
3 garlic cloves, minced or pressed
½ small onion, finely chopped (about ½ cup)
1½ cups cooked white rice
½ cup diced roasted red peppers
¼ cup chopped parsley
¼ teaspoon freshly ground black pepper
½ teaspoon cumin
¾ cup panko bread crumbs

1. Cut the peppers in half through the stem and remove the seeds and ribs. You can either leave the stem attached or cut it out, as you like. Brush the peppers inside and out with 1 tablespoon of olive oil. Sprinkle the insides with ¼ teaspoon of kosher salt. Place the peppers cut-side up in the baking pan.
2. Pour the beans with their liquid into a large bowl. Using a potato masher, lightly mash the beans. Add the remaining ¼ teaspoon of kosher salt, 1 tablespoon of olive oil, the garlic, onion, rice, roasted red peppers, parsley, black pepper, and cumin. Stir to combine. Spoon the mixture into the bell pepper halves.
3. In a small bowl, stir together the panko and remaining 2 tablespoons of olive oil. Top the peppers with the panko mixture.
4. Place the pan on the roast position. Select Roast, set temperature to 375ºF (191ºC), and set time to 18 minutes.
5. After about 12 minutes, remove the pan from the grill. If the panko is browning unevenly, rotate the pan 180 degrees. Return the pan to the grill and continue cooking.
6. When cooking is complete, the peppers should be slightly wrinkled, and the panko should be deep golden brown.

Asparagus and Potato Platter

Prep time: 5 minutes | Cook time: 26 to 30 minutes | Serves 5

4 medium potatoes, cut into wedges
Cooking spray
1 bunch asparagus, trimmed
2 tablespoons olive oil
Salt and pepper, to taste
Cheese Sauce:
¼ cup crumbled cottage cheese
¼ cup buttermilk
1 tablespoon whole-grain mustard
Salt and black pepper, to taste

1. Spritz the crisper tray with cooking spray.
2. Put the potatoes in the crisper tray.
3. Place the crisper tray on the roast position. Select Roast, set the temperature to 400ºF (204ºC), and set the time to 22 minutes.
4. Cook for 20 to 22 minutes, until golden brown. Shake the crisper tray halfway through the cooking time.
5. When ready, remove the potatoes from the crisper tray to a platter. Cover the potatoes with foil to keep warm. Set aside.
6. Place the asparagus in the crisper tray and drizzle with the olive oil. Sprinkle with salt and pepper.
7. Roast for 6 to 8 minutes, shaking the crisper tray once or twice during cooking, or until the asparagus is cooked to your desired crispiness.
8. Meanwhile, make the cheese sauce by stirring together the cottage cheese, buttermilk, and mustard in a small bowl. Season with salt and pepper.
9. Transfer the asparagus to the platter of potatoes and drizzle with the cheese sauce. Serve immediately.

Chapter 5 Vegetable Sides

Easy Asparagus

Prep time: 5 minutes | Cook time: 5 minutes | Serves 4

1 pound (454 g) fresh asparagus spears, trimmed

1 tablespoon olive oil
Salt and ground black pepper, to taste

1. Combine all the ingredients and transfer to the crisper tray.
2. Place the crisper tray on the air fry position. Select Air Fry, set the temperature to 375ºF (191ºC), and set the time to 5 minutes.
3. Cook for 5 minutes or until soft.
4. Serve hot.

Pesto Parmesan Gnocchi

Prep time: 10 minutes | Cook time: 15 minutes | Serves 4

1 (1-pound / 454-g) package gnocchi
1 medium onion, chopped
3 cloves garlic, minced
1 tablespoon extra-

virgin olive oil
1 (8-ounce / 227-g) jar pesto
1/3 cup grated Parmesan cheese

1. In a large bowl combine the onion, garlic, and gnocchi, and drizzle with the olive oil. Mix thoroughly.
2. Transfer the mixture to the crisper tray.
3. Place the crisper tray on the air fry position. Select Air Fry, set the temperature to 340ºF (171ºC), and set the time to 15 minutes.
4. Cook for 15 minutes, stirring occasionally, making sure the gnocchi become light brown and crispy.
5. Add the pesto and Parmesan cheese, and give everything a good stir before serving.

Corn Pakodas

Prep time: 10 minutes | Cook time: 8 minutes | Serves 5

1 cup flour
1/4 teaspoon baking soda
1/4 teaspoon salt
1/2 teaspoon curry powder
1/2 teaspoon red chili

powder
1/4 teaspoon turmeric powder
1/4 cup water
10 cobs baby corn, blanched
Cooking spray

1. Cover the crisper tray with aluminum foil and spritz with the cooking spray.
2. In a bowl, combine all the ingredients, save for the corn. Stir with a whisk until well combined.
3. Coat the corn in the batter and put inside the crisper tray.
4. Place the crisper tray on the air fry position. Select Air Fry, set the temperature to 425ºF (218ºC), and set the time to 8 minutes.
5. Cook for 8 minutes until a golden brown color is achieved.
6. Serve hot.

Buttered Parmesan Broccoli

Prep time: 5 minutes | Cook time: 4 minutes | Serves 4

1 pound (454 g) broccoli florets
1 medium shallot, minced
2 tablespoons olive oil
2 tablespoons unsalted

butter, melted
2 teaspoons minced garlic
1/4 cup grated Parmesan cheese

1. Combine the broccoli florets with the shallot, olive oil, butter, garlic, and Parmesan cheese in a medium bowl and toss until the broccoli florets are thoroughly coated.
2. Arrange the broccoli florets in the crisper tray in a single layer.
3. Place the crisper tray on the roast position. Select Roast, set the temperature to 360ºF (182ºC), and set the time to 4 minutes.
4. Serve warm.

Sriracha Cauliflower

Prep time: 5 minutes | Cook time: 17 minutes | Serves 4

1/4 cup vegan butter, melted
1/4 cup sriracha sauce
4 cups cauliflower

florets
1 cup bread crumbs
1 teaspoon salt

1. Mix the sriracha and vegan butter in a bowl and pour this mixture over the cauliflower, taking care to cover each floret entirely.
2. In a separate bowl, combine the bread crumbs and salt.
3. Dip the cauliflower florets in the bread crumbs, coating each one well. Transfer to the crisper tray.
4. Place the crisper tray on the air fry position. Select Air Fry, set the temperature to 375ºF (191ºC), and set the time to 17 minutes.
5. Serve hot.

Lemon Broccoli

Prep time: 5 minutes | Cook time: 15 minutes | Serves 6

2 heads broccoli, cut into florets
2 teaspoons extra-virgin olive oil, plus more for coating
1 teaspoon salt
½ teaspoon black pepper
1 clove garlic, minced
½ teaspoon lemon juice

1. Cover the crisper tray with aluminum foil and coat with a light brushing of oil.
2. In a bowl, combine all ingredients, save for the lemon juice, and transfer to the crisper tray.
3. Place the crisper tray on the roast position. Select Roast, set the temperature to 375ºF (191ºC), and set the time to 15 minutes.
4. Serve with the lemon juice.

Parmesan Asparagus Fries

Prep time: 15 minutes | Cook time: 5 to 7 minutes | Serves 4

2 egg whites
¼ cup water
¼ cup plus 2 tablespoons grated Parmesan cheese, divided
¾ cup panko bread
crumbs
¼ teaspoon salt
12 ounces (340 g) fresh asparagus spears, woody ends trimmed
Cooking spray

1. In a shallow dish, whisk together the egg whites and water until slightly foamy. In a separate shallow dish, thoroughly combine ¼ cup of Parmesan cheese, bread crumbs, and salt.
2. Dip the asparagus in the egg white, then roll in the cheese mixture to coat well.
3. Place the asparagus in the crisper tray in a single layer, leaving space between each spear. You may need to work in batches to avoid overcrowding.
4. Spritz the asparagus with cooking spray.
5. Place the crisper tray on the air fry position. Select Air Fry, set the temperature to 390ºF (199ºC), and set the time to 7 minutes.
6. Cook for 5 to 7 minutes until golden brown and crisp.
7. Repeat with the remaining asparagus spears.
8. Sprinkle with the remaining 2 tablespoons of cheese and serve hot.

Garlic Balsamic Asparagus

Prep time: 5 minutes | Cook time: 10 minutes | Serves 4

1 pound (454 g) asparagus, woody ends trimmed
2 tablespoons olive oil
1 tablespoon balsamic vinegar
2 teaspoons minced garlic
Salt and freshly ground black pepper, to taste

1. In a large shallow bowl, toss the asparagus with the olive oil, balsamic vinegar, garlic, salt, and pepper until thoroughly coated.
2. Arrange the asparagus in the crisper tray.
3. Place the crisper tray on the roast position. Select Roast, set the temperature to 400ºF (204ºC), and set the time to 10 minutes.
4. Cook for 10 minutes until crispy. Flip the asparagus with tongs halfway through the cooking time.
5. Serve warm.

Charred Sesame Green Beans

Prep time: 5 minutes | Cook time: 8 minutes | Serves 4

1 tablespoon reduced-sodium soy sauce or tamari
½ tablespoon Sriracha sauce
4 teaspoons toasted sesame oil, divided
12 ounces (340 g) trimmed green beans
½ tablespoon toasted sesame seeds

1. Whisk together the soy sauce, Sriracha sauce, and 1 teaspoon of sesame oil in a small bowl until smooth.
2. Toss the green beans with the remaining sesame oil in a large bowl until evenly coated.
3. Place the green beans in the crisper tray in a single layer. You may need to work in batches to avoid overcrowding.
4. Place the crisper tray on the air fry position. Select Air Fry, set the temperature to 375ºF (191ºC), and set the time to 8 minutes.
5. Cook for 8 minutes until the green beans are lightly charred and tender. Shake the crisper tray halfway through the cooking time.
6. Remove from the crisper tray to a platter. Repeat with the remaining green beans.
7. Pour the prepared sauce over the top of green beans and toss well. Serve sprinkled with the toasted sesame seeds.

Crusted Brussels Sprouts with Sage

Prep time: 5 minutes | Cook time: 15 minutes | Serves 4

1 pound (454 g) Brussels sprouts, halved	1 tablespoon paprika
1 cup bread crumbs	2 tablespoons canola oil
2 tablespoons grated Grana Padano cheese	1 tablespoon chopped sage

1. Line the crisper tray with parchment paper.
2. In a small bowl, thoroughly mix the bread crumbs, cheese, and paprika. In a large bowl, place the Brussels sprouts and drizzle the canola oil over the top. Sprinkle with the bread crumb mixture and toss to coat.
3. Place the Brussels sprouts in the crisper tray.
4. Place the crisper tray on the roast position. Select Roast, set the temperature to 400ºF (204ºC), and set the time to 15 minutes.
5. Cook for 15 minutes, or until the Brussels sprouts are lightly browned and crisp. Shake the crisper tray a few times during cooking to ensure even cooking.
6. Transfer the Brussels sprouts to a plate and sprinkle the sage on top before serving.

Corn Casserole

Prep time: 5 minutes | Cook time: 15 minutes | Serves 4

2 cups frozen yellow corn	¼ cup milk
1 egg, beaten	Pinch salt
3 tablespoons flour	Freshly ground black pepper, to taste
½ cup grated Swiss or Havarti cheese	2 tablespoons butter, cut into cubes
½ cup light cream	Nonstick cooking spray

1. Spritz the baking pan with nonstick cooking spray.
2. Stir together the remaining ingredients except the butter in a medium bowl until well incorporated.
3. Transfer the mixture to the prepared baking pan and scatter with the butter cubes.
4. Place the baking pan on the bake position. Select Bake, set the temperature to 320ºF (160ºC), and set the time to 15 minutes.
5. Cook for 15 minutes, or until the top is golden brown and a toothpick inserted in the center comes out clean.
6. Let the casserole cool for 5 minutes before slicing into wedges and serving.

Rosemary Roasted Red Potatoes

Prep time: 5 minutes | Cook time: 20 to 22 minutes | Serves 4

1½ pounds (680 g) small red potatoes, cut into 1-inch cubes	garlic
2 tablespoons olive oil	1 teaspoon salt, plus additional as needed
2 tablespoons minced fresh rosemary	½ teaspoon freshly ground black pepper, plus additional as needed
1 tablespoon minced	

1. Toss the potato cubes with the olive oil, rosemary, garlic, salt, and pepper in a large bowl until thoroughly coated.
2. Arrange the potato cubes in the crisper tray in a single layer.
3. Place the crisper tray on the roast position. Select Roast, set the temperature to 400ºF (204ºC), and set the time to 22 minutes.
4. Cook for 20 to 22 minutes until the potatoes are tender. Shake the crisper tray a few times during cooking for even cooking.
5. Remove from the crisper tray to a plate. Taste and add additional salt and pepper as needed.

Fried Macaroni Balls

Prep time: 10 minutes | Cook time: 10 minutes | Serves 2

2 cups leftover macaroni	3 large eggs
1 cup shredded Cheddar cheese	1 cup milk
½ cup flour	½ teaspoon salt
1 cup bread crumbs	¼ teaspoon black pepper

1. In a bowl, combine the leftover macaroni and shredded cheese.
2. Pour the flour in a separate bowl. Put the bread crumbs in a third bowl. Finally, in a fourth bowl, mix the eggs and milk with a whisk.
3. With an ice-cream scoop, create balls from the macaroni mixture. Coat them the flour, then in the egg mixture, and lastly in the bread crumbs.
4. Arrange the balls in the crisper tray.
5. Place the crisper tray on the air fry position. Select Air Fry, set the temperature to 365ºF (185ºC), and set the time to 10 minutes.
6. Cook for 10 minutes, giving them an occasional stir. Ensure they crisp up nicely.
7. Serve hot.

Broccoli Gratin

Prep time: 5 minutes | Cook time: 12 to 14 minutes | Serves 2

⅓ cup fat-free milk
1 tablespoon all-purpose or gluten-free flour
½ tablespoon olive oil
½ teaspoon ground sage
¼ teaspoon kosher salt
⅛ teaspoon freshly ground black pepper

2 cups roughly chopped broccoli florets
6 tablespoons shredded Cheddar cheese
2 tablespoons panko bread crumbs
1 tablespoon grated Parmesan cheese
Olive oil spray

1. Spritz the baking pan with olive oil spray.
2. Mix the milk, flour, olive oil, sage, salt, and pepper in a medium bowl and whisk to combine. Stir in the broccoli florets, Cheddar cheese, bread crumbs, and Parmesan cheese and toss to coat.
3. Pour the broccoli mixture into the prepared baking pan.
4. Place the baking pan on the bake position. Select Bake, set the temperature to 330ºF (166ºC), and set the time to 14 minutes.
5. Cook for 12 to 14 minutes until the top is golden brown and the broccoli is tender.
6. Serve immediately.

Cinnamon-Spiced Acorn Squash

Prep time: 5 minutes | Cook time: 15 minutes | Serves 2

1 medium acorn squash, halved crosswise and deseeded
1 teaspoon coconut oil
1 teaspoon light brown

sugar
Few dashes of ground cinnamon
Few dashes of ground nutmeg

1. On a clean work surface, rub the cut sides of the acorn squash with coconut oil. Scatter with the brown sugar, cinnamon, and nutmeg.
2. Put the squash halves in the crisper tray, cut-side up.
3. Place the crisper tray on the air fry position. Select Air Fry, set the temperature to 325ºF (163ºC), and set the time to 15 minutes.
4. Cook for 15 minutes until just tender when pierced in the center with a paring knife.
5. Rest for 5 to 10 minutes and serve warm.

Baked Potatoes with Yogurt and Chives

Prep time: 5 minutes | Cook time: 35 minutes | Serves 4

4 (7-ounce / 198-g) russet potatoes, rinsed
Olive oil spray
½ teaspoon kosher salt, divided
½ cup 2% plain Greek

yogurt
¼ cup minced fresh chives
Freshly ground black pepper, to taste

1. Pat the potatoes dry and pierce them all over with a fork. Spritz the potatoes with olive oil spray. Sprinkle with ¼ teaspoon of the salt.
2. Put the potatoes in the crisper tray.
3. Place the crisper tray on the bake position. Select Bake, set the temperature to 400ºF (204ºC), and set the time to 35 minutes.
4. Cook for 35 minutes, or until a knife can be inserted into the center of the potatoes easily.
5. Remove from the crisper tray and split open the potatoes. Top with the yogurt, chives, the remaining ¼ teaspoon of salt, and finish with the black pepper. Serve immediately.

Spicy Cabbage

Prep time: 5 minutes | Cook time: 7 minutes | Serves 4

1 head cabbage, sliced into 1-inch-thick ribbons
1 tablespoon olive oil
1 teaspoon garlic powder

1 teaspoon red pepper flakes
1 teaspoon salt
1 teaspoon freshly ground black pepper

1. Toss the cabbage with the olive oil, garlic powder, red pepper flakes, salt, and pepper in a large mixing bowl until well coated.
2. Arrange the cabbage in the crisper tray.
3. Place the crisper tray on the roast position. Select Roast, set the temperature to 350ºF (177ºC), and set the time to 7 minutes.
4. Cook for 7 minutes until crisp. Flip the cabbage with tongs halfway through the cooking time.
5. Remove from the crisper tray to a plate and serve warm.

Chapter 6 Fish and Seafood

Breaded Calamari with Lemon

Prep time: 5 minutes | Cook time: 12 minutes | Serves 4

2 large eggs
2 garlic cloves, minced
½ cup cornstarch
1 cup bread crumbs

1 pound (454 g) calamari rings
Cooking spray
1 lemon, sliced

1. In a small bowl, whisk the eggs with minced garlic. Place the cornstarch and bread crumbs into separate shallow dishes.
2. Dredge the calamari rings in the cornstarch, then dip in the egg mixture, shaking off any excess, finally roll them in the bread crumbs to coat well. Let the calamari rings sit for 10 minutes in the refrigerator.
3. Spritz the crisper tray with cooking spray.
4. Put the calamari rings in the crisper tray.
5. Place the crisper tray on the air fry position. Select Air Fry, set the temperature to 390ºF (199ºC), and set the time to 12 minutes.
6. Cook for 12 minutes until cooked through. Shake the crisper tray halfway through the cooking time.
7. Serve the calamari rings with the lemon slices sprinkled on top.

Herbed Scallops with Vegetables

Prep time: 15 minutes | Cook time: 8 to 11 minutes | Serves 4

1 cup frozen peas
1 cup green beans
1 cup frozen chopped broccoli
2 teaspoons olive oil
½ teaspoon dried

oregano
½ teaspoon dried basil
12 ounces (340 g) sea scallops, rinsed and patted dry

1. Put the peas, green beans, and broccoli in a large bowl. Drizzle with the olive oil and toss to coat well. Transfer the vegetables to the crisper tray.
2. Place the crisper tray on the air fry position. Select Air Fry, set the temperature to 400ºF (204ºC), and set the time to 6 minutes.
3. Cook for 4 to 6 minutes, or until they are fork-tender.
4. Remove the vegetables from the crisper tray to a serving bowl. Scatter with the oregano and basil and set aside.
5. Place the scallops in the crisper tray. Air fry for 4 to 5 minutes, or until the scallops are firm and just opaque in the center.
6. Transfer the cooked scallops to the bowl of vegetables and toss well. Serve warm.

Lemon Garlic Tilapia

Prep time: 5 minutes | Cook time: 10 to 15 minutes | Serves 4

1 tablespoon lemon juice
1 tablespoon olive oil
1 teaspoon minced garlic

½ teaspoon chili powder
4 (6-ounce / 170-g) tilapia fillets

1. Line the crisper tray with parchment paper.
2. In a large, shallow bowl, mix together the lemon juice, olive oil, garlic, and chili powder to make a marinade. Place the tilapia fillets in the bowl and coat evenly.
3. Place the fillets in the crisper tray in a single layer, leaving space between each fillet. You may need to cook in more than one batch.
4. Place the crisper tray on the air fry position. Select Air Fry, set the temperature to 380ºF (193ºC), and set the time to 15 minutes.
5. Cook for 10 to 15 minutes until the fish is cooked and flakes easily with a fork.
6. Serve hot.

Coconut Panko Shrimp

Prep time: 15 minutes | Cook time: 15 minutes | Serves 4

½ cup all-purpose flour
2 teaspoons freshly ground black pepper
½ teaspoon sea salt
2 large eggs
¾ cup unsweetened coconut flakes

¼ cup panko bread crumbs
24 peeled, deveined shrimp
Nonstick cooking spray
Sweet chili sauce, for serving

1. In a medium shallow bowl, mix together the flour, black pepper, and salt. In a second medium shallow bowl, whisk the eggs. In a third, combine the coconut flakes and bread crumbs.
2. Dredge each shrimp in the flour mixture, then in the egg. Press each shrimp into the coconut mixture on both sides, leaving the tail uncoated.
3. Place half of the shrimp into the crisper tray and coat them with the cooking spray.
4. Place the crisper tray on the air fry position. Select Air Fry, set the temperature to 400ºF (204ºC), and set the time to 8 minutes.
5. Remove the cooked shrimp and add the remaining uncooked shrimp to the crisper tray. Spray them with the cooking spray and air fry for 7 minutes.
6. Serve with sweet chili sauce.

Honey Sriracha Salmon

Prep time: 10 minutes | Cook time: 8 minutes | Serves 4

1 cup Sriracha
Juice of 2 lemons
¼ cup honey
4 (6-ounce / 170-g)

skinless salmon fillets
Chives, chopped, for garnish

1. Place the sriracha, lemon juice, and honey in a large resealable plastic bag or container. Add the salmon fillets and coat evenly. Refrigerate for 30 minutes.
2. Place the fillets on the grill plate, gently pressing them down to maximize grill marks.
3. Place the grill plate on the grill position. Select Grill, set the temperature to 450ºF (232ºC), and set the time to 8 minutes.
4. After 6 minutes, check the fillets for doneness; the internal temperature should read at least 140ºF (60ºC) on a food thermometer. If necessary, continue cooking up to 2 minutes more.
5. When cooking is complete, remove the fillets from the grill. Plate, and garnish with the chives.

Spanish-Style Garlic Shrimp

Prep time: 10 minutes | Cook time: 10 to 15 minutes | Serves 4

2 teaspoons minced garlic
2 teaspoons lemon juice
2 teaspoons olive oil
½ to 1 teaspoon

crushed red pepper
12 ounces (340 g) medium shrimp, deveined, with tails on
Cooking spray

1. In a medium bowl, mix together the garlic, lemon juice, olive oil, and crushed red pepper to make a marinade.
2. Add the shrimp and toss to coat in the marinade. Cover with plastic wrap and place the bowl in the refrigerator for 30 minutes.
3. Spray the crisper tray lightly with cooking spray.
4. Place the shrimp in the crisper tray.
5. Place the crisper tray on the air fry position. Select Air Fry, set the temperature to 400ºF (204ºC), and set the time to 15 minutes.
6. Cook for 5 minutes. Shake the crisper tray and air fry until the shrimp are cooked through and nicely browned, for an additional 5 to 10 minutes. Cool for 5 minutes before serving.

Garlic Scallops

Prep time: 10 minutes | Cook time: 10 to 15 minutes | Serves 4

2 teaspoons olive oil
1 packet dry zesty Italian dressing mix
1 teaspoon minced garlic

16 ounces (454 g) small scallops, patted dry
Cooking spray

1. Spray the crisper tray lightly with cooking spray.
2. In a large zip-top plastic bag, combine the olive oil, Italian dressing mix, and garlic.
3. Add the scallops, seal the zip-top bag, and coat the scallops in the seasoning mixture.
4. Place the scallops in the crisper tray and lightly spray with cooking spray.
5. Place the crisper tray on the air fry position. Select Air Fry, set the temperature to 400ºF (204ºC), and set the time to 15 minutes.
6. Cook for 5 minutes, shake the crisper tray, and cook for 5 to 10 more minutes, or until the scallops reach an internal temperature of 120ºF (49ºC).
7. Serve immediately.

Blackened Shrimp Tacos

Prep time: 10 minutes | Cook time: 10 to 15 minutes | Serves 4

12 ounces (340 g) medium shrimp, deveined, with tails off
1 teaspoon olive oil
1 to 2 teaspoons Blackened seasoning

8 corn tortillas, warmed
1 (14-ounce / 397-g) bag coleslaw mix
2 limes, cut in half
Cooking spray

1. Spray the crisper tray lightly with cooking spray.
2. Dry the shrimp with a paper towel to remove excess water.
3. In a medium bowl, toss the shrimp with olive oil and Blackened seasoning.
4. Place the shrimp in the crisper tray.
5. Place the crisper tray on the air fry position. Select Air Fry, set the temperature to 400ºF (204ºC), and set the time to 15 minutes.
6. Cook for 5 minutes. Shake the crisper tray, lightly spray with cooking spray, and cook until the shrimp are cooked through and starting to brown, 5 to 10 more minutes.
7. Fill each tortilla with the coleslaw mix and top with the blackened shrimp. Squeeze fresh lime juice over top and serve.

Salmon Patty Bites

Prep time: 15 minutes | Cook time: 10 to 15 minutes | Serves 4

4 (5-ounce / 142-g) cans pink salmon, skinless, boneless in water, drained
2 eggs, beaten
1 cup whole-wheat panko bread crumbs
4 tablespoons finely minced red bell pepper
2 tablespoons parsley flakes
2 teaspoons Old Bay seasoning
Cooking spray

1. Spray the crisper tray lightly with cooking spray.
2. In a medium bowl, mix the salmon, eggs, panko bread crumbs, red bell pepper, parsley flakes, and Old Bay seasoning.
3. Using a small cookie scoop, form the mixture into 20 balls.
4. Place the salmon bites in the crisper tray in a single layer and spray lightly with cooking spray. You may need to cook them in batches.
5. Place the crisper tray on the air fry position. Select Air Fry, set the temperature to 360ºF (182ºC), and set the time to 15 minutes.
6. Cook for 10 to 15 minutes until crispy, shaking the crisper tray a couple of times for even cooking.
7. Serve immediately.

Piri-Piri King Prawn

Prep time: 10 minutes | Cook time: 8 minutes | Serves 2

12 king prawns, rinsed
1 tablespoon coconut oil
Salt and ground black pepper, to taste
1 teaspoon onion powder
1 teaspoon garlic
paste
1 teaspoon curry powder
½ teaspoon piri piri powder
½ teaspoon cumin powder

1. Combine all the ingredients in a large bowl and toss until the prawns are completely coated.
2. Place the prawns in the crisper tray.
3. Place the crisper tray on the air fry position. Select Air Fry, set the temperature to 360ºF (182ºC), and set the time to 8 minutes.
4. Cook for 8 minutes, shaking the crisper tray halfway through, or until the prawns turn pink.
5. Serve hot.

Cod Cakes with Salad Greens

Prep time: 15 minutes | Cook time: 12 minutes | Serves 4

1 pound (454 g) cod fillets, cut into chunks
⅓ cup packed fresh basil leaves
3 cloves garlic, crushed
½ teaspoon smoked paprika
¼ teaspoon salt
¼ teaspoon pepper
1 large egg, beaten
1 cup panko bread crumbs
Cooking spray
Salad greens, for serving

1. In a food processor, pulse cod, basil, garlic, smoked paprika, salt, and pepper until cod is finely chopped, stirring occasionally. Form into 8 patties, about 2 inches in diameter. Dip each first into the egg, then into the panko, patting to adhere. Spray with oil on one side.
2. Working in batches, place half the cakes in the crisper tray, oil-side down; spray with oil.
3. Place the crisper tray on the air fry position. Select Air Fry, set the temperature to 400ºF (204ºC), and set the time to 12 minutes.
4. Cook for 12 minutes, until golden brown and cooked through.
5. Serve cod cakes with salad greens.

Shrimp Caesar Salad

Prep time: 10 minutes | Cook time: 5 minutes | Serves 4

1 pound (454 g) fresh jumbo shrimp
Juice of ½ lemon
3 garlic cloves, minced
Sea salt, to taste
Freshly ground black
pepper, to taste
2 heads romaine lettuce, chopped
¾ cup Caesar dressing
½ cup grated Parmesan cheese

1. In a large bowl, toss the shrimp with the lemon juice, garlic, salt, and pepper. Let marinate for 10 minutes.
2. Place the shrimp on the grill plate.
3. Place the grill plate on the grill position. Select Grill, set the temperature to 450ºF (232ºC), and set the time to 5 minutes.
4. Cook for 5 minutes. (There is no need to flip the shrimp during grilling.)
5. While the shrimp grills, toss the romaine lettuce with the Caesar dressing, then divide evenly among four plates or bowls.
6. When cooking is complete, use tongs to remove the shrimp from the grill and place on top of each salad. Sprinkle with the Parmesan cheese and serve.

Green Curry Shrimp

Prep time: 15 minutes | Cook time: 5 minutes | Serves 4

1 to 2 tablespoons Thai green curry paste
2 tablespoons coconut oil, melted
1 tablespoon half-and-half or coconut milk
1 teaspoon fish sauce
1 teaspoon soy sauce
1 teaspoon minced fresh ginger
1 clove garlic, minced
1 pound (454 g) jumbo raw shrimp, peeled and deveined
¼ cup chopped fresh Thai basil or sweet basil
¼ cup chopped fresh cilantro

1. In the baking pan, combine the curry paste, coconut oil, half-and-half, fish sauce, soy sauce, ginger, and garlic. Whisk until well combined.
2. Add the shrimp and toss until well coated. Marinate at room temperature for 15 to 30 minutes. Transfer to the crisper tray.
3. Place the crisper tray on the air fry position. Select Air Fry, set the temperature to 400°F (204°C), and set the time to 5 minutes.
4. Cook for 5 minutes, stirring halfway through the cooking time.
5. Transfer the shrimp to a serving bowl or platter. Garnish with the basil and cilantro. Serve immediately.

Paprika Shrimp

Prep time: 5 minutes | Cook time: 10 minutes | Serves 4

1 pound (454 g) tiger shrimp
2 tablespoons olive oil
½ tablespoon old bay seasoning
¼ tablespoon smoked paprika
¼ teaspoon cayenne pepper
A pinch of sea salt

1. Toss all the ingredients in a large bowl until the shrimp are evenly coated.
2. Arrange the shrimp in the crisper tray.
3. Place the crisper tray on the air fry position. Select Air Fry, set the temperature to 380°F (193°C), and set the time to 10 minutes.
4. Cook for 10 minutes, shaking the crisper tray halfway through, or until the shrimp are pink and cooked through.
5. Serve hot.

Shrimp and Vegetable Paella

Prep time: 5 minutes | Cook time: 14 to 17 minutes | Serves 4

1 (10-ounce / 284-g) package frozen cooked rice, thawed
1 (6-ounce / 170-g) jar artichoke hearts, drained and chopped
¼ cup vegetable broth
½ teaspoon dried
thyme
½ teaspoon turmeric
1 cup frozen cooked small shrimp
½ cup frozen baby peas
1 tomato, diced

1. Mix together the cooked rice, chopped artichoke hearts, vegetable broth, thyme, and turmeric in the baking pan and stir to combine.
2. Place the baking pan on the bake position. Select Bake, set the temperature to 340°F (171°C), and set the time to 17 minutes.
3. Cook for 9 minutes, or until the rice is heated through.
4. Remove the pan from the grill and fold in the shrimp, baby peas, and diced tomato and mix well.
5. Return to the grill and continue cooking for 5 to 8 minutes, or until the shrimp are done and the paella is bubbling.
6. Cool for 5 minutes before serving.

Crab Ratatouille with Eggplant and Tomatoes

Prep time: 15 minutes | Cook time: 11 to 14 minutes | Serves 4

1½ cups peeled and cubed eggplant
2 large tomatoes, chopped
1 red bell pepper, chopped
1 onion, chopped
1 tablespoon olive oil
½ teaspoon dried basil
½ teaspoon dried thyme
Pinch salt
Freshly ground black pepper, to taste
1½ cups cooked crab meat

1. In the pan, stir together the eggplant, tomatoes, bell pepper, onion, olive oil, basil and thyme. Season with salt and pepper.
2. Place the baking pan on the roast position. Select Roast, set the temperature to 400°F (204°C)., and set the time to 14 minutes.
3. Cook for 9 minutes. Add the crab meat and stir well and cook for another 2 to 5 minutes, or until the vegetables are softened and the ratatouille is bubbling.
4. Serve warm.

Fired Shrimp with Mayonnaise Sauce

Prep time: 5 minutes | Cook time: 7 minutes | Serves 4

Shrimp
12 jumbo shrimp
½ teaspoon garlic salt
Sauce:
4 tablespoons mayonnaise
1 teaspoon grated lemon rind
1 teaspoon Dijon

¼ teaspoon freshly cracked mixed peppercorns
mustard
1 teaspoon chipotle powder
½ teaspoon cumin powder

1. In a medium bowl, season the shrimp with garlic salt and cracked mixed peppercorns.
2. Place the shrimp in the crisper tray.
3. Place the crisper tray on the air fry position. Select Air Fry, set the temperature to 395ºF (202ºC), and set the time to 7 minutes.
4. Cook for 5 minutes. Flip the shrimp and cook for another 2 minutes until they are pink and no longer opaque.
5. Meanwhile, stir together all the ingredients for the sauce in a small bowl until well mixed.
6. Remove the shrimp from the crisper tray and serve alongside the sauce.

Garlic Shrimp with Parsley

Prep time: 10 minutes | Cook time: 5 minutes | Serves 4

18 shrimp, shelled and deveined
2 garlic cloves, peeled and minced
2 tablespoons extra-virgin olive oil
2 tablespoons freshly squeezed lemon juice
½ cup fresh parsley, coarsely chopped

1 teaspoon onion powder
1 teaspoon lemon-pepper seasoning
½ teaspoon hot paprika
½ teaspoon salt
¼ teaspoon cumin powder

1. Toss all the ingredients in a mixing bowl until the shrimp are well coated.
2. Cover and allow to marinate in the refrigerator for 30 minutes.
3. Arrange the shrimp in the crisper tray.
4. Place the crisper tray on the air fry position. Select Air Fry, set the temperature to 400ºF (204ºC), and set the time to 5 minutes.
5. Cook for 5 minutes, or until the shrimp are pink on the outside and opaque in the center.
6. Remove from the crisper tray and serve warm.

Breaded Scallops

Prep time: 5 minutes | Cook time: 6 to 8 minutes | Serves 4

1 egg
3 tablespoons flour
1 cup bread crumbs
1 pound (454 g) fresh

scallops
2 tablespoons olive oil
Salt and black pepper, to taste

1. In a bowl, lightly beat the egg. Place the flour and bread crumbs into separate shallow dishes.
2. Dredge the scallops in the flour and shake off any excess. Dip the flour-coated scallops in the beaten egg and roll in the bread crumbs.
3. Brush the scallops generously with olive oil and season with salt and pepper, to taste.
4. Arrange the scallops in the crisper tray.
5. Place the crisper tray on the air fry position. Select Air Fry, set the temperature to 360ºF (182ºC), and set the time to 8 minutes.
6. Cook for 6 to 8 minutes, or until the scallops are firm and reach an internal temperature of just 145ºF (63ºC) on a meat thermometer. Shake the crisper tray halfway through the cooking time.
7. Let the scallops cool for 5 minutes and serve.

Roasted Cod with Sesame Seeds

Prep time: 5 minutes | Cook time: 7 to 9 minutes | Makes 1 fillet

1 tablespoon reduced-sodium soy sauce
2 teaspoons honey
Cooking spray

6 ounces (170 g) fresh cod fillet
1 teaspoon sesame seeds

1. In a small bowl, combine the soy sauce and honey.
2. Spray the crisper tray with cooking spray, then place the cod in the crisper tray, brush with the soy mixture, and sprinkle sesame seeds on top.
3. Place the crisper tray on the roast position. Select Roast, set the temperature to 360ºF (182ºC), and set the time to 9 minutes.
4. Cook for 7 to 9 minutes, or until opaque.
5. Remove the fish and allow to cool on a wire rack for 5 minutes before serving.

Grilled Swordfish Steaks with Caper Sauce

Prep time: 5 minutes | Cook time: 8 minutes | Serves 4

1 tablespoon freshly squeezed lemon juice	fresh swordfish steaks, about 1-inch thick
1 tablespoon extra-virgin olive oil	4 tablespoons unsalted butter
Sea salt, to taste	1 lemon, sliced crosswise into 8 slices
Freshly ground black pepper, to taste	2 tablespoons capers, drained
4 (8-ounce / 227-g)	

1. In a large shallow bowl, whisk together the lemon juice and oil. Season the swordfish steaks with salt and pepper on each side, and place them in the oil mixture. Turn to coat both sides. Refrigerate for 15 minutes.
2. Place the swordfish on the grill plate.
3. Place the grill plate on the grill position. Select Grill, set the temperature to 450ºF (232ºC), and set the time to 8 minutes.
4. While the swordfish grills, melt the butter in a small saucepan over medium heat. Stir and cook for about 3 minutes, until the butter has slightly browned. Add the lemon slices and capers to the pan, and cook for 1 minute. Turn off the heat.
5. Remove the swordfish from the grill and transfer it to a cutting board. Slice the fish into thick strips, transfer to serving platter, pour the caper sauce over the top, and serve immediately.

Miso-Glazed Cod with Bok Choy

Prep time: 5 minutes | Cook time: 17 minutes | Serves 4

4 (6-ounce / 170-g) cod fillets	wine or mirin
¼ cup miso	2 tablespoons soy sauce
3 tablespoons brown sugar	¼ teaspoon red pepper flakes
1 teaspoon sesame oil, divided	1 pound (454 g) baby bok choy, halved lengthwise
1 tablespoon white	

1. Place the cod, miso, brown sugar, ¾ teaspoon of sesame oil, and white wine in a large resealable plastic bag or container. Move the fillets around to coat evenly with the marinade. Refrigerate for 30 minutes.
2. Place the fillets on the grill plate. Gently press them down to maximize grill marks.

3. Place the grill plate on the grill position. Select Grill, set the temperature to 450ºF (232ºC), and set the time to 8 minutes.
4. Cook for 8 minutes. (There is no need to flip the fish during grilling.)
5. While the cod grills, in a small bowl, whisk together the remaining ¼ teaspoon of sesame oil, soy sauce, and red pepper flakes. Brush the bok choy halves with the soy sauce mixture on all sides.
6. Remove the cod from the grill and set aside on a cutting board to rest. Tent with aluminum foil to keep warm.
7. Place the bok choy on the grill plate, cut-side down. Grill for 9 minutes. (There is no need to flip the bok choy during grilling.)
8. Remove the bok choy from the grill, plate with the cod, and serve.

Spiced Crab Cakes with Mayo

Prep time: 10 minutes | Cook time: 10 minutes | Serves 4

1 egg	½ teaspoon cayenne pepper
½ cup mayonnaise, plus 3 tablespoons	¼ teaspoon paprika
Juice of ½ lemon	¼ teaspoon garlic powder
1 tablespoon minced scallions (green parts only)	¼ teaspoon chili powder
1 teaspoon Old Bay seasoning	¼ teaspoon onion powder
8 ounces (227 g) lump crab meat	¼ teaspoon freshly ground black pepper
1/3 cup bread crumbs	1/8 teaspoon ground nutmeg
Nonstick cooking spray	

1. In a medium bowl, whisk together the egg, 3 tablespoons of mayonnaise, lemon juice, scallions, and Old Bay seasoning. Gently stir in the crab meat, making sure not to break up the meat into small pieces. Add the bread crumbs, and gradually mix them in. Form the mixture into four patties.
2. Place the crab cakes in the crisper tray and coat them with the cooking spray.
3. Place the crisper tray on the air fry position. Select Air Fry, set the temperature to 375ºF (191ºC), and set the time to 10 minutes.
4. While the crab cakes are cooking, in a small bowl, mix the remaining ½ cup of mayonnaise, cayenne pepper, paprika, garlic powder, chili powder, onion powder, black pepper, and nutmeg until fully combined.
5. When cooking is complete, serve the crab cakes with the Cajun aioli spooned on top.

Lemon Shrimp and Zucchini

Prep time: 15 minutes | Cook time: 7 to 8 minutes | Serves 4

1¼ pounds (567 g) extra-large raw shrimp, peeled and deveined
2 medium zucchini (about 8 ounces / 227 g each), halved lengthwise and cut into ½-inch-thick slices
1½ tablespoons olive oil
½ teaspoon garlic salt
1½ teaspoons dried oregano
⅛ teaspoon crushed red pepper flakes (optional)
Juice of ½ lemon
1 tablespoon chopped fresh mint
1 tablespoon chopped fresh dill

1. In a large bowl, combine the shrimp, zucchini, oil, garlic salt, oregano, and pepper flakes (if using) and toss to coat.
2. Working in batches, arrange a single layer of the shrimp and zucchini in the crisper tray.
3. Place the crisper tray on the air fry position. Select Air Fry, set the temperature to 350ºF (177ºC), and set the time to 8 minutes.
4. Cook for 7 to 8 minutes, shaking the crisper tray halfway, until the zucchini is golden and the shrimp are cooked through.
5. Transfer to a serving dish and tent with foil while you air fry the remaining shrimp and zucchini.
6. Top with the lemon juice, mint, and dill and serve.

Coconut Chili Fish Curry

Prep time: 10 minutes | Cook time: 20 to 22 minutes | Serves 4

2 tablespoons sunflower oil, divided
1 pound (454 g) fish, chopped
1 ripe tomato, pureéd
2 red chilies, chopped
1 shallot, minced
1 garlic clove, minced
1 cup coconut milk
1 tablespoon coriander powder
1 teaspoon red curry paste
½ teaspoon fenugreek seeds
Salt and white pepper, to taste

1. Coat the crisper tray with 1 tablespoon of sunflower oil.
2. Place the fish in the crisper tray. Place the crisper tray on the air fry position. Select Air Fry, set the temperature to 380ºF (193ºC), and set the time to 10 minutes.
3. Flip the fish halfway through the cooking time.

4. When done, transfer the cooked fish to the baking pan greased with the remaining 1 tablespoon of sunflower oil. Stir in the remaining ingredients and return to the grill.
5. Reduce the temperature to 350ºF (177ºC) and air fry for another 10 to 12 minutes until heated through.
6. Cool for 5 to 8 minutes before serving.

Tuna Salade Niçoise

Prep time: 10 minutes | Cook time: 15 minutes | Serves 4

10 ounces (283 g) small red potatoes, quartered
8 tablespoons extra-virgin olive oil, divided
1 teaspoon kosher salt or ½ teaspoon fine salt, divided
½ pound (227 g) green beans, trimmed
1 pint cherry tomatoes
3 tablespoons red or white wine vinegar
1 teaspoon Dijon mustard
Freshly ground black pepper
1 (9-ounce / 255-g) bag spring greens, washed and dried if necessary
2 (5-ounce / 142-g) cans oil-packed tuna, drained
2 hard-cooked eggs, peeled and quartered
⅓ cup Nicoise or kalamata olives, pitted

1. Place the potatoes in a large bowl. Drizzle with 1 tablespoon of olive oil and ¼ teaspoon of kosher salt. Place in the baking pan.
2. Place the pan on the roast position. Select Roast, set temperature to 375ºF (191ºC), and set time to 15 minutes.
3. While the potatoes are cooking, place the green beans and cherry tomatoes in the bowl and toss with 1 tablespoon of oil and ¼ teaspoon of kosher salt.
4. After 10 minutes, remove the pan from the grill. Add the green beans and tomatoes to the pan. Return the pan to the grill and continue cooking.
5. While the vegetables cook, make the vinaigrette: In a small jar or bowl, shake or whisk together the remaining 6 tablespoons of olive oil, vinegar, mustard, the remaining ½ teaspoon of kosher salt, and a few grinds of black pepper.
6. When cooking is complete, remove the pan from the grill. Let the vegetables cool for a few minutes.
7. Arrange the greens on a platter and spoon the tuna into the middle of the greens. Surround the tuna with the potatoes, green beans, tomatoes, and egg quarters. Drizzle with the vinaigrette and scatter the olives on top.

Crispy Fish Sticks

Prep time: 10 minutes | Cook time: 10 minutes | Serves 4

1 pound (454 g) cod fillets
¼ cup all-purpose flour
1 large egg
1 teaspoon Dijon mustard
½ cup bread crumbs
1 tablespoon dried parsley
1 teaspoon paprika
½ teaspoon freshly ground black pepper
Nonstick cooking spray

1. Cut the fish fillets into ¾- to 1-inch-wide strips.
2. Place the flour on a plate. In a medium shallow bowl, whisk together the egg and Dijon mustard. In a separate medium shallow bowl, combine the bread crumbs, dried parsley, paprika, and black pepper.
3. One at a time, dredge the cod strips in the flour, shaking off any excess, then coat them in the egg mixture. Finally, dredge them in the bread crumb mixture, and coat on all sides.
4. Spray the crisper tray with the cooking spray. Place the cod fillet strips in the crisper tray, and coat them with the cooking spray.
5. Place the crisper tray on the air fry position. Select Air Fry, set the temperature to 390ºF (199ºC), and set the time to 10 minutes.
6. Remove the fish sticks from the crisper tray and serve.

Honey Lime Salmon with Mango Salsa

Prep time: 10 minutes | Cook time: 8 minutes | Serves 4

2 tablespoons unsalted butter, melted
¹/₃ cup honey
1 tablespoon soy sauce
Juice of 3 limes, divided
Grated zest of ½ lime
3 garlic cloves, minced and divided
4 (6-ounce / 170-g) skinless salmon fillets
1 mango, peeled and
diced
1 avocado, peeled and diced
½ tomato, diced
½ red onion, diced
1 jalapeño pepper, seeded, stemmed, and diced
1 tablespoon extra-virgin olive oil
Sea salt, to taste
Freshly ground black pepper, to taste

1. Place the butter, honey, soy sauce, juice of 2 limes, lime zest, and 2 minced garlic cloves in a large resealable plastic bag or container. Add the salmon fillets and coat evenly with the marinade. Refrigerate for 30 minutes.

2. While the salmon is marinating, in a large bowl, combine the mango, avocado, tomato, onion, remaining minced garlic clove, jalapeño, remaining juice of 1 lime, oil, salt, and pepper. Cover and refrigerate.
3. Place the fillets on the grill plate, gently pressing them down to maximize grill marks.
4. Place the grill plate on the grill position. Select Grill, set the temperature to 450ºF (232ºC), and set the time to 8 minutes.
5. After 6 minutes, check the fillets for doneness; the internal temperature should read at least 140ºF (60ºC) on a food thermometer. If necessary, continue cooking up to 2 minutes more.
6. When cooking is complete, top the fillets with salsa and serve immediately.

Lime-Chili Shrimp Bowl

Prep time: 10 minutes | Cook time: 10 to 15 minutes | Serves 4

2 teaspoons lime juice
1 teaspoon olive oil
1 teaspoon honey
1 teaspoon minced garlic
1 teaspoon chili powder
Salt, to taste
12 ounces (340 g) medium shrimp, peeled and deveined
2 cups cooked brown rice
1 (15-ounce / 425-g) can seasoned black beans, warmed
1 large avocado, chopped
1 cup sliced cherry tomatoes
Cooking spray

1. Spray the crisper tray lightly with cooking spray.
2. In a medium bowl, mix together the lime juice, olive oil, honey, garlic, chili powder, and salt to make a marinade.
3. Add the shrimp and toss to coat evenly in the marinade.
4. Place the shrimp in the crisper tray.
5. Place the crisper tray on the air fry position. Select Air Fry, set the temperature to 400ºF (204ºC), and set the time to 15 minutes.
6. Cook for 5 minutes. Shake the crisper tray and air fry until the shrimp are cooked through and starting to brown, an additional 5 to 10 minutes.
7. To assemble the bowls, spoon ¼ of the rice, black beans, avocado, and cherry tomatoes into each of four bowls. Top with the shrimp and serve.

Tuna Cucumber Salad

Prep time: 10 minutes | Cook time: 6 minutes | Serves 4

2 tablespoons rice wine vinegar
¼ teaspoon sea salt, plus additional for seasoning
½ teaspoon freshly ground black pepper, plus additional for seasoning
6 tablespoons extra-
virgin olive oil
1½ pounds (680 g) ahi tuna, cut into four strips
2 tablespoons sesame oil
1 (10-ounce / 284-g) bag baby greens
½ English cucumber, sliced

1. In a small bowl, whisk together the rice vinegar, ¼ teaspoon of salt, and ½ teaspoon of pepper. Slowly pour in the oil while whisking, until the vinaigrette is fully combined.
2. Season the tuna with salt and pepper, and drizzle with the sesame oil.
3. Place the tuna strips on the grill plate.
4. Place the grill plate on the grill position. Select Grill, set the temperature to 450ºF (232ºC), and set the time to 6 minutes.
5. Cook for 4 to 6 minutes. (There is no need to flip during cooking.)
6. While the tuna cooks, divide the baby greens and cucumber slices evenly among four plates or bowls.
7. When cooking is complete, top each salad with one tuna strip. Drizzle the vinaigrette over the top, and serve immediately.

Cajun Fish Tacos

Prep time: 5 minutes | Cook time: 10 to 15 minutes | Serves 6

2 teaspoons avocado oil
1 tablespoon Cajun seasoning
4 tilapia fillets
1 (14-ounce / 397-g) package coleslaw mix
12 corn tortillas
2 limes, cut into wedges

1. Line the crisper tray with parchment paper.
2. In a medium, shallow bowl, mix the avocado oil and the Cajun seasoning to make a marinade. Add the tilapia fillets and coat evenly.
3. Place the fillets in the crisper tray in a single layer, leaving room between each fillet. You may need to cook in batches.
4. Place the crisper tray on the air fry position. Select Air Fry, set the temperature to 380ºF (193ºC), and set the time to 15 minutes.

5. Cook for 10 to 15 minutes until the fish is cooked and easily flakes with a fork.
6. Assemble the tacos by placing some of the coleslaw mix in each tortilla. Add ⅓ of a tilapia fillet to each tortilla. Squeeze some lime juice over the top of each taco and serve.

Blackened Salmon with Cucumber-Avocado Salsa

Prep time: 10 minutes | Cook time: 5 to 7 minutes | Serves 4

Salmon:
1 tablespoon sweet paprika
½ teaspoon cayenne pepper
1 teaspoon garlic powder
1 teaspoon dried oregano
1 teaspoon dried
thyme
¾ teaspoon kosher salt
⅛ teaspoon freshly ground black pepper
Cooking spray
4 (6 ounces / 170 g each) wild salmon fillets

Cucumber-Avocado Salsa:
2 tablespoons chopped red onion
1½ tablespoons fresh lemon juice
1 teaspoon extra-virgin olive oil
¼ teaspoon plus ⅛
teaspoon kosher salt
Freshly ground black pepper, to taste
4 Persian cucumbers, diced
6 ounces (170 g) Hass avocado, diced

1. For the salmon: In a small bowl, combine the paprika, cayenne, garlic powder, oregano, thyme, salt, and black pepper. Spray both sides of the fish with oil and rub all over. Coat the fish all over with the spices.
2. For the cucumber-avocado salsa: In a medium bowl, combine the red onion, lemon juice, olive oil, salt, and pepper. Let stand for 5 minutes, then add the cucumbers and avocado.
3. Working in batches, arrange the salmon fillets skin side down in the crisper tray.
4. Place the crisper tray on the air fry position. Select Air Fry, set the temperature to 400ºF (204ºC), and set the time to 7 minutes.
5. Cook for 5 to 7 minutes, or until the fish flakes easily with a fork, depending on the thickness of the fish.
6. Serve topped with the salsa.

Cajun-Style Salmon Burgers

Prep time: 10 minutes | Cook time: 10 to 15 minutes | Serves 4

4 (5-ounce / 142-g) cans pink salmon in water, any skin and bones removed, drained
2 eggs, beaten
1 cup whole-wheat bread crumbs

4 tablespoons light mayonnaise
2 teaspoons Cajun seasoning
2 teaspoons dry mustard
4 whole-wheat buns
Cooking spray

1. In a medium bowl, mix the salmon, egg, bread crumbs, mayonnaise, Cajun seasoning, and dry mustard. Cover with plastic wrap and refrigerate for 30 minutes.
2. Spray the crisper tray lightly with cooking spray.
3. Shape the mixture into four ½-inch-thick patties about the same size as the buns.
4. Place the salmon patties in the crisper tray in a single layer and lightly spray the tops with cooking spray. You may need to cook them in batches.
5. Place the crisper tray on the air fry position. Select Air Fry, set the temperature to 360ºF (182ºC), and set the time to 15 minutes.
6. Cook for 6 to 8 minutes. Turn the patties over and lightly spray with cooking spray. Cook until crispy on the outside, for 4 to 7 more minutes.
7. Serve on whole-wheat buns.

Crab and Fish Cakes

Prep time: 20 minutes | Cook time: 10 to 12 minutes | Serves 4

8 ounces (227 g) imitation crab meat
4 ounces (113 g) leftover cooked fish (such as cod, pollock, or haddock)
2 tablespoons minced celery
2 tablespoons minced green onion
2 tablespoons light mayonnaise
1 tablespoon plus 2 teaspoons Worcestershire sauce

¾ cup crushed saltine cracker crumbs
2 teaspoons dried parsley flakes
1 teaspoon prepared yellow mustard
½ teaspoon garlic powder
½ teaspoon dried dill weed, crushed
½ teaspoon Old Bay seasoning
½ cup panko bread crumbs
Cooking spray

1. Pulse the crab meat and fish in a food processor until finely chopped.
2. Transfer the meat mixture to a large bowl, along with the celery, green onion, mayo, Worcestershire sauce, cracker crumbs, parsley flakes, mustard, garlic powder, dill weed, and Old Bay seasoning. Stir to mix well.
3. Scoop out the meat mixture and form into 8 equal-sized patties with your hands.
4. Place the panko bread crumbs on a plate. Roll the patties in the bread crumbs until they are evenly coated on both sides. Spritz the patties with cooking spray.
5. Put the patties in the crisper tray.
6. Place the crisper tray on the bake position. Select Bake, set the temperature to 390ºF (199ºC), and set the time to 12 minutes.
7. Cook for 10 to 12 minutes, flipping them halfway through, or until they are golden brown and cooked through.
8. Divide the patties among four plates and serve.

Goat Cheese Shrimp

Prep time: 15 minutes | Cook time: 7 to 8 minutes | Serves 2

1 pound (454 g) shrimp, deveined
1½ tablespoons olive oil
1½ tablespoons balsamic vinegar
1 tablespoon coconut aminos
½ tablespoon fresh parsley, roughly chopped
Sea salt flakes, to

taste
1 teaspoon Dijon mustard
½ teaspoon smoked cayenne pepper
½ teaspoon garlic powder
Salt and ground black peppercorns, to taste
1 cup shredded goat cheese

1. Except for the cheese, stir together all the ingredients in a large bowl until the shrimp are evenly coated.
2. Arrange the shrimp in the crisper tray.
3. Place the crisper tray on the air fry position. Select Air Fry, set the temperature to 385ºF (196ºC), and set the time to 8 minutes.
4. Cook for 7 to 8 minutes, shaking the crisper tray halfway through, or until the shrimp are pink and cooked through.
5. Serve the shrimp with the shredded goat cheese sprinkled on top.

Bacon-Wrapped Scallops

Prep time: 5 minutes | Cook time: 10 minutes | Serves 4

8 slices bacon, cut in half
16 sea scallops, patted dry
Cooking spray
Salt and freshly

ground black pepper, to taste
16 toothpicks, soaked in water for at least 30 minutes

1. On a clean work surface, wrap half of a slice of bacon around each scallop and secure with a toothpick.
2. Lay the bacon-wrapped scallops in the crisper tray in a single layer. You may need to work in batches to avoid overcrowding.
3. Spritz the scallops with cooking spray and sprinkle the salt and pepper to season.
4. Place the crisper tray on the air fry position. Select Air Fry, set the temperature to 370ºF (188ºC), and set the time to 10 minutes.
5. Cook for 10 minutes, flipping the scallops halfway through, or until the bacon is cooked through and the scallops are firm.
6. Remove the scallops from the crisper tray to a plate and repeat with the remaining scallops. Serve warm.

Shrimp with Potatoes and Kielbasa

Prep time: 10 minutes | Cook time: 15 minutes | Serves 4

1 pound (454 g) small red potatoes
2 ears corn, shucked and cut into rounds 1 to 1½ inches thick
½ cup unsalted butter, melted
2 tablespoons Old Bay or similar seasoning
1 (12- to 13-ounce

/ 340- to 369-g) package kielbasa or other smoked sausages
3 garlic cloves, minced or pressed
1 pound (454 g) medium (21–25 or 25–30 count) shrimp, peeled and deveined

1. If the potatoes are 2 inches or smaller in diameter, cut them in half. If larger, cut in quarters. Place in a large bowl and add the corn pieces.
2. In a small bowl, mix together the butter and Old Bay seasoning. Drizzle half the butter mixture over the potatoes and corn and toss to coat. Place the vegetables in the baking pan, reserving the bowl.
3. Place the pan on the roast position. Select Roast, set temperature to 350ºF (177ºC), and set time to 15 minutes.

4. While the vegetables cook, cut the sausages into 2-inch lengths, then cut each piece in half lengthwise. Stir the garlic into the remaining butter mixture. Place the shrimp and sausage pieces in the vegetable bowl.
5. After 10 minutes, remove the pan from the grill. Place the vegetables in the bowl. Pour the garlic butter over and toss to coat. Place the vegetables, sausage, and shrimp in the pan.
6. Return the pan to the grill and continue cooking. After 5 minutes, check the shrimp. They should be pink and opaque. If they are not quite cooked through, return pan to the grill for 1 minute more.
7. When cooking is complete, remove the pan from the grill and serve.

Tilapia Meunière

Prep time: 10 minutes | Cook time: 20 minutes | Serves 4

10 ounces (283 g) Yukon Gold potatoes, sliced ¼-inch thick
5 tablespoons unsalted butter, melted, divided
1 teaspoon kosher salt or ½ teaspoon fine salt, divided

4 (8-ounce / 227-g) tilapia fillets
½ pound (227 g) green beans, trimmed
Juice of 1 lemon
2 tablespoons chopped fresh parsley

1. Place the potatoes in a large bowl. Drizzle with 2 tablespoons of butter and ¼ teaspoon of kosher salt. Place in the baking pan.
2. Place the pan on the roast position. Select Roast, set temperature to 375ºF (191ºC), and set time to 20 minutes.
3. While the potatoes cook, salt the fish fillets on both sides with ½ teaspoon of kosher salt. Place the green beans in the potato bowl and toss with the remaining ¼ teaspoon of kosher salt and 1 tablespoon of butter.
4. After 10 minutes, remove the pan from the grill and move the potatoes to one side. Place the fish fillets in the center of the pan and add the green beans on the other side. Drizzle the fish with 2 tablespoons of butter. Return the pan to the grill and continue cooking.
5. When cooking is complete, the fish should flake apart with a fork. The beans should be tender and starting to crisp. Remove the pan from the grill. To serve, drizzle the lemon juice over the fish, and sprinkle the parsley over the fish and vegetables.

Baked Flounder Fillets

Prep time: 8 minutes | Cook time: 12 minutes | Serves 2

2 flounder fillets, patted dry
1 egg
½ teaspoon Worcestershire sauce
¼ cup almond flour
¼ cup coconut flour
½ teaspoon coarse sea salt
½ teaspoon lemon pepper
¼ teaspoon chili powder
Cooking spray

1. Spritz the crisper tray with cooking spray.
2. In a shallow bowl, beat together the egg with Worcestershire sauce until well incorporated.
3. In another bowl, thoroughly combine the almond flour, coconut flour, sea salt, lemon pepper, and chili powder.
4. Dredge the fillets in the egg mixture, shaking off any excess, then roll in the flour mixture to coat well.
5. Place the fillets in the crisper tray.
6. Place the crisper tray on the bake position. Select Bake, set the temperature to 390ºF (199ºC), and set the time to 12 minutes.
7. Cook for 7 minutes. Flip the fillets and spray with cooking spray. Continue cooking for 5 minutes, or until the fish is flaky.
8. Serve warm.

Scallops with Mushrooms and Snow Peas

Prep time: 10 minutes | Cook time: 8 minutes | Serves 4

1 pound (454 g) sea scallops
3 tablespoons hoisin sauce
½ cup toasted sesame seeds
6 ounces (170 g) snow peas, trimmed
3 teaspoons vegetable oil, divided
1 teaspoon sesame oil
1 teaspoon soy sauce
1 cup Roasted Mushrooms

1. With a basting brush, coat the flat sides of the scallops with the hoisin sauce. Place the sesame seeds in a flat dish. Place the coated sides of the scallops in the seeds, pressing them into the scallops to adhere. Repeat with the other sides of the scallops, so both flat sides are coated with hoisin sauce and sesame seeds.
2. In a medium bowl, toss the snow peas with 1 teaspoon of vegetable oil, the sesame oil, and soy sauce.

3. Brush the baking pan with the remaining 2 teaspoons of vegetable oil. Place the scallops in the center of the pan. Arrange the snow peas in a single layer around the scallops.
4. Place the pan on the roast position. Select Roast, set temperature to 375ºF (191ºC), and set time to 8 minutes.
5. After 5 minutes, remove the pan from the grill. Using a small spatula, carefully turn the scallops over. Add the mushrooms to the peas and stir to combine. Return the pan to the grill and continue cooking.
6. When cooking is complete, the peas should be sizzling and the scallops just cooked through. Remove the pan from the grill and serve.

Mediterranean Salmon and Veg Dish

Prep time: 10 minutes | Cook time: 15 minutes | Serves 4

4 (6-ounce / 170-g) salmon fillets, with or without skin
1 teaspoon kosher salt or ½ teaspoon fine salt, divided
2 pints cherry or grape tomatoes, halved if large, divided
3 tablespoons extra-virgin olive oil, divided
1 small red bell pepper, seeded and chopped
2 garlic cloves, minced
2 tablespoons chopped fresh basil, divided

1. Sprinkle the salmon on both sides with ½ teaspoon of kosher salt.
2. Place about half of the tomatoes in a large bowl, reserving the remainder. Add the remaining ½ teaspoon of kosher salt, 2 tablespoons of olive oil, the bell pepper, garlic, and 1 tablespoon of basil. Toss to coat the vegetables with the oil. Place the vegetables in the baking pan.
3. Pat the salmon dry with a paper towel. Place the fillets in the pan (skin-side down). Brush them with the remaining 1 tablespoon of olive oil.
4. Place the pan on the roast position. Select Roast, set temperature to 375ºF (191ºC), and set time to 15 minutes.
5. After 7 minutes, remove the pan from the grill and add the remaining tomatoes. Return the pan to the grill and continue cooking for about 6 minutes.
6. When cooking is complete, the fish will flake apart with a fork. If the fish is not done, return the pan to the grill for another minute or so. Remove the pan from the grill. Before serving, sprinkle the remaining 1 tablespoon of basil over the dish.

Teriyaki Salmon

Prep time: 15 minutes | Cook time: 15 minutes | Serves 4

¾ cup teriyaki sauce
4 (6-ounce / 170-g) skinless salmon fillets
4 heads baby bok choy, root ends trimmed off and cut in half lengthwise
through the root
1 tablespoon vegetable oil
1 teaspoon sesame oil
1 tablespoon toasted sesame seeds

1. Set aside ¼ cup of Teriyaki Sauce and pour the rest into a resealable plastic bag. Place the salmon in the bag and seal, squeezing as much air out as possible. Let the salmon marinate for at least 10 minutes (longer if you have the time).
2. Place the bok choy halves in the baking pan. Drizzle the vegetable and sesame oils over the vegetables and toss to coat. Drizzle about a tablespoon of the reserved Teriyaki Sauce over the bok choy, then push them to the sides of the pan.
3. Place the salmon fillets in the middle of the baking pan.
4. Place the pan on the roast position. Select Roast, set temperature to 375ºF (191ºC), and set time to 15 minutes.
5. When cooking is complete, remove the pan from the grill. Brush the salmon with the remaining Teriyaki Sauce. Garnish with the sesame seeds. Serve with steamed rice, if desired.

Air-Fried Scallops

Prep time: 10 minutes | Cook time: 12 minutes | Serves 2

⅓ cup shallots, chopped
1½ tablespoons olive oil
1½ tablespoons coconut aminos
1 tablespoon Mediterranean seasoning mix
½ tablespoon balsamic
vinegar
½ teaspoon ginger, grated
1 clove garlic, chopped
1 pound (454 g) scallops, cleaned
Cooking spray
Belgian endive, for garnish

1. Place all the ingredients except the scallops and Belgian endive in a small skillet over medium heat and stir to combine. Let this mixture simmer for about 2 minutes.
2. Remove the mixture from the skillet to a large bowl and set aside to cool.

3. Add the scallops, coating them all over, then transfer to the refrigerator to marinate for at least 2 hours.
4. Arrange the scallops in the crisper tray in a single layer and spray with cooking spray.
5. Place the crisper tray on the air fry position. Select Air Fry, set the temperature to 345ºF (174ºC), and set the time to 10 minutes.
6. Cook for 10 minutes, flipping the scallops halfway through, or until the scallops are tender and opaque.
7. Serve garnished with the Belgian endive.

Orange Shrimp

Prep time: 20 minutes | Cook time: 10 to 15 minutes | Serves 4

⅓ cup orange juice
3 teaspoons minced garlic
1 teaspoon Old Bay seasoning
¼ to ½ teaspoon
cayenne pepper
1 pound (454 g) medium shrimp, peeled and deveined, with tails off
Cooking spray

1. In a medium bowl, combine the orange juice, garlic, Old Bay seasoning, and cayenne pepper.
2. Dry the shrimp with paper towels to remove excess water.
3. Add the shrimp to the marinade and stir to evenly coat. Cover with plastic wrap and place in the refrigerator for 30 minutes so the shrimp can soak up the marinade.
4. Spray the crisper tray lightly with cooking spray.
5. Place the shrimp into the crisper tray.
6. Place the crisper tray on the air fry position. Select Air Fry, set the temperature to 400ºF (204ºC), and set the time to 15 minutes.
7. Cook for 5 minutes. Shake the crisper tray and lightly spray with olive oil. Cook until the shrimp are opaque and crisp, 5 to 10 more minutes.
8. Serve immediately.

Caesar Shrimp Salad

Prep time: 10 minutes | Cook time: 13 minutes | Serves 4

½ baguette, cut into 1-inch cubes (about 2½ cups)
4 tablespoons extra-virgin olive oil, divided
¼ teaspoon kosher salt or ⅛ teaspoon fine salt
¼ teaspoon granulated garlic
2 romaine lettuce hearts

¾ cup Caesar Dressing or store-bought variety, divided
1 pound (454 g) medium (21–25 or 25–30 count) shrimp, peeled and deveined
2 ounces (57 g) Parmesan cheese, coarsely grated or shaved (about ⅔ cup)

1. For the croutons, place the bread cubes in a medium bowl. Drizzle with 3 tablespoons of olive oil and sprinkle with the salt and granulated garlic. Toss to coat the bread cubes. Place in the crisper tray in a single layer.
2. Place the crisper tray on the air fry position. Select Air Fry, set temperature to 400ºF (204ºC), and set time to 4 minutes.
3. After about 2 minutes, remove the crisper tray and toss the croutons, reinsert the crisper tray in the grill, and continue cooking. When cooking is complete, the croutons will be crisp and golden brown. Remove the crisper tray from the grill and set aside.
4. While the croutons cook, halve the romaine hearts lengthwise (through the root). Trim the end of the root off, but leave enough to keep the halves intact. Brush the cut side of the lettuce with 2 tablespoons of Caesar Dressing.
5. Place the shrimp in a large bowl and toss with the ¼ cup of Caesar Dressing. Set aside.
6. Brush the baking pan with the remaining 1 tablespoon of olive oil. Place the romaine halves cut-side down in the pan. Brush the tops with another 2 tablespoons of Caesar Dressing.
7. Place the pan on the roast position. Select Roast, set temperature to 375ºF (191ºC), and set time to 10 minutes.
8. After 5 minutes, remove the pan and turn over the romaine halves. Spoon the shrimp around the lettuce. Return the pan to the grill and continue cooking.
9. When cooking is complete, the shrimp should be pink and opaque. If they are not quite cooked through, return pan to the grill for 1 minute more.
10. To serve, place a romaine half on each of four plates. Divide the shrimp among the plates and garnish with croutons and Parmesan cheese.

Honey Salmon and Asparagus Platter

Prep time: 10 minutes | Cook time: 15 minutes | Serves 4

4 (6-ounce / 170-g) salmon fillets, with or without skin
1 teaspoon kosher salt or ½ teaspoon fine salt, divided
1 tablespoon honey
2 teaspoons Dijon mustard

2 tablespoons unsalted butter, melted, or extra-virgin olive oil for dairy-free
2 pounds (907 g) asparagus, trimmed
Lemon wedges, for serving

1. Sprinkle the salmon on both sides with ½ teaspoon of kosher salt.
2. In a small bowl, whisk together the honey, mustard, and 1 tablespoon of butter.
3. Place the asparagus in the baking pan. Drizzle with the remaining 1 tablespoon of butter and sprinkle with the remaining ½ teaspoon of salt. Toss to coat. Move the asparagus to the outside of the baking pan.
4. Pat the salmon dry with a paper towel. Place the fillets in the baking pan (skin-side down if using skin-on fillets). Brush with the honey mustard sauce.
5. Place the pan on the roast position. Select Roast, set temperature to 375ºF (191ºC), and set time to 15 minutes.
6. After 7 to 8 minutes, remove the pan from the grill and toss the asparagus. Return the pan to the grill and continue cooking.
7. When cooking is complete, remove the pan from the grill. Place the salmon and asparagus on plate. Squeeze a little lemon juice over the fish and vegetables, and serve.

Catfish Strips

Prep time: 5 minutes | Cook time: 16 to 18 minutes | Serves 4

1 cup buttermilk
5 catfish fillets, cut into 1½-inch strips
Cooking spray

1 cup cornmeal
1 tablespoon Creole, Cajun, or Old Bay seasoning

1. Pour the buttermilk into a shallow baking pan. Place the catfish in the dish and refrigerate for at least 1 hour to help remove any fishy taste.
2. Spray the crisper tray lightly with cooking spray.
3. In a shallow bowl, combine cornmeal and Creole seasoning.
4. Shake any excess buttermilk off the catfish. Place each strip in the cornmeal mixture and coat completely. Press the cornmeal into the catfish gently to help it stick.
5. Place the strips in the crisper tray in a single layer. Lightly spray the catfish with cooking spray. You may need to cook the catfish in more than one batch.
6. Place the crisper tray on the air fry position. Select Air Fry, set the temperature to 400ºF (204ºC), and set the time to 18 minutes.
7. Cook for 8 minutes. Turn the catfish strips over and lightly spray with cooking spray. Cook until golden brown and crispy, for 8 to 10 more minutes.
8. Serve warm.

Cod Sandwich

Prep time: 10 minutes | Cook time: 15 minutes | Serves 4

2 large eggs
10 ounces (284 g) beer (an ale, IPA, or any type you have on hand will work)
1½ teaspoons hot sauce
1½ cups cornstarch
1½ cups all-purpose flour
1 teaspoon sea salt

1 teaspoon freshly ground black pepper
4 (5- or 6-ounce / 142- or 170-g) fresh cod fillets
Nonstick cooking spray
4 soft rolls, sliced
Tartar sauce
Lettuce leaves
Lemon wedges

1. Whisk together the eggs, beer, and hot sauce in a large shallow bowl. In a separate large bowl, whisk together the cornstarch, flour, salt, and pepper.
2. One at a time, coat the cod fillets in the egg mixture, then dredge them in the flour mixture and coat on all sides. Repeat with the remaining cod fillets.
3. Spray the crisper tray with the cooking spray. Place the fish fillets in the crisper tray and coat them with the cooking spray.
4. Place the crisper tray on the air fry position. Select Air Fry, set the temperature to 375ºF (191ºC), and set the time to 15 minutes.
5. After 15 minutes, check the fish for desired crispiness. Remove from the crisper tray.
6. Assemble the sandwiches by spreading tartar sauce on one half of each of the sliced rolls. Add one fish fillet and lettuce leaves, and serve with lemon wedges.

Chapter 7 Poultry

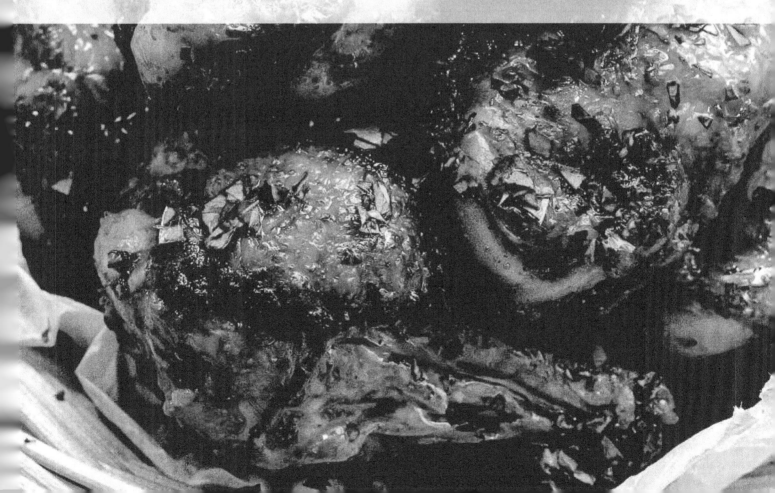

Honey Sriracha Chicken Thighs

Prep time: 5 minutes | Cook time: 17 minutes | Serves 4

1 cup Sriracha
Juice of 2 lemons
¼ cup honey

4 bone-in chicken thighs

1. Place the sriracha, lemon juice, and honey in a large resealable plastic bag or container. Add the chicken thighs and toss to coat evenly. Refrigerate for 30 minutes.
2. Place the chicken thighs onto the grill plate, gently pressing them down to maximize grill marks.
3. Place the grill plate on the grill position. Select Grill, set the temperature to 350ºF (177ºC), and set the time to 14 minutes.
4. After 7 minutes, flip the chicken thighs using tongs. Cook for 7 minutes more.
5. Cooking is complete when the internal temperature of the meat reaches at least 165ºF (74ºC) on a food thermometer. If necessary, continue grilling for 2 to 3 minutes more.
6. When cooking is complete, remove the chicken from the grill, and let it rest for 5 minutes before serving.

BBQ Chicken Drumsticks

Prep time: 10 minutes | Cook time: 20 minutes | Serves 4

2 cups barbecue sauce
Juice of 1 lime
2 tablespoons honey
1 tablespoon hot sauce

Sea salt, to taste
Freshly ground black pepper, to taste
1 pound (454 g) chicken drumsticks

1. In a large bowl, combine the barbecue sauce, lime juice, honey, and hot sauce. Season with salt and pepper. Set aside ½ cup of the sauce. Add the drumsticks to the bowl, and toss until evenly coated.
2. Place the drumsticks on the grill plate.
3. Place the grill plate on the grill position. Select Grill, set the temperature to 350ºF (177ºC), and set the time to 18 minutes.
4. Cook for 18 minutes, basting often during cooking.
5. Cooking is complete when the internal temperature of the meat reaches at least 165ºF (74ºC) on a food thermometer. If necessary, continue grilling for 2 minutes more.

Nutty Chicken Tenders

Prep time: 5 minutes | Cook time: 12 minutes | Serves 4

1 pound (454 g) chicken tenders
1 teaspoon kosher salt
1 teaspoon black pepper
½ teaspoon smoked

paprika
¼ cup coarse mustard
2 tablespoons honey
1 cup finely crushed pecans

1. Place the chicken in a large bowl. Sprinkle with the salt, pepper, and paprika. Toss until the chicken is coated with the spices. Add the mustard and honey and toss until the chicken is coated.
2. Place the pecans on a plate. Working with one piece of chicken at a time, roll the chicken in the pecans until both sides are coated. Lightly brush off any loose pecans. Place the chicken in the crisper tray.
3. Place the crisper tray on the bake position. Select Bake, set the temperature to 350ºF (177ºC), and set the time to 12 minutes.
4. Cook for 12 minutes, or until the chicken is cooked through and the pecans are golden brown.
5. Serve warm.

Blackened Chicken

Prep time: 10 minutes | Cook time: 20 minutes | Serves 4

1 large egg, beaten
¾ cup Blackened seasoning
2 whole boneless, skinless chicken

breasts (about 1 pound / 454 g each), halved
Cooking spray

1. Line the crisper tray with parchment paper.
2. Place the beaten egg in one shallow bowl and the Blackened seasoning in another shallow bowl.
3. One at a time, dip the chicken pieces in the beaten egg and the Blackened seasoning, coating thoroughly.
4. Place the chicken pieces on the parchment and spritz with cooking spray.
5. Place the crisper tray on the air fry position. Select Air Fry, set the temperature to 360ºF (182ºC), and set the time to 20 minutes.
6. Cook for 10 minutes. Flip the chicken, spritz it with cooking spray, and cook for 10 minutes more until the internal temperature reaches 165ºF (74ºC) and the chicken is no longer pink inside.
7. Let sit for 5 minutes before serving.

Spiced Turkey Tenderloin

Prep time: 20 minutes | Cook time: 30 minutes | Serves 4

½ teaspoon paprika
½ teaspoon garlic powder
½ teaspoon salt
½ teaspoon freshly ground black pepper
Pinch cayenne pepper
1½ pounds (680 g) turkey breast tenderloin
Olive oil spray

1. Spray the crisper tray lightly with olive oil spray.
2. In a small bowl, combine the paprika, garlic powder, salt, black pepper, and cayenne pepper. Rub the mixture all over the turkey.
3. Place the turkey in the crisper tray and lightly spray with olive oil spray.
4. Place the crisper tray on the air fry position. Select Air Fry, set the temperature to 370ºF (188ºC), and set the time to 30 minutes.
5. Cook for 15 minutes. Flip the turkey over and lightly spray with olive oil spray. Cook until the internal temperature reaches at least 170ºF (77ºC) for an additional 10 to 15 minutes.
6. Let the turkey rest for 10 minutes before slicing and serving.

Mini Turkey Meatloaves with Carrot

Prep time: 6 minutes | Cook time: 20 to 24 minutes | Serves 4

$^1/_3$ cup minced onion
¼ cup grated carrot
2 garlic cloves, minced
2 tablespoons ground almonds
2 teaspoons olive oil
1 teaspoon dried marjoram
1 egg white
¾ pound (340 g) ground turkey breast

1. In a medium bowl, stir together the onion, carrot, garlic, almonds, olive oil, marjoram, and egg white.
2. Add the ground turkey. With your hands, gently but thoroughly mix until combined.
3. Double 16 foil muffin cup liners to make 8 cups. Divide the turkey mixture evenly among the liners. Transfer to the pan.
4. Place the baking pan on the bake position. Select Bake, set the temperature to 400ºF (204ºC), and set the time to 24 minutes.
5. Cook for 20 to 24 minutes, or until the meatloaves reach an internal temperature of 165ºF (74ºC) on a meat thermometer. Serve immediately.

Whole Chicken Bake

Prep time: 10 minutes | Cook time: 1 hour | Serves 2 to 4

½ cup melted butter
3 tablespoons garlic, minced
Salt, to taste
1 teaspoon ground black pepper
1 (1-pound / 454-g) whole chicken

1. Combine the butter with garlic, salt, and ground black pepper in a small bowl.
2. Brush the butter mixture over the whole chicken, then place the chicken in the baking pan, skin side down.
3. Place the baking pan on the bake position. Select Bake, set the temperature to 350ºF (177ºC), and set the time to 1 hour.
4. Cook for 1 hour, or until an instant-read thermometer inserted in the thickest part of the chicken registers at least 165ºF (74ºC). Flip the chicken halfway through.
5. Remove the chicken from the grill and allow to cool for 15 minutes before serving.

Buffalo Chicken Taquitos

Prep time: 15 minutes | Cook time: 5 to 10 minutes | Serves 6

8 ounces (227 g) fat-free cream cheese, softened
⅛ cup Buffalo sauce
2 cups shredded
cooked chicken
12 (7-inch) low-carb flour tortillas
Olive oil spray

1. Spray the crisper tray lightly with olive oil spray.
2. In a large bowl, mix together the cream cheese and Buffalo sauce until well combined. Add the chicken and stir until combined.
3. Place the tortillas on a clean workspace. Spoon 2 to 3 tablespoons of the chicken mixture in a thin line down the center of each tortilla. Roll up the tortillas.
4. Place the tortillas in the crisper tray, seam-side down. Spray each tortilla lightly with olive oil spray. You may need to cook the taquitos in batches.
5. Place the crisper tray on the air fry position. Select Air Fry, set the temperature to 360ºF (182ºC), and set the time to 10 minutes.
6. Cook for 5 to 10 minutes until golden brown.
7. Serve hot.

Deep Fried Duck Leg Quarters

Prep time: 5 minutes | Cook time: 45 minutes | Serves 4

4 (½-pound / 227-g) skin-on duck leg quarters
2 medium garlic

cloves, minced
½ teaspoon salt
½ teaspoon ground black pepper

1. Spritz the crisper tray with cooking spray.
2. On a clean work surface, rub the duck leg quarters with garlic, salt, and black pepper.
3. Arrange the leg quarters in the crisper tray and spritz with cooking spray.
4. Place the crisper tray on the air fry position. Select Air Fry, set the temperature to 300ºF (149ºC), and set the time to 30 minutes.
5. Flip the leg quarters and increase the temperature to 375ºF (191ºC). Air fry for 15 more minutes or until well browned and crispy.
6. Remove the duck leg quarters from the grill and allow to cool for 10 minutes before serving.

Garlic Lime Grilled Chicken

Prep time: 5 minutes | Cook time: 18 minutes | Serves 4

1½ tablespoons extra-virgin olive oil
3 garlic cloves, minced
¼ teaspoon ground cumin
Sea salt, to taste

Freshly ground black pepper, to taste
Grated zest of 1 lime
Juice of 1 lime
4 boneless, skinless chicken breasts

1. In a large shallow bowl, stir together the oil, garlic, cumin, salt, pepper, zest, and lime juice. Add the chicken breasts and coat well. Cover and marinate in the refrigerator for 30 minutes.
2. Place the chicken breasts on the grill plate.
3. Place the grill plate on the grill position. Select Grill, set the temperature to 350ºF (177ºC), and set the time to 14 minutes.
4. After 7 minutes, flip the chicken and cook for an additional 7 minutes.
5. Check the chicken for doneness. If needed, grill up to 4 minutes more. Cooking is complete when the internal temperature of the chicken reaches at least 165ºF (74ºC) on a food thermometer.
6. Remove from the grill, and place on a cutting board or platter to rest for 5inutes. Serve.

Grilled Herbed Chicken Thighs

Prep time: 10 minutes | Cook time: 13 minutes | Serves 4

Grated zest of 2 lemons
Juice of 2 lemons
3 sprigs fresh rosemary, leaves finely chopped
3 sprigs fresh sage, leaves finely chopped
2 garlic cloves, minced

¼ teaspoon red pepper flakes
¼ cup canola oil
Sea salt
4 (4- to 7-ounce / 113- to 198-g) boneless chicken thighs

1. In a small bowl, whisk together the lemon zest and juice, rosemary, sage, garlic, red pepper flakes, and oil. Season with salt.
2. Place the chicken and lemon-herb mixture in a large resealable plastic bag or container. Toss to coat evenly. Refrigerate the chicken for at least 30 minutes.
3. Place the chicken on the grill plate.
4. Place the grill plate on the grill position. Select Grill, set the temperature to 400ºF (204ºC), and set the time to 13 minutes.
5. Cooking is complete when the internal temperature of the chicken reaches at least 165ºF (74ºC) on a food thermometer.

Teriyaki-Maple Chicken Wings

Prep time: 5 minutes | Cook time: 14 minutes | Serves 4

1 cup maple syrup
⅓ cup soy sauce
¼ cup teriyaki sauce
3 garlic cloves, minced
2 teaspoons garlic powder
2 teaspoons onion

powder
1 teaspoon freshly ground black pepper
2 pounds (907 g) bone-in chicken wings (drumettes and flats)

1. In a large bowl, whisk together the maple syrup, soy sauce, teriyaki sauce, garlic, garlic powder, onion powder, and black pepper. Add the wings, and use tongs to toss and coat.
2. Place the chicken wings on the grill plate.
3. Place the grill plate on the grill position. Select Grill, set the temperature to 350ºF (177ºC), and set the time to 10 minutes.
4. After 5 minutes, flip the wings and cook for an additional 5 minutes.
5. Check the wings for doneness. Cooking is complete when the internal temperature of the meat reaches at least 165ºF (74ºC) on a food thermometer. If needed, grill for up to 4 minutes more.
6. Remove from the grill and serve.

Mayonnaise-Mustard Chicken

Prep time: 10 minutes | Cook time: 15 minutes | Serves 4

6 tablespoons mayonnaise
2 tablespoons coarse-ground mustard
2 teaspoons honey (optional)
2 teaspoons curry
powder
1 teaspoon kosher salt
1 teaspoon cayenne pepper
1 pound (454 g) chicken tenders

1. In a large bowl, whisk together the mayonnaise, mustard, honey (if using), curry powder, salt, and cayenne. Transfer half of the mixture to a serving bowl to serve as a dipping sauce. Add the chicken tenders to the large bowl and toss until well coated.
2. Place the tenders in the crisper tray.
3. Place the crisper tray on the bake position. Select Bake, set the temperature to 350ºF (177ºC), and set the time to 15 minutes.
4. Use a meat thermometer to ensure the chicken has reached an internal temperature of 165ºF (74ºC).
5. Serve the chicken with the dipping sauce.

Rosemary Turkey Scotch Eggs

Prep time: 15 minutes | Cook time: 12 minutes | Serves 4

1 egg
1 cup panko breadcrumbs
½ teaspoon rosemary
1 pound (454 g) ground turkey
4 hard-boiled eggs, peeled
Salt and ground black pepper, to taste
Cooking spray

1. Spritz the crisper tray with cooking spray.
2. Whisk the egg with salt in a bowl. Combine the breadcrumbs with rosemary in a shallow dish.
3. Stir the ground turkey with salt and ground black pepper in a separate large bowl, then divide the ground turkey into four portions.
4. Wrap each hard-boiled egg with a portion of ground turkey. Dredge in the whisked egg, then roll over the breadcrumb mixture.
5. Place the wrapped eggs in the crisper tray and spritz with cooking spray.
6. Place the crisper tray on the air fry position. Select Air Fry, set the temperature to 400ºF (204ºC), and set the time to 12 minutes.
7. Cook for 12 minutes or until golden brown and crunchy. Flip the eggs halfway through.
8. Serve immediately.

Turkey and Cauliflower Meatloaf

Prep time: 15 minutes | Cook time: 50 minutes | Serves 6

2 pounds (907 g) lean ground turkey
1⅓ cups riced cauliflower
2 large eggs, lightly beaten
¼ cup almond flour
⅔ cup chopped yellow or white onion
1 teaspoon ground dried turmeric
1 teaspoon ground cumin
1 teaspoon ground coriander
1 tablespoon minced garlic
1 teaspoon salt
1 teaspoon ground black pepper
Cooking spray

1. Spritz the loaf pan with cooking spray.
2. Combine all the ingredients in a large bowl. Stir to mix well. Pour half of the mixture in the prepared loaf pan and press with a spatula to coat the bottom evenly. Spritz the mixture with cooking spray.
3. Place the loaf pan on the bake position. Select Bake, set the temperature to 350ºF (177ºC), and set the time to 25 minutes.
4. Cook for 25 minutes, or until the meat is well browned and the internal temperature reaches at least 165ºF (74ºC). Repeat with remaining mixture.
5. Remove the loaf pan from the grill and serve immediately.

Cajun Turkey

Prep time: 10 minutes | Cook time: 30 minutes | Serves 4

2 pounds (907 g) turkey thighs, skinless and boneless
1 red onion, sliced
2 bell peppers, sliced
1 habanero pepper, minced
1 carrot, sliced
1 tablespoon Cajun seasoning mix
1 tablespoon fish sauce
2 cups chicken broth
Nonstick cooking spray

1. Spritz the bottom and sides of the pan with nonstick cooking spray.
2. Arrange the turkey thighs in the pan. Add the onion, peppers, and carrot. Sprinkle with Cajun seasoning. Add the fish sauce and chicken broth.
3. Place the baking pan on the roast position. Select Roast, set the temperature to 360ºF (182ºC), and set the time to 30 minutes.
4. Cook for 30 minutes until cooked through. Serve warm.

Strawberry-Glazed Turkey

Prep time: 15 minutes | Cook time: 37 minutes | Serves 2

2 pounds (907 g) turkey breast
1 tablespoon olive oil
Salt and ground black

pepper, to taste
1 cup fresh strawberries

1. Rub the turkey bread with olive oil on a clean work surface, then sprinkle with salt and ground black pepper.
2. Transfer the turkey in the crisper tray.
3. Place the crisper tray on the air fry position. Select Air Fry, set the temperature to 375ºF (191ºC), and set the time to 30 minutes.
4. Cook for 30 minutes or until the internal temperature of the turkey reaches at least 165ºF (74ºC). Flip the turkey breast halfway through.
5. Meanwhile, put the strawberries in a food processor and pulse until smooth.
6. When the cooking of the turkey is complete, spread the puréed strawberries over the turkey. Air fry for 7 more minutes.
7. Serve immediately.

Dill Chicken Strips

Prep time: 15 minutes | Cook time: 10 minutes | Serves 4

2 whole boneless, skinless chicken breasts, halved lengthwise
1 cup Italian dressing
3 cups finely crushed potato chips

1 tablespoon dried dill weed
1 tablespoon garlic powder
1 large egg, beaten
Cooking spray

1. In a large resealable bag, combine the chicken and Italian dressing. Seal the bag and refrigerate to marinate at least 1 hour.
2. In a shallow dish, stir together the potato chips, dill, and garlic powder. Place the beaten egg in a second shallow dish.
3. Remove the chicken from the marinade. Roll the chicken pieces in the egg and the potato chip mixture, coating thoroughly.
4. Place the coated chicken in the baking pan and spritz with cooking spray.
5. Place the baking pan on the bake position. Select Bake, set the temperature to 325ºF (163ºC), and set the time to 10 minutes.
6. Cook for 5 minutes. Flip the chicken, spritz it with cooking spray, and cook for 5 minutes more until the outsides are crispy and the insides are no longer pink. Serve immediately.

Duck Breasts with Marmalade Balsamic Glaze

Prep time: 5 minutes | Cook time: 13 minutes | Serves 4

4 (6-ounce / 170-g) skin-on duck breasts
1 teaspoon salt
¼ cup orange marmalade

1 tablespoon white balsamic vinegar
¾ teaspoon ground black pepper

1. Cut 10 slits into the skin of the duck breasts, then sprinkle with salt on both sides.
2. Place the breasts in the crisper tray, skin side up.
3. Place the crisper tray on the air fry position. Select Air Fry, set the temperature to 400ºF (204ºC), and set the time to 10 minutes.
4. Meanwhile, combine the remaining ingredients in a small bowl. Stir to mix well.
5. When the frying is complete, brush the duck skin with the marmalade mixture. Flip the breast and air fry for 3 more minutes or until the skin is crispy and the breast is well browned.
6. Serve immediately.

Chicken Tenders with Veggies

Prep time: 10 minutes | Cook time: 18 to 20 minutes | Serves 4

1 pound (454 g) chicken tenders
1 tablespoon honey
Pinch salt
Freshly ground black pepper, to taste
½ cup soft fresh bread

crumbs
½ teaspoon dried thyme
1 tablespoon olive oil
2 carrots, sliced
12 small red potatoes

1. In a medium bowl, toss the chicken tenders with the honey, salt, and pepper.
2. In a shallow bowl, combine the bread crumbs, thyme, and olive oil, and mix.
3. Coat the tenders in the bread crumbs, pressing firmly onto the meat.
4. Place the carrots and potatoes in the crisper tray and top with the chicken tenders.
5. Place the crisper tray on the roast position. Select Roast, set the temperature to 380ºF (193ºC), and set the time to 20 minutes.
6. Cook for 18 to 20 minutes, or until the chicken is cooked to 165ºF (74ºC) and the vegetables are tender, shaking the crisper tray halfway during the cooking time.
7. Serve warm.

Asian Turkey Meatballs

Prep time: 10 minutes | Cook time: 11 to 14 minutes | Serves 4

2 tablespoons peanut oil, divided	2 tablespoons low-sodium soy sauce
1 small onion, minced	¼ cup panko bread crumbs
¼ cup water chestnuts, finely chopped	1 egg, beaten
½ teaspoon ground ginger	1 pound (454 g) ground turkey

1. In the baking pan, combine 1 tablespoon of peanut oil and onion.
2. Place the baking pan on the air fry position. Select Air Fry, set the temperature to 400ºF (204ºC), and set the time to 2 minutes.
3. Cook for 1 to 2 minutes or until crisp and tender. Transfer the onion to a medium bowl.
4. Add the water chestnuts, ground ginger, soy sauce, and bread crumbs to the onion and mix well. Add egg and stir well. Mix in the ground turkey until combined.
5. Form the mixture into 1-inch meatballs. Drizzle the remaining 1 tablespoon of oil over the meatballs. Arrange the meatballs in the pan.
6. Bake for 10 to 12 minutes, or until they are 165ºF (74ºC) on a meat thermometer. Rest for 5 minutes before serving.

Honey Rosemary Chicken

Prep time: 10 minutes | Cook time: 20 minutes | Serves 4

¼ cup balsamic vinegar	ground black pepper
¼ cup honey	2 whole boneless, skinless chicken breasts (about 1 pound / 454 g each), halved
2 tablespoons olive oil	
1 tablespoon dried rosemary leaves	
1 teaspoon salt	Cooking spray
½ teaspoon freshly	

1. In a large resealable bag, combine the vinegar, honey, olive oil, rosemary, salt, and pepper. Add the chicken pieces, seal the bag, and refrigerate to marinate for at least 2 hours.
2. Line the crisper tray with parchment paper.
3. Remove the chicken from the marinade and place it on the parchment. Spritz with cooking spray.
4. Place the crisper tray on the bake position. Select Bake, set the temperature to 325ºF (163ºC), and set the time to 20 minutes.
5. Cook for 10 minutes. Flip the chicken, spritz it with cooking spray, and cook for 10 minutes more until the internal temperature reaches 165ºF (74ºC) and the chicken is no longer pink inside. Let sit for 5 minutes before serving.

Orange and Honey Glazed Duck with Apples

Prep time: 5 minutes | Cook time: 15 minutes | Serves 2 to 3

1 pound (454 g) duck breasts (2 to 3 breasts)	orange
	¼ cup honey
Kosher salt and pepper, to taste	2 sprigs thyme, plus more for garnish
Juice and zest of 1	2 firm tart apples, such as Fuji

1. Pat the duck breasts dry and, using a sharp knife, make 3 to 4 shallow, diagonal slashes in the skin. Turn the breasts and score the skin on the diagonal in the opposite direction to create a cross-hatch pattern. Season well with salt and pepper.
2. Place the duck breasts skin-side up in the crisper tray.
3. Place the crisper tray on the roast position. Select Roast, set the temperature to 400ºF (204ºC), and set the time to 13 minutes.
4. Cook for 8 minutes. Flip and cook for 4 more minutes on the second side.
5. While the duck is roasting, prepare the sauce. Combine the orange juice and zest, honey, and thyme in a small saucepan. Bring to a boil, stirring to dissolve the honey, then reduce the heat and simmer until thickened. Core the apples and cut into quarters. Cut each quarter into 3 or 4 slices depending on the size.
6. After the duck has cooked on both sides, turn it and brush the skin with the orange-honey glaze. Roast for 1 more minute. Remove the duck breasts to a cutting board and allow to rest.
7. Toss the apple slices with the remaining orange-honey sauce in a medium bowl. Arrange the apples in a single layer in the crisper tray. Air fry for 10 minutes while the duck breast rests. Slice the duck breasts on the bias and divide them and the apples among 2 or 3 plates.
8. Serve warm, garnished with additional thyme.

Lettuce Chicken Tacos with Peanut Sauce

Prep time: 10 minutes | Cook time: 6 minutes | Serves 4

1 pound (454 g) ground chicken
2 cloves garlic, minced
Peanut Sauce:
¼ cup creamy peanut butter, at room temperature
2 tablespoons tamari
1½ teaspoons hot sauce
2 tablespoons lime
For Serving:
¼ cup diced onions
¼ teaspoon sea salt
Cooking spray

juice
2 tablespoons grated fresh ginger
2 tablespoons chicken broth
2 teaspoons sugar

2 small heads butter lettuce, leaves separated
Lime slices (optional)

1. Spritz the baking pan with cooking spray.
2. Combine the ground chicken, garlic, and onions in the baking pan, then sprinkle with salt. Use a fork to break the ground chicken and combine them well.
3. Place the baking pan on the bake position. Select Bake, set the temperature to 350ºF (177ºC), and set the time to 5 minutes.
4. Cook for 5 minutes, or until the chicken is lightly browned. Stir them halfway through the cooking time.
5. Meanwhile, combine the ingredients for the sauce in a small bowl. Stir to mix well.
6. Pour the sauce in the pan of chicken, then cook for 1 more minute or until heated through.
7. Unfold the lettuce leaves on a large serving plate, then divide the chicken mixture on the lettuce leaves. Drizzle with lime juice and serve immediately.

Turkey Burger

Prep time: 5 minutes | Cook time: 13 minutes | Serves 4

1 pound (454 g) ground turkey
½ red onion, minced
1 jalapeño pepper, seeded, stemmed, and minced
3 tablespoons bread crumbs
1½ teaspoons ground cumin
1 teaspoon paprika
½ teaspoon cayenne
pepper
½ teaspoon sea salt
½ teaspoon freshly ground black pepper
4 burger buns, for serving
Lettuce, tomato, and cheese, if desired, for serving
Ketchup and mustard, if desired, for serving

1. In a large bowl, use your hands to combine the ground turkey, red onion, jalapeño pepper, bread crumbs, cumin, paprika, cayenne pepper, salt, and black pepper. Mix until just combined; be careful not to overwork the burger mixture.
2. Dampen your hands with cool water and form the turkey mixture into four patties.
3. Place the burgers on the grill plate.
4. Place the grill plate on the grill position. Select Grill, set the temperature to 400ºF (204ºC), and set the time to 11 minutes.
5. After 11 minutes, check the burgers for doneness. Cooking is complete when the internal temperature reaches at least 165ºF (74ºC) on a food thermometer. If necessary, continue grilling for up to 2 minutes more.
6. Once the burgers are done cooking, place each patty on a bun. Top with your preferred fixings, such as lettuce, tomato, cheese, ketchup, and/or mustard.

Sweet and Spicy Turkey Meatballs

Prep time: 15 minutes | Cook time: 15 minutes | Serves 6

1 pound (454 g) lean ground turkey
½ cup whole-wheat panko bread crumbs
1 egg, beaten
1 tablespoon soy sauce
¼ cup plus 1 tablespoon hoisin
sauce, divided
2 teaspoons minced garlic
⅛ teaspoon salt
⅛ teaspoon freshly ground black pepper
1 teaspoon sriracha
Olive oil spray

1. Spray the crisper tray lightly with olive oil spray.
2. In a large bowl, mix together the turkey, panko bread crumbs, egg, soy sauce, 1 tablespoon of hoisin sauce, garlic, salt, and black pepper.
3. Using a tablespoon, form the mixture into 24 meatballs.
4. In a small bowl, combine the remaining ¼ cup of hoisin sauce and sriracha to make a glaze and set aside.
5. Place the meatballs in the crisper tray in a single layer. You may need to cook them in batches.
6. Place the crisper tray on the air fry position. Select Air Fry, set the temperature to 350ºF (177ºC), and set the time to 15 minutes.
7. Cook for 8 minutes. Brush the meatballs generously with the glaze and cook until cooked through, an additional 4 to 7 minutes.
8. Serve warm.

Chicken and Veggie Kebabs

Prep time: 15 minutes | Cook time: 14 minutes | Serves 4

2 tablespoons plain Greek yogurt
¼ cup extra-virgin olive oil
Juice of 4 lemons
Grated zest of 1 lemon
4 garlic cloves, minced
2 tablespoons dried oregano
1 teaspoon sea salt
½ teaspoon freshly ground black pepper
1 pound (454 g) boneless, skinless chicken breasts, cut into 2-inch cubes
1 red onion, quartered
1 zucchini, sliced

1. In a large bowl, whisk together the Greek yogurt, oil, lemon juice, zest, garlic, oregano, salt, and pepper until well combined.
2. Place the chicken and half of the marinade into a large resealable plastic bag or container. Move the chicken around to coat evenly. Refrigerate for at least 30 minutes.
3. Assemble the kebabs by threading the chicken on the wood skewers, alternating with the red onion and zucchini. Ensure the ingredients are pushed almost completely down to the end of the skewers.
4. Place the skewers on the grill plate.
5. Place the grill plate on the grill position. Select Grill, set the temperature to 350ºF (177ºC), and set the time to 14 minutes.
6. Cook for 10 to 14 minutes, occasionally basting the kebabs with the remaining marinade while cooking.
7. Cooking is complete when the internal temperature of the chicken reaches 165ºF (74ºC) on a food thermometer.

Parmesan Chicken

Prep time: 10 minutes | Cook time: 20 minutes | Serves 4

1 egg
2 tablespoons lemon juice
2 teaspoons minced garlic
½ teaspoon salt
½ teaspoon freshly ground black pepper
4 boneless, skinless chicken breasts, thin cut
Olive oil spray
½ cup whole-wheat bread crumbs
¼ cup grated Parmesan cheese

1. In a medium bowl, whisk together the egg, lemon juice, garlic, salt, and pepper. Add the chicken breasts, cover, and refrigerate for up to 1 hour.
2. In a shallow bowl, combine the bread crumbs and Parmesan cheese.
3. Spray the crisper tray lightly with olive oil spray.
4. Remove the chicken breasts from the egg mixture, then dredge them in the bread crumb mixture, and place in the crisper tray in a single layer. Lightly spray the chicken breasts with olive oil spray. You may need to cook the chicken in batches.
5. Place the crisper tray on the air fry position. Select Air Fry, set the temperature to 360ºF (182ºC), and set the time to 20 minutes.
6. Cook for 8 minutes. Flip the chicken over, lightly spray with olive oil spray, and cook for an additional 7 to 12 minutes, until the chicken reaches an internal temperature of 165ºF (74ºC).
7. Serve warm.

Turkey Stuffed Bell Peppers

Prep time: 20 minutes | Cook time: 15 minutes | Serves 4

½ pound (227 g) lean ground turkey
4 medium bell peppers
1 (15-ounce / 425-g) can black beans, drained and rinsed
1 cup shredded reduced-fat Cheddar cheese
1 cup cooked long-grain brown rice
1 cup mild salsa
1¼ teaspoons chili powder
1 teaspoon salt
½ teaspoon ground cumin
½ teaspoon freshly ground black pepper
Olive oil spray
Chopped fresh cilantro, for garnish

1. In a large skillet over medium-high heat, cook the turkey, breaking it up with a spoon, until browned, about 5 minutes. Drain off any excess fat.
2. Cut about ½ inch off the tops of the peppers and then cut in half lengthwise. Remove and discard the seeds and set the peppers aside.
3. In a large bowl, combine the browned turkey, black beans, Cheddar cheese, rice, salsa, chili powder, salt, cumin, and black pepper. Spoon the mixture into the bell peppers.
4. Lightly spray the crisper tray with olive oil spray.
5. Place the stuffed peppers in the crisper tray.
6. Place the crisper tray on the air fry position. Select Air Fry, set the temperature to 360ºF (182ºC), and set the time to 15 minutes.
7. Cook for 10 to 15 minutes until heated through.
8. Garnish with cilantro and serve.

Teriyaki Chicken Skewers with Pineapple

Prep time: 15 minutes | Cook time: 14 minutes | Serves 4

1 pound (454 g) boneless, skinless chicken breasts, cut into 2-inch cubes
1 cup teriyaki sauce, divided

2 green bell peppers, seeded and cut into 1-inch cubes
2 cups fresh pineapple, cut into 1-inch cubes

1. Place the chicken and ½ cup of teriyaki sauce in a large resealable plastic bag or container. Toss to coat evenly. Refrigerate for at least 30 minutes.
2. Assemble the kebabs by threading the chicken onto the wood skewers, alternating with the peppers and pineapple. Ensure the ingredients are pushed almost completely down to the end of the skewers.
3. Place the skewers on the grill plate.
4. Place the grill plate on the grill position. Select Grill, set the temperature to 350ºF (177ºC), and set the time to 14 minutes.
5. Cook for 10 to 14 minutes, occasionally basting the kebabs with the remaining ½ cup of teriyaki sauce while cooking.
6. Cooking is complete when the internal temperature of the chicken reaches 165ºF (74ºC) on a food thermometer.

Lime Chicken Kebabs

Prep time: 15 minutes | Cook time: 14 minutes | Serves 4

1 tablespoon ground cumin
1 tablespoon garlic powder
1 tablespoon chili powder
2 teaspoons paprika
¼ teaspoon sea salt
¼ teaspoon freshly ground black pepper
1 pound (454 g)

boneless, skinless chicken breasts, cut in 2-inch cubes
2 tablespoons extra-virgin olive oil, divided
2 red bell peppers, seeded and cut into 1-inch cubes
1 red onion, quartered
Juice of 1 lime

1. In a small mixing bowl, combine the cumin, garlic powder, chili powder, paprika, salt, and pepper, and mix well.
2. Place the chicken, 1 tablespoon oil, and half of the spice mixture into a large resealable plastic bag or container. Toss to coat evenly.

3. Place the bell pepper, onion, remaining 1 tablespoon of oil, and remaining spice mixture into a large resealable plastic bag or container. Toss to coat evenly. Refrigerate the chicken and vegetables for at least 30 minutes.
4. Assemble the kebabs by threading the chicken onto the wood skewers, alternating with the peppers and onion. Ensure the ingredients are pushed almost completely down to the end of the skewers.
5. Place the skewers on the grill plate.
6. Place the grill plate on the grill position. Select Grill, set the temperature to 400ºF (204ºC), and set the time to 14 minutes.
7. Cooking is complete when the internal temperature of the chicken reaches 165ºF (74ºC). When cooking is complete, remove from the heat, and drizzle with lime juice.

Ginger Chicken Thighs

Prep time: 10 minutes | Cook time: 10 minutes | Serves 4

¼ cup julienned peeled fresh ginger
2 tablespoons vegetable oil
1 tablespoon honey
1 tablespoon soy sauce
1 tablespoon ketchup
1 teaspoon garam masala
1 teaspoon ground turmeric

¼ teaspoon kosher salt
½ teaspoon cayenne pepper
Vegetable oil spray
1 pound (454 g) boneless, skinless chicken thighs, cut crosswise into thirds
¼ cup chopped fresh cilantro, for garnish

1. In a small bowl, combine the ginger, oil, honey, soy sauce, ketchup, garam masala, turmeric, salt, and cayenne. Whisk until well combined. Place the chicken in a resealable plastic bag and pour the marinade over. Seal the bag and massage to cover all of the chicken with the marinade. Marinate at room temperature for 30 minutes or in the refrigerator for up to 24 hours.
2. Spray the crisper tray with vegetable oil spray and add the chicken and as much of the marinade and julienned ginger as possible.
3. Place the crisper tray on the bake position. Select Bake, set the temperature to 350ºF (177ºC), and set the time to 10 minutes.
4. Use a meat thermometer to ensure the chicken has reached an internal temperature of 165ºF (74ºC).
5. To serve, garnish with cilantro.

Hoisin Turkey Burgers

Prep time: 10 minutes | Cook time: 20 minutes | Serves 4

1 pound (454 g) lean ground turkey
¼ cup whole-wheat bread crumbs
¼ cup hoisin sauce
2 tablespoons soy sauce
4 whole-wheat buns
Olive oil spray

1. In a large bowl, mix together the turkey, bread crumbs, hoisin sauce, and soy sauce.
2. Form the mixture into 4 equal patties. Cover with plastic wrap and refrigerate the patties for 30 minutes.
3. Spray the crisper tray lightly with olive oil spray.
4. Place the patties in the crisper tray in a single layer. Spray the patties lightly with olive oil spray.
5. Place the crisper tray on the air fry position. Select Air Fry, set the temperature to 370°F (188°C), and set the time to 20 minutes.
6. Cook for 10 minutes. Flip the patties over, lightly spray with olive oil spray, and cook for an additional 5 to 10 minutes, until golden brown.
7. Place the patties on buns and top with your choice of low-calorie burger toppings like sliced tomatoes, onions, and cabbage slaw. Serve immediately.

Dill Pickle Chicken Wings

Prep time: 5 minutes | Cook time: 26 minutes | Serves 4

2 pounds (907 g) bone-in chicken wings (drumettes and flats)
1½ cups dill pickle juice
1½ tablespoons vegetable oil
½ tablespoon dried dill
¾ teaspoon garlic powder
Sea salt, to taste
Freshly ground black pepper, to taste

1. Place the chicken wings in a large shallow bowl. Pour the pickle juice over the top, ensuring all of the wings are coated and as submerged as possible. Cover and refrigerate for 2 hours.
2. Rinse the brined chicken wings under cool water, then pat them dry with a paper towel. Place in a large bowl.
3. In a small bowl, whisk together the oil, dill, garlic powder, salt, and pepper. Drizzle over the wings and toss to fully coat them.
4. Place the wings in the crisper tray, spreading them out evenly.
5. Place the crisper tray on the air fry position. Select Air Fry, set the temperature to 390°F (199°C), and set the time to 22 minutes.
6. After 11 minutes, flip the wings with tongs. Cook for 11 minutes more.
7. Check the wings for doneness. Cooking is complete when the internal temperature of the chicken reaches at least 165°F (74°C) on a food thermometer. If needed, air fry for 4 more minutes.
8. Remove the wings from the crisper tray and serve immediately.

Rosemary Turkey Breast

Prep time: 20 minutes | Cook time: 30 minutes | Serves 6

½ teaspoon dried rosemary
2 minced garlic cloves
2 teaspoons salt
1 teaspoon ground black pepper
¼ cup olive oil
2½ pounds (1.1 kg)
turkey breast
¼ cup pure maple syrup
1 tablespoon stone-ground brown mustard
1 tablespoon melted vegan butter

1. Combine the rosemary, garlic, salt, ground black pepper, and olive oil in a large bowl. Stir to mix well.
2. Dunk the turkey breast in the mixture and wrap the bowl in plastic. Refrigerate for 2 hours to marinate.
3. Remove the bowl from the refrigerator and let sit for half an hour before cooking.
4. Spritz the crisper tray with cooking spray.
5. Remove the turkey from the marinade and place in the crisper tray.
6. Place the crisper tray on the air fry position. Select Air Fry, set the temperature to 400°F (204°C), and set the time to 20 minutes.
7. Cook for 20 minutes or until well browned. Flip the breast halfway through.
8. Meanwhile, combine the remaining ingredients in a small bowl. Stir to mix well.
9. Pour half of the butter mixture over the turkey breast in the crisper tray. Air fry for 10 more minutes. Flip the breast and pour the remaining half of butter mixture over halfway through.
10. Transfer the turkey on a plate and slice to serve.

China Spicy Turkey Thighs

Prep time: 10 minutes | Cook time: 25 minutes | Serves 6

2 pounds (907 g) turkey thighs
1 teaspoon Chinese five-spice powder
¼ teaspoon Sichuan pepper
1 teaspoon pink Himalayan salt
1 tablespoon Chinese rice vinegar
1 tablespoon mustard
1 tablespoon chili sauce
2 tablespoons soy sauce
Cooking spray

1. Spritz the crisper tray with cooking spray.
2. Rub the turkey thighs with five-spice powder, Sichuan pepper, and salt on a clean work surface.
3. Put the turkey thighs in the crisper tray and spritz with cooking spray. You may need to work in batches to avoid overcrowding.
4. Place the crisper tray on the air fry position. Select Air Fry, set the temperature to 360°F (182°C), and set the time to 22 minutes.
5. Cook for 22 minutes or until well browned. Flip the thighs at least three times during the cooking.
6. Meanwhile, heat the remaining ingredients in a saucepan over medium-high heat. Cook for 3 minutes or until the sauce is thickened and reduces to two thirds.
7. Transfer the thighs onto a plate and baste with sauce before serving.

Chicken Piccata

Prep time: 5 minutes | Cook time: 22 minutes | Serves 2

2 large eggs
½ cup all-purpose flour
½ teaspoon freshly ground black pepper
2 boneless, skinless chicken breasts
4 tablespoons unsalted butter
Juice of 1 lemon
1 tablespoon capers, drained

1. In a medium shallow bowl, whisk the eggs until they are fully beaten.
2. In a separate medium shallow bowl, combine the flour and black pepper, using a fork to distribute the pepper evenly throughout.
3. Dredge the chicken in the flour to coat it completely, then dip it into the egg, then back in the flour.
4. Place the chicken in the crisper tray.
5. Place the crisper tray on the air fry position. Select Air Fry, set the temperature to 375°F (191°C), and set the time to 18 minutes.

6. While the chicken is cooking, melt the butter in a skillet over medium heat. Add the lemon juice and capers, and bring to a simmer. Reduce the heat to low, and simmer for 4 minutes.
7. After 18 minutes, check the chicken. Cooking is complete when the internal temperature of the meat reaches at least 165°F (74°C) on a food thermometer. If necessary, continue cooking for up to 3 minutes more.
8. Plate the chicken, and drizzle the butter sauce over each serving.

Gnocchi with Chicken and Spinach

Prep time: 10 minutes | Cook time: 13 minutes | Serves 4

1 (1-pound / 454-g) package shelf-stable gnocchi
1¼ cups low-sodium chicken stock
½ teaspoon kosher salt or ¼ teaspoon fine salt
1 pound (454 g) chicken breast, cut into 1-inch chunks
1 cup heavy (whipping) cream
2 tablespoons sun-dried tomato purée
1 garlic clove, minced or smashed
1 cup frozen spinach, thawed and drained
1 cup grated Parmesan cheese

1. Place the gnocchi in an even layer in the baking pan. Pour the chicken stock over the gnocchi.
2. Place the pan on the bake position. Select Bake, set temperature to 450°F (232°C), and set time to 7 minutes.
3. While the gnocchi are cooking, sprinkle the salt over the chicken pieces. In a small bowl, mix together the cream, tomato purée, and garlic.
4. When cooking is complete, blot off any remaining stock, or drain the gnocchi and return it to the pan. Top the gnocchi with the spinach and chicken. Pour the cream mixture over the ingredients in the pan.
5. Place the pan on the roast position. Select Roast, set temperature to 400°F (204°C), and set time to 6 minutes.
6. After 4 minutes, remove the pan from the grill and gently stir the ingredients. Return the pan to the grill and continue cooking.
7. When cooking is complete, the gnocchi should be tender and the chicken should be cooked through. Remove the pan from the grill. Stir in the Parmesan cheese until it's melted, and serve.

Spiced Breaded Chicken Cutlets

Prep time: 5 minutes | Cook time: 11 minutes | Serves 2

½ pound (227 g) boneless, skinless chicken breasts, horizontally sliced in half, into cutlets
½ tablespoon extra-virgin olive oil
⅛ cup bread crumbs

¼ teaspoon sea salt
¼ teaspoon freshly ground black pepper
¼ teaspoon paprika
¼ teaspoon garlic powder
⅛ teaspoon onion powder

1. Brush each side of the chicken cutlets with the oil.
2. Combine the bread crumbs, salt, pepper, paprika, garlic powder, and onion powder in a medium shallow bowl. Dredge the chicken cutlets in the bread crumb mixture, turning several times, to ensure the chicken is fully coated.
3. Place the chicken in the crisper tray.
4. Place the crisper tray on the air fry position. Select Air Fry, set the temperature to 375°F (191°C), and set the time to 9 minutes.
5. Cook for 9 minutes. Cooking is complete when the internal temperature of the meat reaches at least 165°F (74°C) on a food thermometer. If needed, air fry for 2 minutes more.
6. Remove the chicken cutlets and serve immediately.

Crispy Chicken Strips

Prep time: 15 minutes | Cook time: 20 minutes | Serves 4

1 tablespoon olive oil
1 pound (454 g) boneless, skinless chicken tenderloins
1 teaspoon salt
½ teaspoon freshly ground black pepper
½ teaspoon paprika

½ teaspoon garlic powder
½ cup whole-wheat seasoned bread crumbs
1 teaspoon dried parsley
Cooking spray

1. Spray the crisper tray lightly with cooking spray.
2. In a medium bowl, toss the chicken with the salt, pepper, paprika, and garlic powder until evenly coated.
3. Add the olive oil and toss to coat the chicken evenly.
4. In a separate, shallow bowl, mix together the bread crumbs and parsley.

5. Coat each piece of chicken evenly in the bread crumb mixture.
6. Place the chicken in the crisper tray in a single layer and spray it lightly with cooking spray. You may need to cook them in batches.
7. Place the crisper tray on the air fry position. Select Air Fry, set the temperature to 370°F (188°C), and set the time to 20 minutes.
8. Cook for 10 minutes. Flip the chicken over, lightly spray it with cooking spray, and cook for an additional 8 to 10 minutes, until golden brown. Serve.

Chicken and Brussels Sprout Curry

Prep time: 10 minutes | Cook time: 20 minutes | Serves 4

1 pound (454 g) boneless, skinless chicken thighs
1 teaspoon kosher salt or ½ teaspoon fine salt, divided
¼ cup unsalted butter, melted

1 tablespoon curry powder
2 medium sweet potatoes, peeled and cut in 1-inch cubes
12 ounces (340 g) Brussels sprouts, halved

1. Salt the chicken thighs with ½ teaspoon of kosher salt. Place them in the center of the baking pan.
2. In a small bowl, stir together the butter and curry powder.
3. Place the sweet potatoes and Brussels sprouts in a large bowl. Drizzle half the curry butter over the vegetables and add the remaining ½ teaspoon of kosher salt. Toss to coat. Transfer the vegetables to the baking pan and arrange in a single layer around the chicken. Brush half of the remaining curry butter over the chicken.
4. Place the pan on the roast position. Select Roast, set temperature to 400°F (204°C), and set time to 20 minutes.
5. After 10 minutes, remove the pan from the grill and turn over the chicken thighs. Baste them with the remaining curry butter. Return the pan to the grill and continue cooking.
6. Cooking is complete when the sweet potatoes are tender and the chicken is cooked through and reads 165°F (74°C) on a meat thermometer.

Italian Chicken Parm Sandwiches

Prep time: 12 minutes | Cook time: 13 minutes | Serves 4

2 (8-ounce / 227-g) boneless, skinless chicken breasts
1 teaspoon kosher salt or ½ teaspoon fine salt, divided
1 cup all-purpose flour
1 teaspoon Italian seasoning or ½ teaspoon each dried oregano and dried basil
2 large eggs
2 tablespoons plain yogurt
2 cups panko bread crumbs
1⅓ cups grated Parmesan cheese, divided
2 tablespoons extra-virgin olive oil
4 ciabatta rolls or other sturdy buns, split in half
½ cup marinara sauce
½ cup shredded Mozzarella cheese

1. Lay the chicken breasts on a cutting board and cut each one in half parallel to the board so that you have 4 fairly even, flat fillets. Place a piece of plastic wrap over the chicken pieces and use a rolling pin or small skillet to gently pound them to an even thickness, about ½-inch thick. Season the chicken on both sides with ½ teaspoon of kosher salt.
2. Place the flour on a plate and add the remaining ½ teaspoon of kosher salt and the Italian seasoning. Mix with a fork to distribute evenly. In a wide bowl, whisk together the eggs with the yogurt. In a small bowl combine the panko, 1 cup of Parmesan cheese, and olive oil. Place this in a shallow bowl or plate.
3. Lightly dredge both sides of the chicken pieces in the seasoned flour, and then dip them in the egg wash to coat completely, letting the excess drip off. Finally, dredge the chicken in the bread crumbs. Carefully place the breaded chicken pieces in the crisper tray.
4. Place the crisper tray on the air fry position. Select Air Fry, set temperature to 375°F (191°C), and set time to 10 minutes.
5. After 5 minutes, remove the crisper tray from the grill. Carefully turn the chicken over. Return the crisper tray to the grill and continue cooking. When cooking is complete, remove the crisper tray and pan from the grill.
6. Open the rolls in the baking pan, and spread each half with 1 tablespoon of marinara sauce. Place a chicken breast piece on the bottoms of the buns and sprinkle the remaining ⅓ cup of Parmesan cheese over the chicken pieces. Divide the Mozzarella among the top halves of the buns.
7. Place the pan on the broil position. Select Broil, set temperature to 450°F (232°C), and set time to 3 minutes.
8. Check the sandwiches after 2 minutes; when cooking is complete, the Mozzarella cheese should be melted and bubbling slightly.
9. Remove the pan from the grill. Close the sandwiches and serve. Add additional marinara sauce if desired.

Bacon-Wrapped Turkey

Prep time: 10 minutes | Cook time: 25 minutes | Serves 4

2 (12-ounce / 340-g) turkey tenderloins
1 teaspoon kosher salt or ½ teaspoon fine salt, divided
6 slices bacon (not thick cut)
3 tablespoons balsamic vinegar
2 tablespoons honey
1 tablespoon Dijon mustard
½ teaspoon dried thyme
6 large carrots, peeled and cut into ¼-inch rounds
1 tablespoon extra-virgin olive oil

1. Sprinkle the turkey with ¾ teaspoon of the salt (if your tenderloins are brined, omit this step). Wrap each tenderloin with 3 strips of bacon, securing the bacon with toothpicks if necessary. Place the turkey in the baking pan.
2. In a small bowl, mix together the balsamic vinegar, honey, mustard, and thyme.
3. Place the carrots in a medium bowl and drizzle with the oil. Add 1 tablespoon of the balsamic mixture and ¼ teaspoon of kosher salt and toss to coat. Place these in the pan around the turkey tenderloins. Baste the tenderloins with about one-half of the remaining balsamic mixture.
4. Place the pan on the roast position. Select Roast, set temperature to 375°F (191°C), and set time to 25 minutes.
5. After 13 minutes, remove the pan from the grill. Gently stir the carrots. Turn over the tenderloins and baste them with the remaining balsamic mixture. Return the pan to the grill and continue cooking.
6. When cooking is complete, the carrots should be tender and the center of the tenderloins should register 155°F (68°C) on a meat thermometer (the temperature will continue to rise). Remove the pan from the grill. Slice the turkey and serve with the carrots.

Potato Cheese Crusted Chicken

Prep time: 15 minutes | Cook time: 22 to 25 minutes | Serves 4

¼ cup buttermilk
1 large egg, beaten
1 cup instant potato flakes
¼ cup grated Parmesan cheese
1 teaspoon salt
½ teaspoon freshly

ground black pepper
2 whole boneless, skinless chicken breasts (about 1 pound / 454 g each), halved
Cooking spray

1. Line the crisper tray with parchment paper.
2. In a shallow bowl, whisk the buttermilk and egg until blended. In another shallow bowl, stir together the potato flakes, cheese, salt, and pepper.
3. One at a time, dip the chicken pieces in the buttermilk mixture and the potato flake mixture, coating thoroughly.
4. Place the coated chicken on the parchment and spritz with cooking spray.
5. Place the crisper tray on the bake position. Select Bake, set the temperature to 325ºF (163ºC), and set the time to 25 minutes.
6. Cook for 15 minutes. Flip the chicken, spritz it with cooking spray, and cook for 7 to 10 minutes more until the outside is crispy and the inside is no longer pink. Serve immediately.

Chicken with Corn and Potatoes

Prep time: 10 minutes | Cook time: 25 minutes | Serves 4

4 bone-in, skin-on chicken thighs
2 teaspoons kosher salt or 1 teaspoon fine salt, divided
1 cup Bisquick or similar baking mix
½ cup unsalted butter, melted, divided
1 pound (454 g)

small red potatoes, quartered
3 ears corn, shucked and cut into rounds 1- to 1½-inches thick
$1/3$ cup heavy (whipping) cream
½ teaspoon freshly ground black pepper

1. Sprinkle the chicken on all sides with 1 teaspoon of kosher salt. Place the baking mix in a shallow dish. Brush the thighs on all sides with ¼ cup of butter, then dredge them in the baking mix, coating them all on sides. Place the chicken in the center of the baking pan.
2. Place the potatoes in a large bowl with 2 tablespoons of butter and toss to coat. Place them on one side of the chicken in the pan.

3. Place the corn in a medium bowl and drizzle with the remaining 2 tablespoons of butter. Sprinkle with ¼ teaspoon of kosher salt and toss to coat. Place in the pan on the other side of the chicken.
4. Place the pan on the roast position. Select Roast, set temperature to 375ºF (191ºC), and set time to 25 minutes.
5. After 20 minutes, remove the pan from the grill and transfer the potatoes back to the bowl. Return the pan to grill and continue cooking.
6. As the chicken continues cooking, add the cream, black pepper, and remaining ¾ teaspoon of kosher salt to the potatoes. Lightly mash the potatoes with a potato masher or fork.
7. When cooking is complete, the corn will be tender and the chicken cooked through, reading 165ºF (74ºC) on a meat thermometer. Remove the pan from the grill and serve the chicken with the smashed potatoes and corn on the side.

Thai Sweet-and-Spicy Drumsticks

Prep time: 5 minutes | Cook time: 25 minutes | Serves 4

8 skin-on chicken drumsticks
1 teaspoon kosher salt or ½ teaspoon fine salt, divided
1 pound (454 g) green

beans, trimmed
2 garlic cloves, minced
2 tablespoons vegetable oil
$1/3$ cup Thai sweet chili sauce

1. Salt the drumsticks on all sides with ½ teaspoon of kosher salt. Let sit for a few minutes, then blot dry with a paper towel. Place in the baking pan.
2. Place the pan on the roast position. Select Roast, set temperature to 375ºF (191ºC), and set time to 25 minutes.
3. While the chicken cooks, place the green beans in a large bowl. Add the remaining ½ teaspoon kosher salt, the garlic, and oil. Toss to coat.
4. After 15 minutes, remove the pan from the grill. Brush the drumsticks with the sweet chili sauce. Place the green beans in the pan. Return the pan to the grill and continue cooking.
5. When cooking is complete, the green beans should be sizzling and browned in spots and the chicken cooked through, reading 165ºF (74ºC) on a meat thermometer. Serve the chicken with the green beans on the side.

Glazed Duck with Cherry Sauce

Prep time: 20 minutes | Cook time: 32 minutes | Serves 12

1 whole duck (about 5 pounds / 2.3 kg in total), split in half, back and rib bones removed, fat trimmed

Cherry Sauce:
1 tablespoon butter
1 shallot, minced
½ cup sherry
1 cup chicken stock
1 teaspoon white wine vinegar
¾ cup cherry

1 teaspoon olive oil
Salt and freshly ground black pepper, to taste

preserves
1 teaspoon fresh thyme leaves
Salt and freshly ground black pepper, to taste

1. On a clean work surface, rub the duck with olive oil, then sprinkle with salt and ground black pepper to season.
2. Place the duck in the crisper tray, breast side up.
3. Place the crisper tray on the air fry position. Select Air Fry, set the temperature to 400°F (204°C), and set the time to 25 minutes.
4. Cook for 25 minutes or until well browned. Flip the duck during the last 10 minutes.
5. Meanwhile, make the cherry sauce: Heat the butter in a nonstick skillet over medium-high heat or until melted.
6. Add the shallot and sauté for 5 minutes or until lightly browned.
7. Add the sherry and simmer for 6 minutes or until it reduces in half.
8. Add the chicken stick, white wine vinegar, and cherry preserves. Stir to combine well. Simmer for 6 more minutes or until thickened.
9. Fold in the thyme leaves and sprinkle with salt and ground black pepper. Stir to mix well.
10. When cooking of the duck is complete, glaze the duck with a quarter of the cherry sauce, then air fry for another 4 minutes.
11. Flip the duck and glaze with another quarter of the cherry sauce. Air fry for an additional 3 minutes.
12. Transfer the duck on a large plate and serve with remaining cherry sauce.

Braised Chicken with Peppers and Polenta

Prep time: 10 minutes | Cook time: 27 minutes | Serves 4

4 bone-in, skin-on chicken thighs (about 1½ pounds / 680 g)
1½ teaspoon kosher salt or ¾ teaspoon fine salt, divided
Cooking oil spray
1 link sweet or hot Italian sausage (about ¼ pound / 113 g), whole
8 ounces (227 g) miniature bell peppers, halved and seeded (or 1 large red bell pepper, thinly sliced)

1 small onion, thinly sliced
2 garlic cloves, minced
1 tablespoon extra-virgin olive oil
4 hot or sweet pickled cherry peppers, seeded and quartered, along with 2 tablespoons pickling liquid from the jar
¼ cup low-sodium chicken stock
4 (1-inch) slices polenta

1. Salt the chicken thighs on both sides with 1 teaspoon of kosher salt. Spray the baking pan with cooking oil spray and place the thighs skin-side down in the pan. Add the sausage.
2. Place the pan on the roast position. Select Roast, set temperature to 375°F (191°C), and set time to 27 minutes.
3. While the chicken and sausage cook, place the bell peppers, onion, and garlic in a large bowl. Sprinkle with the remaining ½ teaspoon of kosher salt and add the olive oil. Toss to coat.
4. After 10 minutes, remove the pan from the grill and turn over the chicken thighs and sausage. Add the pepper mixture to the pan. Return the pan to the grill and continue cooking.
5. After another 10 minutes, remove the pan from the grill and add the pickled peppers, pickling liquid, and stock. Stir the pickled peppers into the peppers and onion. Push them to the side and add the polenta slices in a single layer. Return the pan to the grill and continue cooking.
6. When cooking is complete, the peppers and onion should be soft, the polenta warmed through, and the chicken should read 165°F (74°C) on a meat thermometer. Remove the pan from the grill. Slice the sausage into thin pieces and stir it into the pepper mixture. Place a slice of polenta on each of four plates and spoon the peppers over. Top with a chicken thigh.

Chicken Thighs with Radish Slaw

Prep time: 10 minutes | Cook time: 27 minutes | Serves 4

4 bone-in, skin-on chicken thighs
1½ teaspoon kosher salt or ¾ teaspoon fine salt, divided
1 tablespoon smoked or sweet paprika
½ teaspoon granulated garlic
½ teaspoon dried oregano
¼ teaspoon freshly ground black pepper
Cooking oil spray
3 cups shredded cabbage or coleslaw mix
½ small red or white onion, thinly sliced
4 large radishes, julienned (optional)
3 tablespoons red or white wine vinegar
2 tablespoons extra-virgin olive oil

1. Salt the chicken thighs on both sides with 1 teaspoon of kosher salt. In a small bowl, combine the paprika, garlic, oregano, and black pepper. Sprinkle half this mixture over the skin sides of the thighs. Spray the baking pan with cooking oil spray and place the thighs skin-side down in the pan. Sprinkle the remaining spice mixture over the other sides of the chicken pieces.
2. Place the pan on the roast position. Select Roast, set temperature to 375ºF (191ºC), and set time to 27 minutes.
3. After 10 minutes, remove the pan from the grill and turn over the chicken thighs. Return the pan to the grill and continue cooking.
4. While the chicken cooks, place the cabbage, onion, and radishes (if using) in a large bowl. Sprinkle with the remaining ½ teaspoon of kosher salt, vinegar, and olive oil. Toss to coat.
5. After another 9 to 10 minutes, remove the pan from the grill and place the chicken thighs on a cutting board or plate. Place the cabbage mixture in the pan and toss it with the chicken fat and spices on the bottom of the pan. Spread out the cabbage into an even layer and place the chicken on it, skin-side up. Return the pan to the grill and continue cooking. Cook for another 7 to 8 minutes.
6. When cooking is complete, the cabbage is just becoming tender. Remove the pan from the grill. Taste and adjust the seasoning if necessary. Serve.

Southwestern Chicken Skewers

Prep time: 17 minutes | Cook time: 10 minutes | Serves 4

1 pound (454 g) boneless, skinless chicken breast, cut into 1½-inch chunks
1 large onion, cut into large chunks
1 red bell pepper, seeded and cut into 1-inch pieces
1 green bell pepper, seeded and cut into 1-inch pieces
3 tablespoons vegetable oil, divided
2 tablespoons Southwestern Seasoning or store-
bought southwestern or fajita seasoning
2 teaspoons kosher salt or 1 teaspoon fine salt, divided
2 cups corn, fresh or frozen, thawed and drained
¼ teaspoon granulated garlic
1 tablespoon mayonnaise
1 teaspoon freshly squeezed lime juice
3 tablespoons grated Parmesan cheese

Special Equipment:
12 (9- to 12-inch) wooden skewers, soaked in water for at least 30 minutes

1. Place the chicken, onion, and bell peppers in a large bowl. Add 2 tablespoons of oil, the Southwestern Seasoning, and 1½ teaspoons of kosher salt (omit if using a store-bought seasoning mix that includes salt). Toss to coat evenly.
2. Alternate the chicken and vegetables on the skewers, making about 12 skewers (if you use the larger skewers, you'll probably only need 8).
3. Place the corn in a medium bowl, and add the remaining 1 tablespoon of oil. Add the remaining ½ teaspoon of kosher salt and the garlic, and toss to coat. Place the corn in an even layer in the baking pan and place the skewers on top.
4. Place the pan on the roast position. Select Roast, set temperature to 375ºF (191ºC), and set time to 10 minutes.
5. After about 5 minutes, remove the pan from the grill and turn the skewers. Return the pan to the grill and continue cooking.
6. When cooking is complete, remove the pan from the grill. Place the skewers on a platter and cover with aluminum foil to stay warm. Place the corn back into the bowl and add the mayonnaise, lime juice, and Parmesan cheese. Stir to combine.

Chicken and Roasted Tomato Shawarma

Prep time: 10 minutes | Cook time: 18 minutes | Serves 4

1½ pounds (680 g) boneless, skinless chicken thighs
1¼ teaspoon kosher salt or ⅜ teaspoon fine salt, divided
2 tablespoons plus 1 teaspoon extra-virgin olive oil, divided
⅔ cup plus 2 tablespoons plain Greek yogurt, divided
2 tablespoons freshly squeezed lemon juice
(about 1 medium lemon)
4 garlic cloves, pressed or minced, divided
1 generous tablespoon Shawarma seasoning
4 pita breads, cut in half
1 pint cherry tomatoes
½ small cucumber
1 tablespoon chopped fresh parsley

1. Sprinkle the chicken thighs on both sides with 1 teaspoon of kosher salt. Place in a resealable plastic bag and set aside while you make the marinade.
2. In a small bowl, mix together 2 tablespoons of olive oil, 2 tablespoons of yogurt, the lemon juice, 3 pressed garlic cloves, and Shawarma Seasoning until thoroughly combined. Pour the marinade over the chicken. Seal the bag, squeezing out as much air as possible. and massage the chicken to coat the it with the sauce. Set aside.
3. Wrap 2 pita breads each in two pieces of aluminum foil and place in the baking pan.
4. Place the pan on the bake position. Select Bake, set temperature to 300ºF (149ºC), and set time to 6 minutes.
5. After 3 minutes, remove the pan from the grill and turn over the foil packets. Return the pan to the grill and continue cooking. When cooking is complete, remove the pan from the grill and place the foil-wrapped pitas on the top of the grill to keep warm.
6. Remove the chicken from the marinade, letting the excess drip off into the bag. Place them in the baking pan. Arrange the tomatoes around the sides of the chicken. Discard the marinade.
7. Place the pan on the broil position. Select Broil, set temperature to 450ºF (232ºC), and set time to 12 minutes.
8. After 6 minutes, remove the pan from the grill and turn over the chicken. Return the pan to the grill and continue cooking.
9. While the chicken cooks, peel and seed the cucumber. Grate or finely chop it. Wrap it in a paper towel to remove as much moisture as possible. Place the cucumber in a small bowl. Add the remaining ⅔ cup of yogurt, ¼ teaspoon kosher salt, 1 teaspoon of olive oil, 1 pressed garlic clove, and parsley. Whisk until combined.
10. When cooking is complete, the chicken should be browned, crisp along its edges, and sizzling. Remove the pan from the grill and place the chicken on a cutting board. Cut each thigh into several pieces. Unwrap the pitas. Spread a tablespoon or two of sauce into a pita half. Add some chicken and add 2 or 3 roasted tomatoes. Serve.

Pecan-Crusted Turkey Cutlets

Prep time: 10 minutes | Cook time: 10 to 12 minutes | Serves 4

¾ cup panko bread crumbs
¼ teaspoon salt
¼ teaspoon pepper
¼ teaspoon dry mustard
¼ teaspoon poultry seasoning
½ cup pecans
¼ cup cornstarch
1 egg, beaten
1 pound (454 g) turkey cutlets, ½-inch thick
Salt and pepper, to taste
Cooking spray

1. Place the panko crumbs, salt, pepper, mustard, and poultry seasoning in a food processor. Process until crumbs are finely crushed. Add pecans and process just until nuts are finely chopped.
2. Place cornstarch in a shallow dish and beaten egg in another. Transfer coating mixture from food processor into a third shallow dish.
3. Sprinkle turkey cutlets with salt and pepper to taste.
4. Dip cutlets in cornstarch and shake off excess, then dip in beaten egg and finally roll in crumbs, pressing to coat well. Spray both sides with cooking spray.
5. Place 2 cutlets in crisper tray in a single layer.
6. Place the crisper tray on the air fry position. Select Air Fry, set the temperature to 360ºF (182ºC), and set the time to 12 minutes.
7. Cook for 10 to 12 minutes. Repeat with the remaining cutlets.
8. Serve warm.

Chapter 8 Meats

Korean Beef Tips

Prep time: 5 minutes | Cook time: 13 minutes | Serves 4

4 garlic cloves, minced
½ apple, peeled and grated
3 tablespoons sesame oil
3 tablespoons brown sugar

⅓ cup soy sauce
1 teaspoon freshly ground black pepper
Sea salt
1½ pounds (680 g) beef tips

1. In a medium bowl, combine the garlic, apple, sesame oil, sugar, soy sauce, pepper, and salt until well mixed.
2. Place the beef tips in a large shallow bowl and pour the marinade over them. Cover and refrigerate for 30 minutes.
3. Place the steak tips on the grill plate.
4. Place the grill plate on the grill position. Select Grill, set the temperature to 350ºF (177ºC), and set the time to 11 minutes.
5. Cooking is complete to medium doneness when the internal temperature of the meat reaches 145ºF (63ºC) on a food thermometer. If desired, grill for up to 2 minutes more.
6. Remove the steak, and set it on a cutting board to rest for 5 minutes. Serve.

Cumin-Chili Flank Steak

Prep time: 10 minutes | Cook time: 8 minutes | Serves 2

1 tablespoon chili powder
1 teaspoon dried oregano
2 teaspoons ground cumin

1 teaspoon sea salt
¼ teaspoon freshly ground black pepper
2 (8-ounce / 227-g) flank steaks

1. In a small bowl, mix together the chili powder, oregano, cumin, salt, and pepper. Use your hands to rub the spice mixture on all sides of the steaks.
2. Place the steaks on the grill plate. Gently press the steaks down to maximize grill marks.
3. Place the grill plate on the grill position. Select Grill, set the temperature to 400ºF (204ºC), and set the time to 8 minutes.
4. After 4 minutes, flip the steaks, and cook for 4 minutes more.
5. Remove the steaks from the grill, and transfer them to a cutting board. Let rest for 5 minutes before slicing and serving.

Meatball Sandwiches with Mozzarella and Basil

Prep time: 5 minutes | Cook time: 10 minutes | Serves 4

12 frozen meatballs
8 slices Mozzarella cheese
4 sub rolls, halved

lengthwise
½ cup marinara sauce, warmed
12 fresh basil leaves

1. Place the meatballs in the crisper tray.
2. Place the crisper tray on the air fry position. Select Air Fry, set the temperature to 350ºF (177ºC), and set the time to 10 minutes.
3. After 5 minutes, shake the crisper tray of meatballs. Place the crisper tray back in the grill to resume cooking.
4. While the meatballs are cooking, place two slices of Mozzarella cheese on each sub roll. Use a spoon to spread the marinara sauce on top of the cheese slices. Press three leaves of basil into the sauce on each roll.
5. When cooking is complete, place three meatballs on each sub roll. Serve immediately.

Gochujang-Glazed Baby Back Ribs

Prep time: 10 minutes | Cook time: 22 minutes | Serves 4

¼ cup gochujang paste
¼ cup soy sauce
¼ cup freshly squeezed orange juice
2 tablespoons apple cider vinegar
2 tablespoons sesame oil

6 garlic cloves, minced
1½ tablespoons brown sugar
1 tablespoon grated fresh ginger
1 teaspoon salt
4 (8- to 10-ounce / 227- to 284-g) baby back ribs

1. In a medium bowl, add the gochujang paste, soy sauce, orange juice, vinegar, oil, garlic, sugar, ginger, and salt, and stir to combine.
2. Place the baby back ribs on a baking sheet and coat all sides with the sauce. Cover with aluminum foil and refrigerate for 6 hours.
3. Place the ribs on the grill plate.
4. Place the grill plate on the grill position. Select Grill, set the temperature to 350ºF (177ºC), and set the time to 22 minutes.
5. After 11 minutes, flip the ribs and cook for an additional 11 minutes.
6. When cooking is complete, serve immediately.

Pepperoni and Bell Pepper Pockets

Prep time: 5 minutes | Cook time: 8 minutes | Serves 4

4 bread slices, 1-inch thick
Olive oil, for misting
24 slices pepperoni
1 ounce (28 g) roasted

red peppers, drained and patted dry
1 ounce (28 g) Pepper Jack cheese, cut into 4 slices

1. Spray both sides of bread slices with olive oil.
2. Stand slices upright and cut a deep slit in the top to create a pocket (almost to the bottom crust, but not all the way through).
3. Stuff each bread pocket with 6 slices of pepperoni, a large strip of roasted red pepper, and a slice of cheese.
4. Put bread pockets in crisper tray, standing up.
5. Place the crisper tray on the air fry position. Select Air Fry, set the temperature to 360ºF (182ºC), and set the time to 8 minutes.
6. Cook for 8 minutes, until filling is heated through and bread is lightly browned.
7. Serve hot.

Crispy Pork Tenderloin

Prep time: 5 minutes | Cook time: 10 minutes | Serves 6

2 large egg whites
1½ tablespoons Dijon mustard
2 cups crushed pretzel crumbs

1½ pounds (680 g) pork tenderloin, cut into ¼-pound (113-g) sections
Cooking spray

1. Spritz the crisper tray with cooking spray.
2. Whisk the egg whites with Dijon mustard in a bowl until bubbly. Pour the pretzel crumbs in a separate bowl.
3. Dredge the pork tenderloin in the egg white mixture and press to coat. Shake the excess off and roll the tenderloin over the pretzel crumbs.
4. Arrange the well-coated pork tenderloin in batches in a single layer in the crisper tray and spritz with cooking spray.
5. Place the crisper tray on the air fry position. Select Air Fry, set the temperature to 350ºF (177ºC), and set the time to 10 minutes.
6. Cook for 10 minutes or until the pork is golden brown and crispy. Flip the pork halfway through. Repeat with remaining pork sections.
7. Serve immediately.

Asian Steak Kebabs

Prep time: 5 minutes | Cook time: 12 minutes | Serves 4

¾ cup soy sauce
5 garlic cloves, minced
3 tablespoons sesame oil
½ cup canola oil
⅓ cup sugar
¼ teaspoon dried ground ginger
2 (10- to 12-ounce / 284- to 340-g) New

York strip steaks, cut in 2-inch cubes
1 cup whole white mushrooms
1 red bell pepper, seeded, and cut into 2-inch cubes
1 red onion, cut into 2-inch wedges

1. In a medium bowl, whisk together the soy sauce, garlic, sesame oil, canola oil, sugar, and ginger until well combined. Add the steak and toss to coat. Cover and refrigerate for at least 30 minutes.
2. Assemble the skewers in the following order: steak, mushroom, bell pepper, onion. Ensure the ingredients are pushed almost completely down to the end of the wood skewers.
3. Place the skewers on the grill plate.
4. Place the grill plate on the grill position. Select Grill, set the temperature to 350ºF (177ºC), and set the time to 12 minutes.
5. After 8 minutes, check the steak for desired doneness, grilling up to 4 minutes more if desired.
6. When cooking is complete, serve immediately.

Barbecue Pork Ribs

Prep time: 5 minutes | Cook time: 30 minutes | Serves 4

1 tablespoon barbecue dry rub
1 teaspoon mustard
1 tablespoon apple

cider vinegar
1 teaspoon sesame oil
1 pound (454 g) pork ribs, chopped

1. Combine the dry rub, mustard, apple cider vinegar, and sesame oil, then coat the ribs with this mixture. Refrigerate the ribs for 20 minutes.
2. When the ribs are ready, place them in the crisper tray.
3. Place the crisper tray on the air fry position. Select Air Fry, set the temperature to 360ºF (182ºC), and set the time to 30 minutes.
4. Cook for 15 minutes. Flip them and cook on the other side for a further 15 minutes.
5. Serve immediately.

Rosemary Rack of Lamb

Prep time: 5 minutes | Cook time: 14 minutes | Serves 2

3 tablespoons extra-virgin olive oil
1 garlic clove, minced
1 tablespoon fresh rosemary, chopped

½ rack lamb (4 bones)
Sea salt, to taste
Freshly ground black pepper, to taste

1. Combine the oil, garlic, and rosemary in a large bowl. Season the rack of lamb with the salt and pepper, then place the lamb in the bowl, using tongs to turn and coat fully in the oil mixture. Cover and refrigerate for 2 hours.
2. Place the lamb on the grill plate.
3. Place the grill plate on the grill position. Select Grill, set the temperature to 400ºF (204ºC), and set the time to 12 minutes.
4. After 6 minutes, flip the lamb and continue cooking for 6 minutes more.
5. Cooking is complete when the internal temperature of the lamb reaches 145ºF (63ºC) on a food thermometer. If needed, grill for up to 2 minutes more.

Spaghetti Squash Lasagna

Prep time: 5 minutes | Cook time: 1 hour 15 minutes | Serves 6

2 large spaghetti squash, cooked (about 2¾ pounds / 1.2 kg)
4 pounds (1.8 kg) ground beef
1 (2½-pound / 1.1-

kg) large jar Marinara sauce
25 slices Mozzarella cheese
30 ounces whole-milk ricotta cheese

1. Slice the spaghetti squash and place it face down inside the baking pan. Fill with water until covered.
2. Place the baking pan on the bake position. Select Bake, set the temperature to 375ºF (191ºC), and set the time to 45 minutes.
3. Cook for 45 minutes until skin is soft.
4. Sear the ground beef in a skillet over medium-high heat for 5 minutes or until browned, then add the marinara sauce and heat until warm. Set aside.
5. Scrape the flesh off the cooked squash to resemble strands of spaghetti.
6. Layer the lasagna in a large greased pan in alternating layers of spaghetti squash, beef sauce, Mozzarella, ricotta. Repeat until all the ingredients have been used.
7. Bake for 30 minutes.
8. Serve.

Korean-Style BBQ Beef

Prep time: 5 minutes | Cook time: 5 minutes | Serves 4

⅓ cup soy sauce
2 tablespoons sesame oil
2½ tablespoons brown sugar
3 garlic cloves, minced
½ teaspoon freshly

ground black pepper
1 pound (454 g) rib eye steak, thinly sliced
2 scallions, thinly sliced, for garnish
Toasted sesame seeds, for garnish

1. In a small bowl, whisk together the soy sauce, sesame oil, brown sugar, garlic, and black pepper until fully combined.
2. Place the beef into a large shallow bowl, and pour the sauce over the slices. Cover and refrigerate for 1 hour.
3. Place the beef onto the grill plate.
4. Place the grill plate on the grill position. Select Grill, set the temperature to 350ºF (177ºC), and set the time to 5 minutes.
5. After 4 minutes, check the steak for desired doneness, grilling for up to 1 minute more, if desired.
6. When cooking is complete, top with scallions and sesame seeds and serve immediately.

Golden Wasabi Spam

Prep time: 5 minutes | Cook time: 12 minutes | Serves 3

⅔ cup all-purpose flour
2 large eggs
1½ tablespoons wasabi paste

2 cups panko breadcrumbs
6 ½-inch-thick spam slices
Cooking spray

1. Spritz the crisper tray with cooking spray.
2. Pour the flour in a shallow plate. Whisk the eggs with wasabi in a large bowl. Pour the panko in a separate shallow plate.
3. Dredge the spam slices in the flour first, then dunk in the egg mixture, and then roll the spam over the panko to coat well. Shake the excess off.
4. Arrange the spam slices in a single layer in the crisper tray and spritz with cooking spray.
5. Place the crisper tray on the air fry position. Select Air Fry, set the temperature to 400ºF (204ºC), and set the time to 12 minutes.
6. Cook for 12 minutes or until the spam slices are golden and crispy. Flip the spam slices halfway through.
7. Serve immediately.

Lamb Satay

Prep time: 5 minutes | Cook time: 8 minutes | Serves 2

¼ teaspoon cumin
1 teaspoon ginger
½ teaspoons nutmeg
Salt and ground black

pepper, to taste
2 boneless lamb
steaks
Cooking spray

1. Combine the cumin, ginger, nutmeg, salt and pepper in a bowl.
2. Cube the lamb steaks and massage the spice mixture into each one.
3. Leave to marinate for 10 minutes, then transfer onto metal skewers.
4. Place the skewers in the crisper tray and spritz with cooking spray.
5. Place the crisper tray on the air fry position. Select Air Fry, set the temperature to 400ºF (204ºC), and set the time to 8 minutes.
6. Take care when removing them from the grill and serve.

Walliser Schnitzel

Prep time: 5 minutes | Cook time: 14 minutes | Serves 2

½ cup pork rinds
½ tablespoon fresh
parsley
½ teaspoon fennel
seed
½ teaspoon mustard
$1/_3$ tablespoon cider
vinegar

1 teaspoon garlic salt
$1/_3$ teaspoon ground
black pepper
2 eggs
2 pork schnitzel,
halved
Cooking spray

1. Spritz the crisper tray with cooking spray.
2. Put the pork rinds, parsley, fennel seeds, and mustard in a food processor. Pour in the vinegar and sprinkle with salt and ground black pepper. Pulse until well combined and smooth.
3. Pour the pork rind mixture in a large bowl. Whisk the eggs in a separate bowl.
4. Dunk the pork schnitzel in the whisked eggs, then dunk in the pork rind mixture to coat well. Shake the excess off.
5. Arrange the schnitzel in the crisper tray and spritz with cooking spray.
6. Place the crisper tray on the air fry position. Select Air Fry, set the temperature to 350ºF (177ºC), and set the time to 14 minutes.
7. Cook for 14 minutes or until golden and crispy. Flip the schnitzel halfway through.
8. Serve immediately.

Miso Marinated Steak

Prep time: 5 minutes | Cook time: 12 minutes | Serves 4

¾ pound (340 g) flank
steak
1½ tablespoons sake
1 tablespoon brown
miso paste

1 teaspoon honey
2 cloves garlic,
pressed
1 tablespoon olive oil

1. Put all the ingredients in a Ziploc bag. Shake to cover the steak well with the seasonings and refrigerate for at least 1 hour.
2. Coat all sides of the steak with cooking spray. Put the steak in the crisper tray.
3. Place the crisper tray on the air fry position. Select Air Fry, set the temperature to 400ºF (204ºC), and set the time to 12 minutes.
4. Cook for 12 minutes, turning the steak twice during the cooking time, then serve immediately.

Bourbon-Glazed Pork Chops

Prep time: 5 minutes | Cook time: 35 minutes | Serves 4

2 cups ketchup
¾ cup bourbon
¼ cup apple cider
vinegar
¼ cup soy sauce
1 cup packed brown
sugar
3 tablespoons

Worcestershire sauce
½ tablespoon dry
mustard powder
4 boneless pork chops
Sea salt, to taste
Freshly ground black
pepper, to taste

1. In a medium saucepan over high heat, combine the ketchup, bourbon, vinegar, soy sauce, sugar, Worcestershire sauce, and mustard powder. Stir to combine and bring to a boil.
2. Reduce the heat to low and simmer, uncovered and stirring occasionally, for 20 minutes. The barbecue sauce will thicken while cooking. Once thickened, remove the pan from the heat and set aside.
3. Place the pork chops on the grill plate.
4. Place the grill plate on the grill position. Select Grill, set the temperature to 350ºF (177ºC), and set the time to 15 minutes.
5. After 8 minutes, flip the pork chops and baste the cooked side with the barbecue sauce. Cook for 5 minutes more.
6. Flip the pork chops again, basting both sides with the barbecue sauce. Cook for the final 2 minutes.
7. When cooking is complete, season with salt and pepper and serve immediately.

Honey Glazed Pork Tenderloin

Prep time: 5 minutes | Cook time: 15 to 20 minutes | Serves 4

2 tablespoons honey
1 tablespoon soy sauce
½ teaspoon garlic powder
½ teaspoon sea salt
1 (1½-pound / 680-g) pork tenderloin

1. In a small bowl, combine the honey, soy sauce, garlic powder, and salt.
2. Place the pork tenderloin on the grill plate. Baste all sides with the honey glaze.
3. Place the grill plate on the grill position. Select Grill, set the temperature to 350ºF (177ºC), and set the time to 15 minutes.
4. After 8 minutes, flip the pork tenderloin and baste with any remaining glaze. Cook for 7 minutes more.
5. Cooking is complete when the internal temperature of the pork reaches 145ºF (63ºC) on a food thermometer. If needed, grill for up to 5 minutes more.
6. Remove the pork, and set it on a cutting board to rest for 5 minutes. Slice and serve.

Vietnamese Pork Chops

Prep time: 15 minutes | Cook time: 12 minutes | Serves 2

1 tablespoon chopped shallot
1 tablespoon chopped garlic
1 tablespoon fish sauce
3 tablespoons lemongrass
1 teaspoon soy sauce
1 tablespoon brown sugar
1 tablespoon olive oil
1 teaspoon ground black pepper
2 pork chops

1. Combine shallot, garlic, fish sauce, lemongrass, soy sauce, brown sugar, olive oil, and pepper in a bowl. Stir to mix well.
2. Put the pork chops in the bowl. Toss to coat well. Place the bowl in the refrigerator to marinate for 2 hours.
3. Remove the pork chops from the bowl and discard the marinade. Transfer the chops into the crisper tray.
4. Place the crisper tray on the air fry position. Select Air Fry, set the temperature to 400ºF (204ºC), and set the time to 12 minutes.
5. Cook for 12 minutes or until lightly browned. Flip the pork chops halfway through the cooking time.
6. Remove the pork chops from the crisper tray and serve hot.

Citrus Pork Loin Roast

Prep time: 10 minutes | Cook time: 45 minutes | Serves 8

1 tablespoon lime juice
1 tablespoon orange marmalade
1 teaspoon coarse brown mustard
1 teaspoon curry powder
1 teaspoon dried lemongrass
2 pound (907 g) boneless pork loin roast
Salt and ground black pepper, to taste
Cooking spray

1. Mix the lime juice, marmalade, mustard, curry powder, and lemongrass.
2. Rub mixture all over the surface of the pork loin. Season with salt and pepper.
3. Spray the crisper tray with cooking spray and place pork roast diagonally in the crisper tray.
4. Place the crisper tray on the air fry position. Select Air Fry, set the temperature to 360ºF (182ºC), and set the time to 45 minutes.
5. Cook for 45 minutes, until the internal temperature reaches at least 145ºF (63ºC).
6. Wrap roast in foil and let rest for 10 minutes before slicing.
7. Serve immediately.

Swedish Beef Meatballs

Prep time: 10 minutes | Cook time: 12 minutes | Serves 8

1 pound (454 g) ground beef
1 egg, beaten
2 carrots, shredded
2 bread slices, crumbled
1 small onion, minced
½ teaspoons garlic salt
Pepper and salt, to taste
1 cup tomato sauce
2 cups pasta sauce

1. In a bowl, combine the ground beef, egg, carrots, crumbled bread, onion, garlic salt, pepper and salt.
2. Divide the mixture into equal amounts and shape each one into a small meatball.
3. Put them in the crisper tray.
4. Place the crisper tray on the air fry position. Select Air Fry, set the temperature to 400ºF (204ºC), and set the time to 7 minutes.
5. Transfer the meatballs to a dish and top with the tomato sauce and pasta sauce.
6. Set the dish into the pan and allow to air fry at 320ºF (160ºC) for 5 more minutes. Serve hot.

Mushroom and Beef Meatloaf

Prep time: 10 minutes | Cook time: 25 minutes | Serves 4

1 pound (454 g) ground beef
1 egg, beaten
1 mushrooms, sliced
1 tablespoon thyme
1 small onion, chopped
3 tablespoons bread crumbs
Ground black pepper, to taste

1. Put all the ingredients into a large bowl and combine entirely.
2. Transfer the meatloaf mixture into the loaf pan.
3. Place the loaf pan on the bake position. Select Bake, set the temperature to 400ºF (204ºC), and set the time to 25 minutes.
4. Slice up before serving.

Steak Salad with Blue Cheese Dressing

Prep time: 5 minutes | Cook time: 16 minutes | Serves 4 to 6

4 (8-ounce / 227-g) skirt steaks
Sea salt, to taste
Freshly ground black pepper, to taste
6 cups chopped romaine lettuce
¾ cup cherry
tomatoes, halved
¼ cup blue cheese, crumbled
1 cup croutons
2 avocados, peeled and sliced
1 cup blue cheese dressing

1. Season the steaks on both sides with the salt and pepper.
2. Place 2 steaks on the grill plate. Gently press the steaks down to maximize grill marks.
3. Place the grill plate on the grill position. Select Grill, set the temperature to 400ºF (204ºC), and set the time to 8 minutes.
4. After 4 minutes, flip the steaks and cook for an additional 4 minutes.
5. Remove the steaks from the grill and transfer to them a cutting board. Tent with aluminum foil.
6. Repeat step 3 with the remaining 2 steaks.
7. While the second set of steaks is cooking, assemble the salad by tossing together the lettuce, tomatoes, blue cheese crumbles, and croutons. Top with the avocado slices.
8. Once the second set of steaks has finished cooking, slice all four of the steaks into thin strips, and place on top of the salad. Drizzle with the blue cheese dressing and serve.

Balsamic London Broil

Prep time: 15 minutes | Cook time: 25 minutes | Serves 8

2 pounds (907 g) London broil
3 large garlic cloves, minced
3 tablespoons balsamic vinegar
3 tablespoons whole-
grain mustard
2 tablespoons olive oil
Sea salt and ground black pepper, to taste
½ teaspoons dried hot red pepper flakes

1. Wash and dry the London broil. Score its sides with a knife.
2. Mix the remaining ingredients. Rub this mixture into the broil, coating it well. Allow to marinate for a minimum of 3 hours.
3. Place the meat in the crisper tray.
4. Place the crisper tray on the air fry position. Select Air Fry, set the temperature to 400ºF (204ºC), and set the time to 25 minutes.
5. Cook for 15 minutes. Turn it over and cook for an additional 10 minutes before serving.

Char Siew

Prep time: 10 minutes | Cook time: 20 minutes | Serves 4 to 6

1 strip of pork shoulder butt with a good amount of fat
Marinade:
1 teaspoon sesame oil
4 tablespoons raw honey
1 teaspoon low-sodium dark soy sauce
1 teaspoon light soy
marbling
Olive oil, for brushing the pan

sauce
1 tablespoon rose wine
2 tablespoons Hoisin sauce

1. Combine all the marinade ingredients together in a Ziploc bag. Put pork in bag, making sure all sections of pork strip are engulfed in the marinade. Chill for 3 to 24 hours.
2. Take out the strip 30 minutes before planning to roast.
3. Put foil on the pan and brush with olive oil. Put marinated pork strip onto prepared pan.
4. Place the baking pan on the roast position. Select Roast, set the temperature to 350ºF (177ºC), and set the time to 20 minutes.
5. Glaze with marinade every 5 to 10 minutes.
6. Remove strip and leave to cool a few minutes before slicing.
7. Serve immediately.

Mint Lamb Ribs

Prep time: 5 minutes | Cook time: 18 minutes | Serves 4

2 tablespoons mustard	Salt and ground black
1 pound (454 g) lamb	pepper, to taste
ribs	¼ cup mint leaves,
1 teaspoon rosemary,	chopped
chopped	1 cup Greek yogurt

1. Use a brush to apply the mustard to the lamb ribs, and season with rosemary, salt, and pepper. Transfer to the crisper tray.
2. Place the crisper tray on the air fry position. Select Air Fry, set the temperature to 350°F (177°C), and set the time to 18 minutes.
3. Meanwhile, combine the mint leaves and yogurt in a bowl.
4. Remove the lamb ribs from the grill when cooked and serve with the mint yogurt.

Apple-Glazed Pork

Prep time: 15 minutes | Cook time: 19 minutes | Serves 4

1 sliced apple	3 tablespoons olive oil,
1 small onion, sliced	divided
2 tablespoons apple	¼ teaspoon smoked
cider vinegar, divided	paprika
½ teaspoon thyme	4 pork chops
½ teaspoon rosemary	Salt and ground black
¼ teaspoon brown	pepper, to taste
sugar	

1. Combine the apple slices, onion, 1 tablespoon of vinegar, thyme, rosemary, brown sugar, and 2 tablespoons of olive oil in the baking pan. Stir to mix well.
2. Place the baking pan on the bake position. Select Bake, set the temperature to 350°F (177°C), and set the time to 4 minutes.
3. Meanwhile, combine the remaining vinegar and olive oil, and paprika in a large bowl. Sprinkle with salt and ground black pepper. Stir to mix well. Dredge the pork in the mixture and toss to coat well.
4. Remove the baking pan from the grill and put in the pork. Air fry for 10 minutes to lightly brown the pork. Flip the pork chops halfway through.
5. Remove the pork from the grill and baste with baked apple mixture on both sides. Put the pork back to the grill and air fry for an additional 5 minutes. Flip halfway through.
6. Serve immediately.

Teriyaki Pork and Mushroom Rolls

Prep time: 10 minutes | Cook time: 8 minutes | Serves 6

4 tablespoons brown	flour
sugar	2-inch ginger, chopped
4 tablespoons mirin	6 (4-ounce / 113-g)
4 tablespoons soy	pork belly slices
sauce	6 ounces (170 g)
1 teaspoon almond	Enoki mushrooms

1. Mix the brown sugar, mirin, soy sauce, almond flour, and ginger together until brown sugar dissolves.
2. Take pork belly slices and wrap around a bundle of mushrooms. Brush each roll with teriyaki sauce. Chill for half an hour.
3. Add marinated pork rolls to the crisper tray.
4. Place the crisper tray on the air fry position. Select Air Fry, set the temperature to 350°F (177°C), and set the time to 8 minutes.
5. Flip the rolls halfway through.
6. Serve immediately.

Lechon Kawali

Prep time: 10 minutes | Cook time: 30 minutes | Serves 4

1 pound (454 g) pork	sauce
belly, cut into three	1 teaspoon kosher salt
thick chunks	1 teaspoon ground
6 garlic cloves	black pepper
2 bay leaves	3 cups water
2 tablespoons soy	Cooking spray

1. Put all the ingredients in a pressure cooker, then put the lid on and cook on high for 15 minutes.
2. Natural release the pressure and release any remaining pressure, transfer the tender pork belly on a clean work surface. Allow to cool under room temperature until you can handle.
3. Generously spritz the crisper tray with cooking spray.
4. Cut each chunk into two slices, then put the pork slices in the crisper tray.
5. Place the crisper tray on the air fry position. Select Air Fry, set the temperature to 400°F (204°C), and set the time to 15 minutes.
6. Cook for 15 minutes or until the pork fat is crispy. Spritz the pork with more cooking spray, if necessary.
7. Serve immediately.

Cheesy Beef Meatballs

Prep time: 5 minutes | Cook time: 18 minutes | Serves 6

1 pound (454 g) ground beef	garlic
½ cup grated Parmesan cheese	½ cup Mozzarella cheese
1 tablespoon minced	1 teaspoon freshly ground pepper

1. In a bowl, mix all the ingredients together.
2. Roll the meat mixture into 5 generous meatballs. Transfer to the crisper tray.
3. Place the crisper tray on the air fry position. Select Air Fry, set the temperature to 400ºF (204ºC), and set the time to 18 minutes.
4. Serve immediately.

Beef and Vegetable Cubes

Prep time: 15 minutes | Cook time: 17 minutes | Serves 4

2 tablespoons olive oil	¼ teaspoon ground cumin
1 tablespoon apple cider vinegar	1 pound (454 g) top round steak, cut into cubes
1 teaspoon fine sea salt	4 ounces (113 g) broccoli, cut into florets
½ teaspoons ground black pepper	4 ounces (113 g) mushrooms, sliced
1 teaspoon shallot powder	1 teaspoon dried basil
¾ teaspoon smoked cayenne pepper	1 teaspoon celery seeds
½ teaspoons garlic powder	

1. Massage the olive oil, vinegar, salt, black pepper, shallot powder, cayenne pepper, garlic powder, and cumin into the cubed steak, ensuring to coat each piece evenly.
2. Allow to marinate for a minimum of 3 hours.
3. Put the beef cubes in the crisper tray.
4. Place the crisper tray on the air fry position. Select Air Fry, set the temperature to 365ºF (185ºC), and set the time to 12 minutes.
5. When the steak is cooked through, place it in a bowl.
6. Wipe the grease from the crisper tray and pour in the vegetables. Season them with basil and celery seeds.
7. Increase the temperature of the grill to 400ºF (204ºC) and air fry for 5 to 6 minutes. When the vegetables are hot, serve them with the steak.

Smoked Beef

Prep time: 10 minutes | Cook time: 45 minutes | Serves 8

2 pounds (907 g) roast beef, at room temperature	black pepper
2 tablespoons extra-virgin olive oil	1 teaspoon smoked paprika
1 teaspoon sea salt flakes	Few dashes of liquid smoke
1 teaspoon ground	2 jalapeño peppers, thinly sliced

1. With kitchen towels, pat the beef dry.
2. Massage the extra-virgin olive oil, salt, black pepper, and paprika into the meat. Cover with liquid smoke.
3. Put the beef in the pan.
4. Place the baking pan on the roast position. Select Roast, set the temperature to 330ºF (166ºC), and set the time to 45 minutes.
5. Cook for 30 minutes. Flip the roast over and allow to cook for another 15 minutes.
6. When cooked through, serve topped with sliced jalapeños.

Pork Meatballs with Red Chili

Prep time: 5 minutes | Cook time: 15 minutes | Serves 4

1 pound (454 g) ground pork	grated ginger root
2 cloves garlic, finely minced	1 teaspoon turmeric powder
1 cup scallions, finely chopped	1 tablespoon oyster sauce
1½ tablespoons Worcestershire sauce	1 small sliced red chili, for garnish
½ teaspoon freshly	Cooking spray

1. Spritz the crisper tray with cooking spray.
2. Combine all the ingredients, except for the red chili in a large bowl. Toss to mix well.
3. Shape the mixture into equally sized balls, then arrange them in the crisper tray and spritz with cooking spray.
4. Place the crisper tray on the air fry position. Select Air Fry, set the temperature to 350ºF (177ºC), and set the time to 15 minutes.
5. Cook for 15 minutes or until the balls are lightly browned. Flip the balls halfway through.
6. Serve the pork meatballs with red chili on top.

Potato and Prosciutto Salad

Prep time: 10 minutes | Cook time: 7 minutes | Serves 8

Salad:

4 pounds (1.8 kg) potatoes, boiled and cubed	diced
	2 cups shredded Cheddar cheese
15 slices prosciutto,	

Dressing:

15 ounces (425 g) sour cream	1 teaspoon salt
2 tablespoons mayonnaise	1 teaspoon black pepper
	1 teaspoon dried basil

1. Put the potatoes, prosciutto, and Cheddar in the baking pan.
2. Place the baking pan on the air fry position. Select Air Fry, set the temperature to 350ºF (177ºC), and set the time to 7 minutes.
3. In a separate bowl, mix the sour cream, mayonnaise, salt, pepper, and basil using a whisk.
4. Coat the salad with the dressing and serve.

Pork Sausage with Cauliflower Mash

Prep time: 5 minutes | Cook time: 27 minutes | Serves 6

1 pound (454 g) cauliflower, chopped	1 teaspoon cumin powder
6 pork sausages, chopped	½ teaspoon tarragon
½ onion, sliced	½ teaspoon sea salt
3 eggs, beaten	½ teaspoon ground black pepper
1/3 cup Colby cheese	Cooking spray

1. Spritz the baking pan with cooking spray.
2. In a saucepan over medium heat, boil the cauliflower until tender. Place the boiled cauliflower in a food processor and pulse until puréed. Transfer to a large bowl and combine with remaining ingredients until well blended.
3. Pour the cauliflower and sausage mixture into the baking pan.
4. Place the baking pan on the bake position. Select Bake, set the temperature to 365ºF (185ºC), and set the time to 27 minutes.
5. Cook for 27 minutes, or until lightly browned.
6. Divide the mixture among six serving dishes and serve warm.

Homemade Teriyaki Pork Ribs

Prep time: 5 minutes | Cook time: 30 minutes | Serves 4

¼ cup soy sauce	dried ginger
¼ cup honey	4 (8-ounce / 227-g)
1 teaspoon garlic powder	boneless country-style pork ribs
1 teaspoon ground	Cooking spray

1. Spritz the crisper tray with cooking spray.
2. Make the teriyaki sauce: Combine the soy sauce, honey, garlic powder, and ginger in a bowl. Stir to mix well.
3. Brush the ribs with half of the teriyaki sauce, then arrange the ribs in the crisper tray. Spritz with cooking spray. You may need to work in batches to avoid overcrowding.
4. Place the crisper tray on the air fry position. Select Air Fry, set the temperature to 350ºF (177ºC), and set the time to 30 minutes.
5. Cook for 30 minutes or until the internal temperature of the ribs reaches at least 145ºF (63ºC). Brush the ribs with remaining teriyaki sauce and flip halfway through.
6. Serve immediately.

Citrus Carnitas

Prep time: 1 hour 10 minutes | Cook time: 25 minutes | Serves 6

2½ pounds (1.1 kg) boneless country-style pork ribs, cut into 2-inch pieces	1 teaspoon ground cumin
3 tablespoons olive brine	1 tablespoon minced garlic
1 tablespoon minced fresh oregano leaves	1 teaspoon salt
1/3 cup orange juice	1 teaspoon ground black pepper
	Cooking spray

1. Combine all the ingredients in a large bowl. Toss to coat the pork ribs well. Wrap the bowl in plastic and refrigerate for at least an hour to marinate.
2. Spritz the crisper tray with cooking spray.
3. Arrange the marinated pork ribs in a single layer in the crisper tray and spritz with cooking spray.
4. Place the crisper tray on the air fry position. Select Air Fry, set the temperature to 400ºF (204ºC), and set the time to 25 minutes.
5. Cook for 25 minutes or until well browned. Flip the ribs halfway through.
6. Serve immediately.

Beef Schnitzel

Prep time: 5 minutes | Cook time: 12 minutes | Serves 1

½ cup friendly bread crumbs
2 tablespoons olive oil
Pepper and salt, to taste
1 egg, beaten
1 thin beef schnitzel

1. In a shallow dish, combine the bread crumbs, oil, pepper, and salt.
2. In a second shallow dish, place the beaten egg.
3. Dredge the schnitzel in the egg before rolling it in the bread crumbs.
4. Put the coated schnitzel in the crisper tray.
5. Place the crisper tray on the air fry position. Select Air Fry, set the temperature to 350ºF (177ºC), and set the time to 12 minutes.
6. Flip the schnitzel halfway through.
7. Serve immediately.

Smoky Paprika Pork and Vegetable Kabobs

Prep time: 25 minutes | Cook time: 15 minutes | Serves 4

1 pound (454 g) pork tenderloin, cubed
1 teaspoon smoked paprika
Salt and ground black pepper, to taste
1 green bell pepper,
cut into chunks
1 zucchini, cut into chunks
1 red onion, sliced
1 tablespoon oregano
Cooking spray

Special Equipment:
Small bamboo skewers, soaked in water for 20 minutes to keep them from burning while cooking

1. Spritz the crisper tray with cooking spray.
2. Add the pork to a bowl and season with the smoked paprika, salt and black pepper. Thread the seasoned pork cubes and vegetables alternately onto the soaked skewers.
3. Arrange the skewers in the prepared crisper tray and spray with cooking spray.
4. Place the crisper tray on the air fry position. Select Air Fry, set the temperature to 350ºF (177ºC), and set the time to 15 minutes.
5. Cook for 15 minutes, or until the pork is well browned and the vegetables are tender, flipping once halfway through.
6. Transfer the skewers to the serving dishes and sprinkle with oregano. Serve hot.

Pork and Water Chestnut Lettuce Cups

Prep time: 10 minutes | Cook time: 12 minutes | Serves 4

1 medium pork tenderloin (about 1 pound / 454 g), silver skin and external fat trimmed
⅔ cup Asian Sauce, divided
1 teaspoon cornstarch
1 medium jalapeño, seeded and minced
1 can diced water chestnuts
½ large (or 1 very
small) red bell pepper, seeded and chopped
2 scallions, chopped, white and green parts separated
1 head butter lettuce or Boston lettuce
½ cup roasted, chopped almonds or peanuts (optional)
¼ cup coarsely chopped cilantro (optional)

1. Cut the tenderloin into ¼-inch slices and place them in the baking pan. Baste with about 3 tablespoons of Asian-Style Sauce. Stir the cornstarch into the remaining sauce and set aside.
2. Place the pan on the roast position. Select Roast, set temperature to 375ºF (191ºC), and set time to 12 minutes.
3. After 5 minutes, remove the pan from the grill. Place the pork slices on a cutting board. Place the jalapeño, water chestnuts, red pepper, and the white parts of the scallions in the baking pan and pour the remaining sauce over. Stir to coat the vegetables with the sauce. Return the pan to the grill and continue cooking.
4. While the vegetables cook, chop the pork into small pieces. Separate the lettuce leaves, discarding any tough outer leaves and setting aside the small inner leaves for another use. You'll want 12 to 18 leaves, depending on size and your appetites.
5. After 5 minutes, remove the pan from the grill. Add the pork to the vegetables, stirring to combine. Return the pan to the grill and continue cooking for the remaining 2 minutes, until the pork is warmed back up and the sauce has reduced slightly.
6. When cooking is complete, remove the pan from the grill. Place the pork and vegetables in a medium serving bowl and stir in half the green parts of the scallions. To serve, spoon some of the pork and vegetables into each of the lettuce leaves. Top with the remaining scallion greens and garnish with the nuts and cilantro (if using).

Pork, Pepper, and Pineapple Kebabs

Prep time: 10 minutes | Cook time: 12 minutes | Serves 4

¼ teaspoon kosher salt or ⅛ teaspoon fine salt
1 medium pork tenderloin (about 1 pound / 454 g), cut into 1½-inch chunks
1 red bell pepper, seeded and cut into 1-inch pieces
1 green bell pepper, seeded and cut into 1-inch pieces
2 cups fresh pineapple chunks
¾ cup teriyaki sauce

Special Equipment:
12 (9- to 12-inch) wooden skewers soaked in water for about 30 minutes

1. Sprinkle the salt over the pork cubes.
2. Alternate the pork, bell peppers, and pineapple on the skewers, making about 12 skewers (if you use the larger skewers, you'll probably only need 8). Liberally brush the skewers with about half of the teriyaki sauce. Transfer to the baking pan.
3. Place the pan on the roast position. Select Roast, set temperature to 375ºF (191ºC), and set time to 10 minutes.
4. After about 5 minutes, remove the pan from the grill. Turn over the skewers and brush with the remaining teriyaki sauce. Return the pan to the grill and continue cooking.
5. When cooking is complete, the vegetables should be tender and browned in spots, and the pork browned and cooked through. Remove the pan from the grill and serve.

Fillet Mignon with Pineapple Salsa

Prep time: 15 minutes | Cook time: 8 minutes | Serves 4

4 (6- to 8-ounce / 170- to 227-g) fillet mignon steaks
1 tablespoon canola oil, divided
Sea salt, to taste
Freshly ground black pepper, to taste
½ medium pineapple, cored and diced
1 medium red onion, diced
1 jalapeño pepper, seeded, stemmed, and diced
1 tablespoon freshly squeezed lime juice
¼ cup chopped fresh cilantro leaves
Chili powder
Ground coriander

1. Rub each filet on all sides with ½ tablespoon of the oil, then season with the salt and pepper.
2. Add the fillets to the grill plate.

3. Place the grill plate on the grill position. Select Grill, set temperature to 400ºF (204ºC), and set time to 8 minutes.
4. After 4 minutes, flip the fillets. Continue cooking for an additional 4 minutes, or until the fillets' internal temperature reads 125ºF (52ºC) on a food thermometer. Remove the fillets from the grill; they will continue to cook (called carry-over cooking) to a food-safe temperature even after you've removed them from the grill.
5. Let the fillets rest for a total of 10 minutes; this allows the natural juices to redistribute into the steak.
6. While the fillets rest, in a medium bowl, combine the pineapple, onion, and jalapeño. Stir in the lime juice and cilantro, then season to taste with the chili powder and coriander.
7. Plate the fillets, and pile the salsa on top of each before serving.

Grapes with Italian Sausages and Polenta

Prep time: 10 minutes | Cook time: 20 minutes | Serves 6

2 pounds (907 g) seedless red grapes
3 shallots, sliced
2 teaspoons fresh thyme or 1 teaspoon dried thyme
2 tablespoons extra-virgin olive oil
½ teaspoon kosher salt or ¼ teaspoon fine salt
Freshly ground black pepper
6 links (about 1½ pounds / 680 g) hot or sweet Italian sausage
3 tablespoons sherry vinegar or balsamic vinegar
6 (1-inch-thick) slices polenta

1. Place the grapes in a large bowl. Add the shallots, thyme, olive oil, salt, and pepper. Gently toss. Place the grapes in the baking pan. Arrange the sausage links evenly in the pan.
2. Place the pan on the roast position. Select Roast, set temperature to 375ºF (191ºC), and set time to 20 minutes.
3. After 10 minutes, remove the pan. Turn over the sausages and sprinkle the vinegar over the sausages and grapes. Gently toss the grapes and move them to one side of the pan. Place the polenta slices in the pan. Return the pan to the grill and continue cooking.
4. When cooking is complete, the grapes should be very soft and the sausages browned.

Lamb Rack with Pistachio

Prep time: 10 minutes | Cook time: 20 minutes | Serves 2

½ cup finely chopped pistachios
1 teaspoon chopped fresh rosemary
3 tablespoons panko breadcrumbs
2 teaspoons chopped fresh oregano
1 tablespoon olive oil
Salt and freshly ground black pepper, to taste
1 lamb rack, bones fat trimmed and frenched
1 tablespoon Dijon mustard

1. Put the pistachios, rosemary, breadcrumbs, oregano, olive oil, salt, and black pepper in a food processor. Pulse to combine until smooth.
2. Rub the lamb rack with salt and black pepper on a clean work surface, then place it in the crisper tray.
3. Place the crisper tray on the air fry position. Select Air Fry, set the temperature to 380ºF (193ºC), and set the time to 12 minutes.
4. Cook for 12 minutes or until lightly browned. Flip the lamb halfway through the cooking time.
5. Transfer the lamb to a plate and brush with Dijon mustard on the fat side, then sprinkle with the pistachios mixture over the lamb rack to coat well.
6. Put the lamb rack back to the crisper tray. Air fry for 8 more minutes or until the internal temperature of the rack reaches at least 145ºF (63ºC).
7. Remove the lamb rack from the grill with tongs and allow to cool for 5 minutes before sling to serve.

Broccoli with Steak

Prep time: 10 minutes | Cook time: 15 minutes | Serves 4

12 ounces (340 g) broccoli florets (about 4 cups)
1 pound (454 g) sirloin or flat iron steak, cut into thin strips
½ teaspoon kosher salt or ¼ teaspoon fine salt
¾ cup Asian Sauce
1 teaspoon sriracha or chile-garlic sauce
3 tablespoons freshly squeezed orange juice
1 teaspoon cornstarch
1 medium onion, thinly sliced

1. Place a large piece of aluminum foil in the baking pan. Place the broccoli on top and sprinkle with 3 tablespoons of water. Seal the broccoli in the foil in a single layer.

2. Place the pan on the roast position. Select Roast, set temperature to 375ºF (191ºC), and set time to 6 minutes.
3. While the broccoli steams, sprinkle the steak with the salt. In a small bowl, whisk together the Asian-Style Sauce, sriracha, orange juice, and cornstarch. Place the onion and beef in a large bowl.
4. When cooking is complete, remove the pan from the grill. Open the packet of broccoli and use tongs to transfer the broccoli to the bowl with the beef and onion, discarding the foil and remaining water. Pour the sauce over the beef and vegetables and toss to coat. Place the mixture in the baking pan.
5. Place the pan on the roast position. Select Roast, set temperature to 375ºF (191ºC), and set time to 9 minutes.
6. After about 4 minutes, remove the pan from the grill and gently toss the ingredients. Return the pan to grill and continue cooking.
7. When cooking is complete, the sauce should be thickened, the vegetables tender, and the beef barely pink in the center. Serve plain or with steamed rice.

Tonkatsu

Prep time: 5 minutes | Cook time: 10 minutes per batch | Serves 4

⅔ cup all-purpose flour
2 large egg whites
1 cup panko breadcrumbs
4 (4-ounce / 113-g) center-cut boneless pork loin chops (about ½ inch thick)
Cooking spray

1. Spritz the crisper tray with cooking spray.
2. Pour the flour in a bowl. Whisk the egg whites in a separate bowl. Spread the breadcrumbs on a large plate.
3. Dredge the pork loin chops in the flour first, press to coat well, then shake the excess off and dunk the chops in the eggs whites, and then roll the chops over the breadcrumbs. Shake the excess off.
4. Arrange the pork chops in batches in a single layer in the crisper tray and spritz with cooking spray.
5. Place the crisper tray on the air fry position. Select Air Fry, set the temperature to 375ºF (191ºC), and set the time to 10 minutes.
6. Cook for 10 minutes or until the pork chops are lightly browned and crunchy. Flip the chops halfway through. Repeat with remaining chops.
7. Serve immediately.

Spicy Pork with Candy Onions

Prep time: 10 minutes | Cook time: 52 minutes | Serves 4

2 teaspoons sesame oil
1 teaspoon dried sage, crushed
1 teaspoon cayenne pepper
1 rosemary sprig, chopped
1 thyme sprig, chopped

Sea salt and ground black pepper, to taste
2 pounds (907 g) pork leg roast, scored
½ pound (227 g) candy onions, sliced
4 cloves garlic, finely chopped
2 chili peppers, minced

1. In a mixing bowl, combine the sesame oil, sage, cayenne pepper, rosemary, thyme, salt and black pepper until well mixed. In another bowl, place the pork leg and brush with the seasoning mixture.
2. Place the seasoned pork leg in the baking pan.
3. Place the baking pan on the air fry position. Select Air Fry, set the temperature to 400ºF (204ºC), and set the time to 52 minutes.
4. Cook for 40 minutes, or until lightly browned, flipping halfway through. Add the candy onions, garlic and chili peppers to the pan and cook for another 12 minutes.
5. Transfer the pork leg to a plate. Let cool for 5 minutes and slice. Spread the juices left in the pan over the pork and serve warm with the candy onions.

Pork Chops with Carrots and Mushrooms

Prep time: 10 minutes | Cook time: 15 to 18 minutes | Serves 4

2 carrots, cut into sticks
1 cup mushrooms, sliced
2 garlic cloves, minced
2 tablespoons olive oil
1 pound (454 g) boneless pork chops
1 teaspoon dried

oregano
1 teaspoon dried thyme
1 teaspoon cayenne pepper
Salt and ground black pepper, to taste
Cooking spray

1. Spritz the crisper tray with cooking spray.
2. In a mixing bowl, toss together the carrots, mushrooms, garlic, olive oil and salt until well combined.
3. Add the pork chops to a different bowl and season with oregano, thyme, cayenne pepper, salt and black pepper.

4. Lower the vegetable mixture in the prepared crisper tray. Place the seasoned pork chops on top.
5. Place the crisper tray on the air fry position. Select Air Fry, set the temperature to 360ºF (182ºC), and set the time to 18 minutes.
6. Cook for 15 to 18 minutes, or until the pork is well browned and the vegetables are tender, flipping the pork and shaking the crisper tray once halfway through.
7. Transfer the pork chops to the serving dishes and let cool for 5 minutes. Serve warm with vegetable on the side.

Jalapeño Popper Burgers

Prep time: 5 minutes | Cook time: 9 minutes | Serves 4

2 jalapeño peppers, seeded, stemmed, and minced
½ cup shredded Cheddar cheese
4 ounces (113 g) cream cheese, at room temperature
4 slices bacon, cooked and crumbled
2 pounds (907 g) ground beef

½ teaspoon chili powder
¼ teaspoon paprika
¼ teaspoon freshly ground black pepper
4 hamburger buns
4 slices pepper Jack cheese
Lettuce, sliced tomato, and sliced red onion, for topping (optional)

1. In a medium bowl, combine the peppers, Cheddar cheese, cream cheese, and bacon until well combined.
2. Form the ground beef into 8¼-inch-thick patties. Spoon some of the filling mixture onto four of the patties, then place a second patty on top of each to make four burgers. Use your fingers to pinch the edges of the patties together to seal in the filling. Reshape the patties with your hands as needed.
3. Combine the chili powder, paprika, and pepper in a small bowl. Sprinkle the mixture onto both sides of the burgers.
4. Place the burgers on the grill plate.
5. Place the grill plate on the grill position. Select Grill, set the temperature to 400ºF (204ºC), and set the time to 4 minutes.
6. Cook for 4 minutes without flipping. Cooking is complete when the internal temperature of the beef reaches at least 145ºF (63ºC) on a food thermometer. If needed, grill for up to 5 more minutes.
7. Place the burgers on the hamburger buns and top with pepper Jack cheese. Add lettuce, tomato, and red onion, if desired.

Mushroom and Italian Sausage Calzones

Prep time: 10 minutes | Cook time: 24 minutes | Serves 4

2 links Italian sausages (about ½ pound / 227 g)
1 pound (454 g) store-bought pizza dough or frozen bread dough, thawed
3 tablespoons extra-

virgin olive oil, divided
¼ cup marinara sauce
½ cup Roasted Mushrooms
1 cup shredded Mozzarella cheese or Mozzarella blend

1. Place the sausages in the baking pan.
2. Place the pan on the roast position. Select Roast, set temperature to 375ºF (191ºC), and set time to 12 minutes.
3. After 6 minutes, remove the pan from the grill and turn over the sausages. Return the pan to the grill and continue cooking.
4. While the sausages cook, divide the pizza dough into 4 equal pieces. One at a time, place a piece of dough onto a square of parchment paper 9 inches in diameter. Brush the dough on both sides with ¾ teaspoon of olive oil, then top the dough with another piece of parchment. Press the dough into a 7-inch circle. Remove the top piece of parchment and set aside. Repeat with the remaining pieces of dough.
5. When cooking is complete, remove the pan from the grill. Place the sausages on a cutting board. Let them cool for several minutes, then slice into ¼-inch rounds and cut each round into 4 pieces. (Don't worry if the very center of the sausage isn't cooked; it will cook again inside the calzones.)
6. One at a time, spread a tablespoon of marinara sauce over half of a dough circle, leaving a ½-inch border at the edges. Cover with a quarter of the sausage pieces and add a quarter of the mushrooms. Sprinkle with ¼ cup of cheese. Pull the other side of the dough over the filling and pinch the edges together to seal. Transfer from the parchment to the baking pan. Repeat with the other rounds of dough, sauce, sausage, mushrooms, and cheese.
7. Brush the tops of the calzones with 1 tablespoon of olive oil.
8. Place the pan on the roast position. Select Roast, set temperature to 450ºF (232ºC), and set time to 12 minutes.
9. After 6 minutes, remove the pan from the grill. The calzones should be golden brown. Turn over the calzones and brush the tops with the remaining 1 tablespoon of olive oil. Return the pan to the grill and continue cooking.
10. When cooking is complete, the crust should be a deep golden brown on both sides. Remove the pan from the grill. The center will be molten; let cool for several minutes before serving.

Bacon-Wrapped Sausage with Tomato Relish

Prep time: 1 hour 15 minutes | Cook time: 32 minutes | Serves 4

8 pork sausages
Relish:
8 large tomatoes, chopped
1 small onion, peeled
1 clove garlic, peeled
1 tablespoon white wine vinegar
3 tablespoons chopped

8 bacon strips

parsley
1 teaspoon smoked paprika
2 tablespoons sugar
Salt and ground black pepper, to taste

1. Purée the tomatoes, onion, and garlic in a food processor until well mixed and smooth.
2. Pour the purée in a saucepan and drizzle with white wine vinegar. Sprinkle with salt and ground black pepper. Simmer over medium heat for 10 minutes.
3. Add the parsley, paprika, and sugar to the saucepan and cook for 10 more minutes or until it has a thick consistency. Keep stirring during the cooking. Refrigerate for an hour to chill.
4. Wrap the sausage with bacon strips and secure with toothpicks, then place them in the crisper tray.
5. Place the crisper tray on the air fry position. Select Air Fry, set the temperature to 350ºF (177ºC), and set the time to 12 minutes.
6. Cook for 12 minutes or until the bacon is crispy and browned. Flip the bacon-wrapped sausage halfway through.
7. Transfer the bacon-wrapped sausage on a plate and baste with the relish or just serve with the relish alongside.

Scratch Meatball Hoagies

Prep time: 15 minutes | Cook time: 24 minutes | Serves 4

1 large egg
¼ cup whole milk
24 saltines, crushed but not pulverized
1 pound (454 g) ground chuck
1 pound (454 g) Italian sausage, casings removed
4 tablespoons grated Parmesan cheese, divided
1 teaspoon kosher salt or ½ teaspoon fine salt
4 hoagie or sub rolls, split
1 cup marinara sauce
¾ cup shredded Mozzarella cheese

1. In a large bowl, whisk the egg into the milk, then stir in the crackers. Let sit for 5 minutes to hydrate.
2. With your hands, break the ground chuck and sausage into the milk mixture, alternating beef and sausage. When you've added half of the meat, sprinkle 2 tablespoons of the grated Parmesan and the salt over it, then continue breaking up the meat until it's all in the bowl. Gently mix everything together. Try not to overwork the meat, but get it all combined.
3. Form the mixture into balls about the size of a golf ball. You should get about 24 meatballs. Flatten the balls slightly to prevent them from rolling, then arrange them in the baking pan, about 2 inches apart.
4. Place the pan on the roast position. Select Roast, set temperature to 400°F (204°C), and set time to 20 minutes.
5. After 10 minutes, remove the pan from the grill and turn over the meatballs. Return the pan to the grill and continue cooking.
6. When cooking is complete, remove the pan from the grill. Place the meatballs on a rack. Wipe off the baking pan (it doesn't have to be completely clean; you just want to remove the fat from the meatballs. If you can't help yourself, you can wash it.)
7. Open the rolls, cut-side up, in the baking pan. Place 3 to 4 meatballs on the base of each roll, and top each sandwich with ¼ cup of marinara sauce. Divide the Mozzarella among the top halves of the buns and sprinkle the remaining 2 tablespoons of Parmesan cheese over the Mozzarella.
8. Place the pan on the broil position. Select Broil, set temperature to 450°F (232°C), and set time to 4 minutes.
9. Check the sandwiches after 2 minutes; the Mozzarella cheese should be melted and bubbling slightly.
10. When cooking is complete, remove the pan from the grill. Close the sandwiches and serve.

Braised Pork with Butternut Squash

Prep time: 15 minutes | Cook time: 13 minutes | Serves 4

4 boneless pork loin chops, ¾- to 1-inch thick
1 teaspoon kosher salt or ½ teaspoon fine salt, divided
2 tablespoons Dijon mustard
2 tablespoons brown sugar
1 pound (454 g) butternut squash, cut into 1-inch cubes
1 large Gala or
Braeburn apple, peeled and cut into 12 to 16 wedges
1 medium onion, thinly sliced
½ teaspoon dried thyme
¼ teaspoon freshly ground black pepper
1 tablespoon unsalted butter, melted
½ cup low-sodium chicken stock

1. Sprinkle the pork chops on both sides with ½ teaspoon of kosher salt. In a small bowl, whisk together the mustard and brown sugar. Baste about half of the mixture on one side of the pork chops. Place the chops, basted-side up, in the baking pan.
2. Place the squash in a large bowl. Add the apple, onion, thyme, remaining ½ teaspoon of kosher salt, pepper, and butter and toss to coat. Arrange the squash-fruit mixture around the chops in the pan. Pour the chicken stock over the mixture, avoiding the chops.
3. Place the pan on the roast position. Select Roast, set temperature to 350°F (177°C), and set time to 13 minutes.
4. After about 7 minutes, remove the pan from the grill. Gently toss the squash mixture and turn over the chops. Baste the chops with the remaining mustard mixture. Return the pan to the grill and continue cooking.
5. When cooking is complete, the pork chops should register at least 145°F (63°C) in the center on a meat thermometer, and the squash and apples should be tender. If necessary, continue cooking for up to 3 minutes more.
6. Remove the pan from the grill. Spoon the squash and apples onto four plates, and place a pork chop on top. If you like, sprinkle with a little fresh thyme or parsley.

Tandoori Lamb Chops with Red Potatoes

Prep time: 10 minutes | Cook time: 20 minutes | Serves 4

8 (½-inch thick) lamb loin chops (about 2 pounds / 907 g)
2 teaspoons kosher salt or 1 teaspoon fine salt, divided
¾ cup plain whole milk yogurt
1 tablespoon freshly grated ginger (1- or 2-inch piece) or 1 teaspoon ground ginger

2 garlic cloves, minced or smashed
1 teaspoon smoked paprika
½ teaspoon cayenne pepper
1 teaspoon curry powder
12 ounces (340 g) small red potatoes, quartered
Cooking oil spray

1. Salt the lamb chops on both sides with 1 teaspoon of kosher salt and let sit while you prepare the marinade.
2. In a large bowl, whisk together the yogurt, ginger, garlic, paprika, cayenne pepper, curry powder, and remaining 1 teaspoon of kosher salt. Pour all but 2 tablespoons of the marinade into a resealable plastic bag, leaving those 2 tablespoons in the bowl. Place the lamb chops in the bag. Squeeze out as much air as possible and squish the bag around to coat the chops with the marinade. Set aside.
3. Add the potatoes to the bowl with the remaining marinade and toss to coat. Spray the baking pan with cooking oil spray. Place the potatoes in the pan.
4. Place the pan on the roast position. Select Roast, set temperature to 375°F (191°C), and set time to 10 minutes.
5. When cooking is complete, remove the pan from the grill. Remove the chops from the marinade, draining off all but a thin coat (and discarding the marinade and plastic bag), and place them in the baking pan.
6. Place the pan on the broil position. Select Broil, set temperature to 450°F (232°C), and set time to 10 minutes.
7. After 5 minutes, remove the pan from the grill and turn over the chops and potatoes. Return the pan to the grill and continue cooking.
8. When cooking is complete, the lamb should read 145°F (63°C) for medium rare on a meat thermometer; continue cooking for an additional few minutes if you want it more well done. Remove the pan from the grill and serve.

Steak and Bell Pepper Fajitas

Prep time: 10 minutes | Cook time: 15 minutes | Serves 4

8 (6-inch) flour or corn tortillas
1 pound (454 g) top sirloin steak, sliced ¼-inch thick
1 red bell pepper, seeded and sliced ½-inch thick
1 green bell pepper, seeded and sliced ½-inch thick
1 jalapeño, seeded and sliced thin

1 medium onion, sliced ½-inch thick
2 tablespoons vegetable oil
2 tablespoons Mexican seasoning
1 teaspoon kosher salt or ½ teaspoon fine salt
Salsa
1 small avocado, sliced

1. Place a large sheet of aluminum foil in the baking pan. Place the tortillas on the foil in two stacks and wrap in the foil.
2. Place the pan on the roast position. Select Roast, set temperature to 325°F (163°C), and set time to 6 minutes.
3. After 3 minutes, remove the pan from the grill and flip the packet of tortillas over. Return the pan to the grill and continue cooking.
4. While the tortillas warm, place the steak, bell peppers, jalapeño, and onion in a large bowl and drizzle the oil over. Sprinkle with the Mexican seasoning and salt, and toss to coat.
5. When cooking is complete, remove the pan from the grill and place the packet of tortillas on top of the grill to keep warm. Place the beef and peppers mixture in the baking pan, spreading out into a single layer as much as possible.
6. Place the pan on the roast position. Select Roast, set temperature to 375°F (191°C), and set time to 9 minutes.
7. After about 5 minutes, remove the pan from the grill and stir the ingredients. Return the pan to the grill and continue cooking.
8. When cooking is complete, the vegetables will be soft and browned in places, and the beef will be browned on the outside and barely pink inside. Remove the pan from the grill. Unwrap the tortillas and spoon the fajita mixture into the tortillas. Serve with salsa and avocado slices.

Chapter 9 Desserts

Apple Pear Crisp

Prep time: 10 minutes | Cook time: 20 minutes | Serves 6

½ pound (227 g) apples, cored and chopped
½ pound (227 g) pears, cored and chopped
1 cup flour
1 cup sugar
1 tablespoon butter
1 teaspoon ground

cinnamon
¼ teaspoon ground cloves
1 teaspoon vanilla extract
¼ cup chopped walnuts
Whipped cream, for serving

1. Lightly grease the baking pan and place the apples and pears inside.
2. Combine the rest of the ingredients, minus the walnuts and the whipped cream, until a coarse, crumbly texture is achieved.
3. Pour the mixture over the fruits and spread it evenly. Top with the chopped walnuts.
4. Place the baking pan on the bake position. Select Bake, set the temperature to 340ºF (171ºC), and set the time to 20 minutes.
5. Cook for 20 minutes or until the top turns golden brown.
6. Serve at room temperature with whipped cream.

Chocolate S'mores

Prep time: 5 minutes | Cook time: 3 minutes | Serves 12

12 whole cinnamon graham crackers
2 (1.55-ounce / 44-g)

chocolate bars, broken into 12 pieces
12 marshmallows

1. Halve each graham cracker into 2 squares.
2. Put 6 graham cracker squares in the crisper tray. Do not stack. Put a piece of chocolate into each.
3. Place the crisper tray on the bake position. Select Bake, set the temperature to 350ºF (177ºC), and set the time to 3 minutes.
4. Cook for 2 minutes. Open the grill and add a marshmallow onto each piece of melted chocolate. Cook for 1 additional minute.
5. Remove the cooked s'mores from the grill, then repeat steps 2 and 3 for the remaining 6 s'mores.
6. Top with the remaining graham cracker squares and serve.

Chocolate Coconut Cake

Prep time: 5 minutes | Cook time: 15 minutes | Serves 10

1¼ cups unsweetened bakers' chocolate
1 stick butter
1 teaspoon liquid stevia
1/₃ cup shredded

coconut
2 tablespoons coconut milk
2 eggs, beaten
Cooking spray

1. Lightly spritz the baking pan with cooking spray.
2. Place the chocolate, butter, and stevia in a microwave-safe bowl. Microwave for about 30 seconds until melted. Let the chocolate mixture cool to room temperature.
3. Add the remaining ingredients to the chocolate mixture and stir until well incorporated. Pour the batter into the prepared baking pan.
4. Place the baking pan on the bake position. Select Bake, set the temperature to 330ºF (166ºC), and set the time to 15 minutes.
5. Cook for 15 minutes, or until a toothpick inserted in the center comes out clean.
6. Remove from the pan and allow to cool for about 10 minutes before serving.

Fudge Pie

Prep time: 15 minutes | Cook time: 25 to 30 minutes | Serves 8

1½ cups sugar
½ cup self-rising flour
1/₃ cup unsweetened cocoa powder
3 large eggs, beaten
12 tablespoons (1½ sticks) butter, melted

1½ teaspoons vanilla extract
1 (9-inch) unbaked pie crust
¼ cup confectioners' sugar (optional)

1. Thoroughly combine the sugar, flour, and cocoa powder in a medium bowl. Add the beaten eggs and butter and whisk to combine. Stir in the vanilla.
2. Pour the prepared filling into the pie crust and transfer to the pan.
3. Place the baking pan on the bake position. Select Bake, set the temperature to 350ºF (177ºC), and set the time to 30 minutes.
4. Cook for 25 to 30 minutes until just set.
5. Allow the pie to cool for 5 minutes. Sprinkle with the confectioners' sugar, if desired. Serve warm.

Peanut Butter-Chocolate Bread Pudding

Prep time: 10 minutes | Cook time: 10 to 12 minutes | Serves 8

1 egg
1 egg yolk
¾ cup chocolate milk
3 tablespoons brown sugar
3 tablespoons peanut butter

2 tablespoons cocoa powder
1 teaspoon vanilla
5 slices firm white bread, cubed
Nonstick cooking spray

1. Spritz the baking pan with nonstick cooking spray.
2. Whisk together the egg, egg yolk, chocolate milk, brown sugar, peanut butter, cocoa powder, and vanilla until well combined.
3. Fold in the bread cubes and stir to mix well. Allow the bread soak for 10 minutes.
4. When ready, transfer the egg mixture to the prepared baking pan.
5. Place the baking pan on the bake position. Select Bake, set the temperature to 330°F (166°C), and set the time to 12 minutes.
6. Cook for 10 to 12 minutes, or until the pudding is just firm to the touch.
7. Serve at room temperature.

Apple Cranberry Peach Crisp

Prep time: 10 minutes | Cook time: 12 minutes | Serves 8

1 apple, peeled and chopped
2 peaches, peeled and chopped
1/3 cup dried cranberries

2 tablespoons honey
1/3 cup brown sugar
¼ cup flour
½ cup oatmeal
3 tablespoons softened butter

1. In the baking pan, combine the apple, peaches, cranberries, and honey, and mix well.
2. In a medium bowl, combine the brown sugar, flour, oatmeal, and butter, and mix until crumbly. Sprinkle this mixture over the fruit in the pan.
3. Place the baking pan on the bake position. Select Bake, set the temperature to 370°F (188°C), and set the time to 12 minutes.
4. Cook for 10 to 12 minutes or until the fruit is bubbly and the topping is golden brown. Serve warm.

Curried Fruit

Prep time: 5 minutes | Cook time: 5 minutes | Serves 6 to 8

2 peaches
2 firm pears
2 plums
2 tablespoons melted

butter
1 tablespoon honey
2 to 3 teaspoons curry powder

1. Cut the peaches in half, remove the pits, and cut each half in half again. Cut the pears in half, core them, and remove the stem. Cut each half in half again. Do the same with the plums.
2. Spread a large sheet of heavy-duty foil on the work surface. Arrange the fruit on the foil and drizzle with the butter and honey. Sprinkle with the curry powder.
3. Wrap the fruit in the foil, making sure to leave some air space in the packet.
4. Put the foil package in the crisper tray.
5. Place the crisper tray on the bake position. Select Bake, set the temperature to 325°F (163°C), and set the time to 8 minutes.
6. Cook for 5 to 8 minutes, shaking the crisper tray once during the cooking time, until the fruit is soft.
7. Serve immediately.

Pineapple Chocolate Cake

Prep time: 10 minutes | Cook time: 35 to 40 minutes | Serves 4

2 cups flour
4 ounces (113 g) butter, melted
¼ cup sugar
½ pound (227 g) pineapple, chopped

½ cup pineapple juice
1 ounce (28 g) dark chocolate, grated
1 large egg
2 tablespoons skimmed milk

1. Grease a cake tin with a little oil or butter.
2. In a bowl, combine the butter and flour to create a crumbly consistency.
3. Add the sugar, chopped pineapple, juice, and grated dark chocolate and mix well.
4. In a separate bowl, combine the egg and milk. Add this mixture to the flour mixture and stir well until a soft dough forms.
5. Pour the mixture into the cake tin.
6. Place the cake tin on the bake position. Select Bake, set the temperature to 370°F (188°C), and set the time to 40 minutes.
7. Cook for 35 to 40 minutes.
8. Serve immediately.

Chocolate Cookies

Prep time: 10 minutes | Cook time: 9 minutes | Serves 4

Nonstick baking spray with flour
3 tablespoons softened butter
1/3 cup plus 1 tablespoon brown sugar
1 egg yolk
½ cup flour
2 tablespoons ground white chocolate
¼ teaspoon baking soda
½ teaspoon vanilla
¾ cup chocolate chips

1. In a medium bowl, beat the butter and brown sugar together until fluffy. Stir in the egg yolk.
2. Add the flour, white chocolate, baking soda, and vanilla, and mix well. Stir in the chocolate chips.
3. Line the baking pan with parchment paper. Spray the parchment paper with nonstick baking spray with flour.
4. Spread the batter into the prepared pan, leaving a ½-inch border on all sides.
5. Place the baking pan on the bake position. Select Bake, set the temperature to 350ºF (177ºC), and set the time to 9 minutes.
6. Cook for 9 minutes or until the cookie is light brown and just barely set.
7. Remove the pan from the grill and lct cool for 10 minutes. Remove the cookie from the pan, remove the parchment paper, and let cool on a wire rack.
8. Serve immediately.

Cinnamon Candied Apples

Prep time: 15 minutes | Cook time: 12 minutes | Serves 4

1 cup packed light brown sugar
2 teaspoons ground cinnamon
2 medium Granny Smith apples, peeled and diced

1. Thoroughly combine the brown sugar and cinnamon in a medium bowl.
2. Add the apples to the bowl and stir until well coated. Transfer the apples to the baking pan.
3. Place the baking pan on the bake position. Select Bake, set the temperature to 350ºF (177ºC), and set the time to 12 minutes.
4. Cook for 9 minutes. Stir the apples once and cook for an additional 3 minutes until softened.
5. Serve warm.

Black Forest Pie

Prep time: 10 minutes | Cook time: 15 minutes | Serves 6

3 tablespoons milk or dark chocolate chips
2 tablespoons thick, hot fudge sauce
2 tablespoons chopped dried cherries
1 (10-by-15-inch) sheet frozen puff pastry, thawed
1 egg white, beaten
2 tablespoons sugar
½ teaspoon cinnamon

1. In a small bowl, combine the chocolate chips, fudge sauce, and dried cherries.
2. Roll out the puff pastry on a floured surface. Cut into 6 squares with a sharp knife.
3. Divide the chocolate chip mixture into the center of each puff pastry square. Fold the squares in half to make triangles. Firmly press the edges with the tines of a fork to seal.
4. Brush the triangles on all sides sparingly with the beaten egg white. Sprinkle the tops with sugar and cinnamon.
5. Put in the crisper tray.
6. Place the crisper tray on the bake position. Select Bake, set the temperature to 350ºF (177ºC), and set the time to 15 minutes.
7. Cook for 15 minutes or until the triangles are golden brown. The filling will be hot, so cool for at least 20 minutes before serving.

Chia Pudding

Prep time: 5 minutes | Cook time: 4 minutes | Serves 2

1 cup chia seeds
1 cup unsweetened coconut milk
1 teaspoon liquid stevia
1 tablespoon coconut oil
1 teaspoon butter, melted

1. Mix together the chia seeds, coconut milk, and stevia in a large bowl. Add the coconut oil and melted butter and stir until well blended.
2. Divide the mixture evenly between the ramekins, filling only about 2/3 of the way. Transfer to the pan.
3. Place the baking pan on the bake position. Select Bake, set the temperature to 360ºF (182ºC), and set the time to 4 minutes.
4. Allow to cool for 5 minutes and serve warm.

Blueberry Cobbler

Prep time: 15 minutes | Cook time: 30 minutes | Serves 6

4 cups fresh blueberries
1 teaspoon grated lemon zest
1 cup sugar, plus 2 tablespoons
1 cup all-purpose flour, plus 2 tablespoons
Juice of 1 lemon

2 teaspoons baking powder
¼ teaspoon salt
6 tablespoons unsalted butter
¾ cup whole milk
⅛ teaspoon ground cinnamon

1. In a medium bowl, combine the blueberries, lemon zest, 2 tablespoons of sugar, 2 tablespoons of flour, and lemon juice.
2. In a medium bowl, combine the remaining 1 cup of flour and 1 cup of sugar, baking powder, and salt. Cut the butter into the flour mixture until it forms an even crumb texture. Stir in the milk until a dough forms.
3. Meanwhile, pour the blueberry mixture into the baking pan, spreading it evenly across the pan. Gently pour the batter over the blueberry mixture, then sprinkle the cinnamon over the top.
4. Place the baking pan on the bake position. Select Bake, set the temperature to 350ºF (177ºC), and set the time to 30 minutes.
5. Cook for 30 minutes, until lightly golden.
6. When cooking is complete, serve warm.

Lemon Ricotta Cake

Prep time: 5 minutes | Cook time: 25 minutes | Serves 6

17.5 ounces (496 g) ricotta cheese
5.4 ounces (153 g) sugar
3 eggs, beaten

3 tablespoons flour
1 lemon, juiced and zested
2 teaspoons vanilla extract

1. In a large mixing bowl, stir together all the ingredients until the mixture reaches a creamy consistency.
2. Pour the mixture into the baking pan.
3. Place the baking pan on the bake position. Select Bake, set the temperature to 320ºF (160ºC), and set the time to 25 minutes.
4. Cook for 25 minutes until a toothpick inserted in the center comes out clean.
5. Allow to cool for 10 minutes on a wire rack before serving.

Marshmallow Banana Boat

Prep time: 10 minutes | Cook time: 6 minutes | Serves 4

4 ripe bananas
1 cup mini marshmallows

½ cup chocolate chips
½ cup peanut butter chips

1. Slice each banana lengthwise while still in its peel, making sure not to cut all the way through. Using both hands, pull the banana peel open like you would a book, revealing the banana inside. Divide the marshmallows, chocolate chips, and peanut butter chips among the bananas, stuffing them inside the skin.
2. Place the stuffed banana on the grill plate.
3. Place the grill plate on the grill position. Select Grill, set the temperature to 350ºF (177ºC), and set the time to 6 minutes.
4. Cook for 4 to 6 minutes, until the chocolate is melted and the marshmallows are toasted.

Blackberry Chocolate Cake

Prep time: 10 minutes | Cook time: 22 minutes | Serves 8

½ cup butter, at room temperature
2 ounces (57 g) Swerve
4 eggs
1 cup almond flour
1 teaspoon baking soda

⅓ teaspoon baking powder
½ cup cocoa powder
1 teaspoon orange zest
⅓ cup fresh blackberries

1. With an electric mixer or hand mixer, beat the butter and Swerve until creamy.
2. One at a time, mix in the eggs and beat again until fluffy.
3. Add the almond flour, baking soda, baking powder, cocoa powder, orange zest and mix well. Add the butter mixture to the almond flour mixture and stir until well blended. Fold in the blackberries.
4. Scrape the batter to the baking pan.
5. Place the baking pan on the bake position. Select Bake, set the temperature to 335ºF (168ºC), and set the time to 22 minutes.
6. Check the cake for doneness: If a toothpick inserted into the center of the cake comes out clean, it's done.
7. Allow the cake cool on a wire rack to room temperature. Serve immediately.

Blackberry Crisp

Prep time: 5 minutes | Cook time: 15 minutes | Serves 1

2 tablespoons lemon juice	¼ teaspoon xantham gum
⅓ cup powdered erythritol	2 cup blackberries
	1 cup crunchy granola

1. In a bowl, combine the lemon juice, erythritol, xantham gum, and blackberries. Transfer to the baking pan and cover with aluminum foil.
2. Place the baking pan on the bake position. Select Bake, set the temperature to 350ºF (177ºC), and set the time to 12 minutes.
3. Take care when removing the pan from the grill. Give the blackberries a stir and top with the granola.
4. Return the pan to the grill and bake at 320ºF (160ºC) for an additional 3 minutes. Serve once the granola has turned brown and enjoy.

Chocolate Coconut Brownies

Prep time: 15 minutes | Cook time: 15 minutes | Serves 8

½ cup coconut oil	¼ teaspoon coconut extract
2 ounces (57 g) dark chocolate	½ teaspoons vanilla extract
1 cup sugar	1 tablespoon honey
2½ tablespoons water	½ cup flour
4 whisked eggs	½ cup desiccated coconut
¼ teaspoon ground cinnamon	Sugar, for dusting
½ teaspoons ground anise star	

1. Melt the coconut oil and dark chocolate in the microwave.
2. Combine with the sugar, water, eggs, cinnamon, anise, coconut extract, vanilla, and honey in a large bowl.
3. Stir in the flour and desiccated coconut. Incorporate everything well.
4. Lightly grease the baking pan with butter. Transfer the mixture to the pan.
5. Place the baking pan on the bake position. Select Bake, set the temperature to 355ºF (179ºC), and set the time to 15 minutes.
6. Remove from the grill and allow to cool slightly.
7. Take care when taking it out of the baking pan. Slice it into squares.
8. Dust with sugar before serving.

Corn Biscuits

Prep time: 15 minutes | Cook time: 15 minutes | Serves 6

1½ cups all-purpose flour, plus additional for dusting	½ teaspoon sea salt
½ cup yellow cornmeal	⅓ cup vegetable shortening
2½ teaspoons baking powder	⅔ cup buttermilk
	Nonstick cooking spray

1. In a large bowl, combine the flour, cornmeal, baking powder, and salt.
2. Add the shortening, and cut it into the flour mixture, until well combined and the dough resembles a coarse meal. Add the buttermilk and stir together just until moistened.
3. Dust a clean work surface with flour. Knead the mixture on the floured surface until a cohesive dough forms. Roll out the dough to an even thickness, then cut into biscuits with a 2-inch biscuit cutter.
4. Coat the crisper tray with cooking spray. Place 6 to 8 biscuits in the crisper tray, well spaced, and spray each with cooking spray.
5. Place the crisper tray on the air fry position. Select Air Fry, set the temperature to 350ºF (177ºC), and set the time to 15 minutes.
6. Cook for 12 to 15 minutes, until golden brown.
7. Gently remove the biscuits from the crisper tray, and place them on a wire rack to cool. Repeat with the remaining dough.

Creamy Pumpkin Pudding

Prep time: 10 minutes | Cook time: 15 minutes | Serves 4

3 cups pumpkin purée	1 teaspoon clove
3 tablespoons honey	1 teaspoon nutmeg
1 tablespoon ginger	1 cup full-fat cream
1 tablespoon cinnamon	2 eggs
	1 cup sugar

1. In a bowl, stir all the ingredients together to combine.
2. Scrape the mixture into the greased baking pan.
3. Place the baking pan on the bake position. Select Bake, set the temperature to 390ºF (199ºC), and set the time to 15 minutes.
4. Serve warm.

Classic Pound Cake

Prep time: 5 minutes | Cook time: 30 minutes | Serves 8

1 stick butter, at room temperature	powder
	¼ teaspoon salt
1 cup Swerve	1 teaspoon vanilla
4 eggs	essence
1½ cups coconut flour	A pinch of ground star
½ cup buttermilk	anise
½ teaspoon baking soda	A pinch of freshly grated nutmeg
½ teaspoon baking	Cooking spray

1. Spray the baking pan with cooking spray.
2. With an electric mixer or hand mixer, beat the butter and Swerve until creamy. One at a time, mix in the eggs and whisk until fluffy. Add the remaining ingredients and stir to combine.
3. Transfer the batter to the prepared baking pan.
4. Place the baking pan on the bake position. Select Bake, set the temperature to 320ºF (160ºC), and set the time to 30 minutes.
5. Cook for 30 minutes until the center of the cake is springy. Rotate the pan halfway through the cooking time.
6. Allow the cake to cool in the pan for 10 minutes before removing and serving.

Walnut and Pistachio Baklava

Prep time: 10 minutes | Cook time: 16 minutes | Serves 10

1 cup shelled raw pistachios	tablespoons honey, divided
1 cup walnut pieces	1 teaspoon ground
½ cup unsalted butter, melted	cinnamon
	2 (1.9-ounce / 54-
3 tablespoons granulated sugar	g) packages frozen miniature phyllo tart
¼ cup plus 2	shells

1. Place the pistachios and walnuts in the crisper tray in an even layer.
2. Place the crisper tray on the air fry position. Select Air Fry, set temperature to 350ºF (177ºC), and set time to 4 minutes.
3. After 2 minutes, remove the crisper tray and stir the nuts. Return the crisper tray to the grill and continue cooking until the nuts are golden brown and fragrant, 1 to 2 minutes more.

4. While the nuts are toasting, place the butter into a medium bowl. Add the sugar, ¼ cup of honey, and cinnamon. Stir to combine.
5. When the nuts are toasted, remove the crisper tray from the grill and place them on a cutting board and let cool for a couple of minutes. Finely chop the nuts—not so that they're pulverized, but so no large chunks remain. If you have a food processor, a few pulses of the blade should do it. If you have an old-fashioned nut chopper, this is a great time to pull it out. Add the chopped nuts, with all the "nut dust," to the sugar mixture and stir to combine.
6. Place the phyllo cups in the baking pan, which will be cool by now. Evenly fill the phyllo cups with the nut mixture, mounding it up. (You'll think you have too much filling, but you won't; trust me.) As you work, stir the nuts in the bowl frequently so that the syrup is even distributed throughout the filling.
7. Place the pan on the bake position. Select Bake, set temperature to 350ºF (177ºC), and set time to 12 minutes.
8. After about 8 minutes, check the cups, and rotate the pan if the they are not browning evenly. Continue cooking until the cups are dark golden brown and the syrup is bubbling (it might ooze out; don't worry about that).
9. As soon as you remove the baklava from the grill, drizzle each cup with about ⅛ teaspoon or so of the remaining honey over the top. Let cool completely before serving.

Banana Walnut Cake

Prep time: 10 minutes | Cook time: 25 minutes | Serves 6

1 pound (454 g) bananas, mashed	walnuts, chopped
	2.5 ounces (71 g)
8 ounces (227 g) flour	butter, melted
6 ounces (170 g) sugar	2 eggs, lightly beaten
	¼ teaspoon baking
3.5 ounces (99 g)	soda

1. In a bowl, combine the sugar, butter, egg, flour, and baking soda with a whisk. Stir in the bananas and walnuts.
2. Transfer the mixture to the greased baking pan.
3. Place the baking pan on the bake position. Select Bake, set the temperature to 355ºF (179ºC), and set the time to 10 minutes.
4. Reduce the temperature to 330ºF (166ºC) and bake for another 15 minutes. Serve hot.

Graham Cracker Cheesecake

Prep time: 10 minutes | Cook time: 20 minutes | Serves 8

1 cup graham cracker crumbs
3 tablespoons softened butter
1½ (8-ounce / 227-g) packages cream

cheese, softened
⅓ cup sugar
2 eggs
1 tablespoon flour
1 teaspoon vanilla
¼ cup chocolate syrup

1. For the crust, combine the graham cracker crumbs and butter in a small bowl and mix well. Press into the bottom of the baking pan and put in the freezer to set.
2. For the filling, combine the cream cheese and sugar in a medium bowl and mix well. Beat in the eggs, one at a time. Add the flour and vanilla.
3. Remove ⅔ cup of the filling to a small bowl and stir in the chocolate syrup until combined.
4. Pour the vanilla filling into the pan with the crust. Drop the chocolate filling over the vanilla filling by the spoonful. With a clean butter knife, stir the fillings in a zigzag pattern to marbleize them.
5. Place the baking pan on the bake position. Select Bake, set the temperature to 450ºF (232ºC), and set the time to 20 minutes.
6. Cook for 20 minutes or until the cheesecake is just set.
7. Cool on a wire rack for 1 hour, then chill in the refrigerator until the cheesecake is firm.
8. Serve immediately.

Chocolate and Peanut Butter Lava Cupcakes

Prep time: 10 minutes | Cook time: 10 to 13 minutes | Serves 8

Nonstick baking spray with flour
1⅓ cups chocolate cake mix
1 egg
1 egg yolk
¼ cup safflower oil

¼ cup hot water
⅓ cup sour cream
3 tablespoons peanut butter
1 tablespoon powdered sugar

1. Double up 16 foil muffin cups to make 8 cups. Spray each lightly with nonstick spray; set aside.
2. In a medium bowl, combine the cake mix, egg, egg yolk, safflower oil, water, and sour cream, and beat until combined.

3. In a small bowl, combine the peanut butter and powdered sugar and mix well. Form this mixture into 8 balls.
4. Spoon about ¼ cup of the chocolate batter into each muffin cup and top with a peanut butter ball. Spoon remaining batter on top of the peanut butter balls to cover them.
5. Arrange the cups in the pan, leaving some space between each.
6. Place the baking pan on the bake position. Select Bake, set the temperature to 350ºF (177ºC), and set the time to 13 minutes.
7. Cook for 10 to 13 minutes or until the tops look dry and set.
8. Let the cupcakes cool for about 10 minutes, then serve warm.

Ultimate Skillet Brownies

Prep time: 15 minutes | Cook time: 40 minutes | Serves 6

½ cup all-purpose flour
¼ cup unsweetened cocoa powder
¾ teaspoon sea salt
2 large eggs
1 tablespoon water
½ cup granulated sugar
½ cup dark brown

sugar
1 tablespoon vanilla extract
8 ounces (227 g) semisweet chocolate chips, melted
¾ cup unsalted butter, melted
Nonstick cooking spray

1. In a medium bowl, whisk together the flour, cocoa powder, and salt.
2. In a large bowl, whisk together the eggs, water, sugar, brown sugar, and vanilla until smooth.
3. In a microwave-safe bowl, melt the chocolate in the microwave. In a separate microwave-safe bowl, melt the butter.
4. In a separate medium bowl, stir together the chocolate and butter until evenly combined. Whisk into the egg mixture. Then slowly add the dry ingredients, stirring just until incorporated.
5. Lightly grease the baking pan with cooking spray. Pour the batter into the pan, spreading evenly.
6. Place the baking pan on the bake position. Select Bake, set the temperature to 350ºF (177ºC), and set the time to 40 minutes.
7. After 40 minutes, check that baking is complete. A wooden toothpick inserted into the center of the brownies should come out clean.

Ultimate Orange Cake

Prep time: 10 minutes | Cook time: 23 minutes | Serves 8

Nonstick baking spray with flour
1¼ cups all-purpose flour
⅓ cup yellow cornmeal
¾ cup white sugar
1 teaspoon baking soda
¼ cup safflower oil
1¼ cups orange juice, divided
1 teaspoon vanilla
¼ cup powdered sugar

1. Spray the baking pan with nonstick spray and set aside.
2. In a medium bowl, combine the flour, cornmeal, sugar, baking soda, safflower oil, 1 cup of the orange juice, and vanilla, and mix well.
3. Pour the batter into the baking pan.
4. Place the baking pan on the bake position. Select Bake, set the temperature to 350°F (177°C), and set the time to 23 minutes.
5. Cook for 23 minutes or until a toothpick inserted in the center of the cake comes out clean.
6. Remove the cake from the grill and place on a cooling rack. Using a toothpick, make about 20 holes in the cake.
7. In a small bowl, combine remaining ¼ cup of orange juice and the powdered sugar and stir well. Drizzle this mixture over the hot cake slowly so the cake absorbs it.
8. Cool completely, then cut into wedges to serve.

Blueberry and Peach Galette

Prep time: 10 minutes | Cook time: 20 minutes | Serves 6

2 large peaches or nectarines, peeled and cut into ½-inch slices (about 2 cups)
1 pint blueberries, rinsed and picked through (about 2 cups)
⅓ cup plus 2 tablespoons granulated sugar, divided
2 tablespoons unbleached all-purpose flour
¼ teaspoon ground allspice or cinnamon
½ teaspoon grated lemon zest (optional)
Pinch kosher or fine salt
1 (9-inch) refrigerated piecrust (or use homemade)
2 teaspoons unsalted butter, cut into pea-size pieces
1 large egg, beaten

1. In a medium bowl, gently mix the peaches and blueberries with ⅓ cup of sugar, flour, allspice, lemon zest (if using), and salt.

2. In the baking pan, unroll the crust, patching any tears if necessary. Arrange the fruit in the center of the crust, leaving about 1½ inches of space around the edges. Distribute the butter pieces over the fruit. Fold the outside edge of the crust over the outer circle of the fruit, making pleats as necessary. Brush the crust with the egg. Sprinkle the remaining 2 tablespoons of sugar over the crust and fruit.
3. Place the pan on the bake position. Select Bake, set temperature to 350°F (177°C), and set time to 20 minutes.
4. After about 15 minutes, check the galette, rotating the pan if the crust is not browning evenly. The galette is done when the crust is deep golden brown and the fruit is bubbling.
5. Remove the pan from the grill and let cool for 10 minutes, then cut into wedges and serve warm.

Grilled Peaches with Bourbon Butter Sauce

Prep time: 10 minutes | Cook time: 12 minutes | Serves 4

4 tablespoons salted butter
¼ cup bourbon
½ cup brown sugar
4 ripe peaches, halved and pitted
¼ cup candied pecans

1. In a saucepan over medium heat, melt the butter for about 5 minutes. Once the butter is browned, remove the pan from the heat and carefully add the bourbon.
2. Return the saucepan to medium-high heat and add the brown sugar. Bring to a boil and let the sugar dissolve for 5 minutes, stirring occasionally.
3. Pour the bourbon butter sauce into a medium shallow bowl and arrange the peaches cut-side down to coat in the sauce.
4. Place the fruit on the grill plate in a single layer (you may need to do this in multiple batches). Gently press the fruit down to maximize grill marks.
5. Place the grill plate on the grill position. Select Grill, set the temperature to 450°F (232°C), and set the time to 12 minutes.
6. Cook for 10 to 12 minutes without flipping. If working in batches, repeat this step for all the peaches.
7. When cooking is complete, remove the peaches and top each with the pecans. Drizzle with the remaining bourbon butter sauce and serve immediately.

Black and White Brownies

Prep time: 10 minutes | Cook time: 20 minutes | Makes 1 dozen brownies

1 egg
¼ cup brown sugar
2 tablespoons white sugar
2 tablespoons safflower oil
1 teaspoon vanilla
⅓ cup all-purpose flour
¼ cup cocoa powder
¼ cup white chocolate chips
Nonstick cooking spray

1. Spritz the baking pan with nonstick cooking spray.
2. Whisk together the egg, brown sugar, and white sugar in a medium bowl. Mix in the safflower oil and vanilla and stir to combine.
3. Add the flour and cocoa powder and stir just until incorporated. Fold in the white chocolate chips.
4. Scrape the batter into the prepared baking pan.
5. Place the baking pan on the bake position. Select Bake, set the temperature to 340ºF (171ºC), and set the time to 20 minutes.
6. Cook for 20 minutes, or until the brownie springs back when touched lightly with your fingers.
7. Transfer to a wire rack and let cool for 30 minutes before slicing to serve.

Blackberry Cobbler

Prep time: 15 minutes | Cook time: 25 to 30 minutes | Serves 6

3 cups fresh or frozen blackberries
1¾ cups sugar, divided
1 teaspoon vanilla extract
8 tablespoons (1 stick) butter, melted
1 cup self-rising flour
Cooking spray

1. Spritz the baking pan with cooking spray.
2. Mix the blackberries, 1 cup of sugar, and vanilla in a medium bowl and stir to combine.
3. Stir together the melted butter, remaining sugar, and flour in a separate medium bowl.
4. Spread the blackberry mixture evenly in the prepared pan and top with the butter mixture.
5. Place the baking pan on the bake position. Select Bake, set the temperature to 350ºF (177ºC), and set the time to 30 minutes.
6. Cook for 20 to 25 minutes. Check for doneness and cook for another 5 minutes, if needed.

7. Remove from the grill and place on a wire rack to cool to room temperature. Serve immediately.

Churros with Chocolate Sauce

Prep time: 15 minutes | Cook time: 30 minutes | Serves 8

1 cup water
1 stick unsalted butter, cut into 8 pieces
½ cup sugar, plus 1 tablespoon
1 cup all-purpose flour
1 teaspoon vanilla extract
3 large eggs
2 teaspoons ground cinnamon
Nonstick cooking spray
4 ounces (113 g) dark chocolate, chopped
¼ cup Greek yogurt

1. In a medium saucepan over medium-high heat, combine the water, butter, and the 1 tablespoon of sugar. Bring to a simmer. Add the flour, stirring it in quickly. Continue to cook, stirring constantly, until the mixture is thick, about 3 minutes. Transfer to a large bowl.
2. Using a spoon, beat the flour mixture for about 1 minute, until cooled slightly. Stir in the vanilla, then the eggs, one at a time.
3. Transfer the dough to a plastic bag or a piping bag. Let the dough rest for 1 hour at room temperature.
4. Meanwhile, in a medium shallow bowl, combine the cinnamon and remaining ½ cup of sugar.
5. Spray the crisper tray with the nonstick cooking spray. Take the plastic bag with your dough and cut off one corner. Pipe the batter directly into the crisper tray, making 6 (3-inch-long) churros, placed at least ½ inch apart.
6. Place the crisper tray on the air fry position. Select Air Fry, set the temperature to 375ºF (191ºC), and set the time to 10 minutes.
7. Meanwhile, in a small microwave-safe mixing bowl, melt the chocolate in the microwave, stirring it after every 30 seconds, until completely melted and smooth. Add the yogurt and whisk until smooth.
8. After 10 minutes, carefully transfer the churros to the sugar mixture and toss to coat evenly. Repeat piping and air frying with the remaining batter, adding time as needed.
9. Serve the churros with the warm chocolate dipping sauce.

Chocolate and Coconut Cake

Prep time: 5 minutes | Cook time: 15 minutes | Serves 6

½ cup unsweetened chocolate, chopped
½ stick butter, at room temperature
1 tablespoon liquid stevia
1½ cups coconut flour
2 eggs, whisked
½ teaspoon vanilla extract
A pinch of fine sea salt
Cooking spray

1. Place the chocolate, butter, and stevia in a microwave-safe bowl. Microwave for about 30 seconds until melted.
2. Let the chocolate mixture cool for 5 to 10 minutes.
3. Add the remaining ingredients to the bowl of chocolate mixture and whisk to incorporate.
4. Lightly spray the baking pan with cooking spray.
5. Scrape the chocolate mixture into the prepared baking pan.
6. Place the baking pan on the bake position. Select Bake, set the temperature to 330ºF (166ºC), and set the time to 15 minutes.
7. Cook for 15 minutes, or until the top springs back lightly when gently pressed with your fingers.
8. Let the cake cool for 5 minutes and serve.

Sugar-Glazed Biscuit Bites

Prep time: 15 minutes | Cook time: 12 minutes | Serves 8

²/₃ cup all-purpose flour, plus additional for dusting
²/₃ cup whole-wheat flour
2 tablespoons granulated sugar
1 teaspoon baking powder
¼ teaspoon ground cinnamon
¼ teaspoon sea salt
4 tablespoons salted butter, cold and cut into small pieces
¹/₃ cup whole milk
Nonstick cooking spray
2 cups powdered sugar
3 tablespoons water

1. In a large bowl, combine the all-purpose flour, whole-wheat flour, sugar, baking powder, cinnamon, and salt. Add the cold butter pieces, and cut them into the flour mixture using a pastry cutter or a fork, until well-combined and the mixture resembles a course meal. Add the milk to the mixture, and stir together until the dough comes together into a ball.
2. Dust a clean work surface with the all-purpose flour. Place the dough on the floured surface, and knead until the dough is smooth and forms a cohesive ball, about 30 seconds. Cut the dough into 16 equal pieces. Gently roll each piece into a smooth ball.
3. Coat the crisper tray well with cooking spray. Place 8 biscuit bites in the crisper tray, leaving room between each, and spray each with cooking spray.
4. Place the crisper tray on the air fry position. Select Air Fry, set the temperature to 350ºF (177ºC), and set the time to 12 minutes.
5. Cook for 10 to 12 minutes, until golden brown.
6. Meanwhile, in a medium mixing bowl, whisk together the powdered sugar and water until it forms a smooth glaze.
7. Gently remove the bites from the crisper tray, and place them on a wire rack covered with aluminum foil. Repeat step 4 with the remaining biscuit bites.
8. Spoon half the glaze over the bites and let cool 5 minutes, then spoon over the remaining glaze.

Rum Grilled Pineapple Sundaes

Prep time: 15 minutes | Cook time: 8 minutes | Serves 6

½ cup dark rum
½ cup packed brown sugar
1 teaspoon ground cinnamon, plus more
for garnish
1 pineapple, cored and sliced
Vanilla ice cream, for serving

1. In a large shallow bowl or storage container, combine the rum, sugar, and cinnamon. Add the pineapple slices and arrange them in a single layer. Coat with the mixture, then let soak for at least 5 minutes per side.
2. Strain the extra rum sauce from the pineapple.
3. Place the fruit on the grill plate in a single layer (you may need to do this in multiple batches). Gently press the fruit down to maximize grill marks.
4. Place the grill plate on the grill position. Select Grill, set the temperature to 450ºF (232ºC), and set the time to 8 minutes.
5. Cook for about 6 to 8 minutes without flipping. If working in batches, remove the pineapple, and repeat this step for the remaining pineapple slices.
6. When cooking is complete, remove, and top each pineapple ring with a scoop of ice cream. Sprinkle with cinnamon and serve immediately.

Oatmeal and Carrot Cookie Cups

Prep time: 10 minutes | Cook time: 8 minutes | Makes 16 cups

3 tablespoons unsalted butter, at room temperature
¼ cup packed brown sugar
1 tablespoon honey
1 egg white
½ teaspoon vanilla extract

⅓ cup finely grated carrot
½ cup quick-cooking oatmeal
⅓ cup whole-wheat pastry flour
½ teaspoon baking soda
¼ cup dried cherries

1. In a medium bowl, beat the butter, brown sugar, and honey until well combined.
2. Add the egg white, vanilla, and carrot. Beat to combine.
3. Stir in the oatmeal, pastry flour, and baking soda.
4. Stir in the dried cherries.
5. Double up 32 mini muffin foil cups to make 16 cups. Fill each with about 4 teaspoons of dough. Place the cookie cups directly in the pan.
6. Place the baking pan on the bake position. Select Bake, set the temperature to 350ºF (177ºC), and set the time to 8 minutes.
7. Cook for 8 minutes, 8 at a time, or until light golden brown and just set. Serve warm.

Oatmeal and Chocolate Bars

Prep time: 10 minutes | Cook time: 20 minutes | Makes 4 dozen (1-by-1½-inch) bars

1 cup unsalted butter, at room temperature
1 cup dark brown sugar
½ cup granulated sugar
2 large eggs
1 tablespoon vanilla extract
Pinch salt

1½ cups all-purpose flour
1 teaspoon baking soda
1 teaspoon baking powder
2 cups old-fashioned rolled oats
2 cups chocolate chips

1. In a large mixing bowl or stand mixer, beat together the butter, brown sugar, and granulated sugar until creamy and light in color.
2. Add the eggs one at a time, mixing after each addition. Add the vanilla and salt and mix to combine.

3. In a separate bowl, combine the flour, baking soda, baking powder, and oats. Add to the butter mixture and mix until combined. By hand, stir in the chocolate chips. (If you have a stand mixer, you can do this with the machine, but hand mixers usually aren't strong enough to handle these ingredients.)
4. Spread the dough into the baking pan in an even layer. It will fill the entire pan.
5. Place the pan on the bake position. Select Bake, set temperature to 350ºF (177ºC), and set time to 20 minutes.
6. After 15 minutes, check the cookie, rotating the pan if the crust is not browning evenly. Continue cooking for a total of 18 to 20 minutes or until golden brown. Remove the pan from the grill and let cool completely before cutting.

Orange and Anise Cake

Prep time: 5 minutes | Cook time: 20 minutes | Serves 6

1 stick butter, at room temperature
5 tablespoons liquid monk fruit
2 eggs plus 1 egg yolk, beaten
⅓ cup hazelnuts, roughly chopped
3 tablespoons sugar-free orange marmalade
6 ounces (170 g)

unbleached almond flour
1 teaspoon baking soda
½ teaspoon baking powder
½ teaspoon ground cinnamon
½ teaspoon ground allspice
½ ground anise seed
Cooking spray

1. Lightly spritz the baking pan with cooking spray.
2. In a mixing bowl, whisk the butter and liquid monk fruit until the mixture is pale and smooth. Mix in the beaten eggs, hazelnuts, and marmalade and whisk again until well incorporated.
3. Add the almond flour, baking soda, baking powder, cinnamon, allspice, anise seed and stir to mix well.
4. Scrape the batter into the prepared baking pan.
5. Place the baking pan on the bake position. Select Bake, set the temperature to 310ºF (154ºC), and set the time to 20 minutes.
6. Cook for 20 minutes, or until the top of the cake springs back when gently pressed with your fingers.
7. Transfer to a wire rack and let the cake cool to room temperature. Serve immediately.

Lemon Pear Tart

Prep time: 15 minutes | Cook time: 25 minutes | Serves 8

Juice of 1 lemon
3 medium or 2 large ripe or almost ripe pears
1 sheet (½ package) frozen puff pastry, thawed
All-purpose flour, for dusting
4 tablespoons caramel sauce, divided

1. In a large bowl, mix the lemon juice with about 1 quart of water.
2. Peel the pears and remove the stems. Cut them in half through the stem end. Use a melon baller to remove the seeds and cut out the blossom end. Remove any tough fibers between the stem end and the center. As you work, place the pear halves in the acidulated water.
3. Unwrap and unfold the puff pastry on a lightly floured cutting board. Using a rolling pin, roll it very lightly, just to press the folds together. Transfer it to the baking pan.
4. Roll about ½ inch of the pastry edges up to form a ridge around the perimeter. Crimp the corners together so you have a solid rim around the pastry to hold in the liquid as the tart cooks. Brush the bottom of the pastry with 2 tablespoons of caramel sauce. (If the sauce is cold, it may be very stiff. You can microwave it for a few seconds, or set the jar in a bowl of very hot water for a few minutes to make it easier to brush).
5. Remove the pear halves from the water and blot them dry with paper towels. Place one of the halves on the board cut-side down and cut ¼-inch-thick slices radially (think of cutting really thin wedges, rather than slicing straight up and down). Repeat with the remaining halves. Arrange the pear slices over the pastry. You can get as fancy as you like, but I find that three rows of slices fills the tart, looks good, and isn't difficult to achieve. Drizzle the remaining 2 tablespoons of caramel sauce over the pears.
6. Place the pan on the bake position. Select Bake, set temperature to 350ºF (177ºC), and set time to 25 minutes.
7. After 15 minutes, check the tart, rotating the pan if the crust is not browning evenly. Continue cooking.
8. When cooking is complete, the pastry will be golden brown, the pears soft, and the caramel bubbling. Remove the pan from the grill and let the tart cool for about 10 minutes. The tart can be served warm or at room temperature. If there is a lot of liquid floating around the pears, you can blot it off with paper towels, which will keep the crust crisper and won't diminish the flavor.

Shortbread

Prep time: 10 minutes | Cook time: 36 to 40 minutes | Makes 4 dozen cookies

1 cup granulated sugar
1 tablespoon grated lemon zest
1 pound (454 g) unsalted butter, at room temperature
¼ teaspoon fine salt
4 cups all-purpose flour
$1/_3$ cup cornstarch
Cooking oil spray

1. In a stand mixer fitted with the paddle attachment, beat the sugar and lemon zest on medium speed for a minute or two, then let sit for about 5 minutes. (If you don't have a stand mixer, use a hand mixer.) Add the butter and salt, and beat until well blended and fluffy.
2. In a large bowl, whisk together the flour and cornstarch. Gradually add the dry ingredients to the butter mixture and mix just until combined. (If you're using a hand mixer, you may have to finish mixing by hand; the dough is quite stiff.)
3. Spray the baking pan with cooking oil spray and fit in a piece of parchment paper. Press the dough into the pan until very even and smooth.
4. Place the pan on the bake position. Select Bake, set temperature to 325ºF (163ºC), and set time to 36 minutes.
5. After 20 minutes, check the shortbread, rotating the pan if it is not browning evenly. Continue for 16 minutes more, or until light golden brown. This will yield shortbread bars that are crumbly and just slightly soft. For crisper shortbread, bake for an additional 3 to 4 minutes, then turn the grill off and let the shortbread stay in the grill for a few more minutes until it's a few shades darker.
6. When cooking is complete, remove the pan from the grill. These bars are easiest to cut when they're slightly warm. Let cool. If you like, dust the bars with confectioners' sugar or granulated sugar.

Orange Coconut Cake

Prep time: 5 minutes | Cook time: 17 minutes | Serves 6

1 stick butter, melted
¾ cup granulated Swerve
2 eggs, beaten
¾ cup coconut flour
¼ teaspoon salt
¹⁄₃ teaspoon grated nutmeg
¹⁄₃ cup coconut milk
1¼ cups almond flour
½ teaspoon baking powder
2 tablespoons unsweetened orange jam
Cooking spray

1. Coat the baking pan with cooking spray. Set aside.
2. In a large mixing bowl, whisk together the melted butter and granulated Swerve until fluffy.
3. Mix in the beaten eggs and whisk again until smooth. Stir in the coconut flour, salt, and nutmeg and gradually pour in the coconut milk. Add the remaining ingredients and stir until well incorporated.
4. Scrape the batter into the baking pan.
5. Place the baking pan on the bake position. Select Bake, set the temperature to 355ºF (179ºC), and set the time to 17 minutes.
6. Cook for 17 minutes until the top of the cake springs back when gently pressed with your fingers.
7. Remove from the grill to a wire rack to cool. Serve chilled.

Coffee Chocolate Cake

Prep time: 5 minutes | Cook time: 30 minutes | Serves 8

Dry Ingredients:
1½ cups almond flour
½ cup coconut meal
²⁄₃ cup Swerve
1 teaspoon baking powder
¼ teaspoon salt
Wet Ingredients:
1 egg
1 stick butter, melted
½ cup hot strongly brewed coffee
Topping:
½ cup confectioner's Swerve
¼ cup coconut flour
3 tablespoons coconut oil
1 teaspoon ground cinnamon
½ teaspoon ground cardamom

1. In a medium bowl, combine the almond flour, coconut meal, Swerve, baking powder, and salt.
2. In a large bowl, whisk the egg, melted butter, and coffee until smooth.

3. Add the dry mixture to the wet and stir until well incorporated. Transfer the batter to the greased baking pan.
4. Stir together all the ingredients for the topping in a small bowl. Spread the topping over the batter and smooth the top with a spatula.
5. Place the baking pan on the bake position. Select Bake, set the temperature to 330ºF (166ºC), and set the time to 30 minutes.
6. Cook for 30 minutes, or until the cake springs back when gently pressed with your fingers.
7. Rest for 10 minutes before serving.

Chocolate Pecan Pie

Prep time: 20 minutes | Cook time: 25 minutes | Serves 8

1 (9-inch) unbaked pie crust
Filling:
2 large eggs
¹⁄₃ cup butter, melted
1 cup sugar
½ cup all-purpose flour
1 cup milk chocolate chips
1½ cups coarsely chopped pecans
2 tablespoons bourbon

1. Whisk the eggs and melted butter in a large bowl until creamy.
2. Add the sugar and flour and stir to incorporate. Mix in the milk chocolate chips, pecans, and bourbon and stir until well combined.
3. Use a fork to prick holes in the bottom and sides of the pie crust. Pour the prepared filling into the pie crust. Place the pie crust in the pan.
4. Place the baking pan on the bake position. Select Bake, set the temperature to 350ºF (177ºC), and set the time to 25 minutes.
5. Cook for 25 minutes until a toothpick inserted in the center comes out clean.
6. Allow the pie cool for 10 minutes in the crisper tray before serving.

Chapter 10 Fast and Easy Everyday Favorites

Sweet Potato Soufflé

Prep time: 10 minutes | Cook time: 30 minutes | Serves 4

1 sweet potato, baked and mashed
2 tablespoons unsalted butter, divided
1 large egg, separated
¼ cup whole milk
½ teaspoon kosher salt

1. In a medium bowl, combine the sweet potato, 1 tablespoon of melted butter, egg yolk, milk, and salt. Set aside.
2. In a separate medium bowl, whisk the egg white until stiff peaks form.
3. Using a spatula, gently fold the egg white into the sweet potato mixture.
4. Coat the inside of four 3-inch ramekins with the remaining 1 tablespoon of butter, then fill each ramekin halfway full. Place 2 ramekins in the pan.
5. Place the baking pan on the bake position. Select Bake, set the temperature to 330°F (166°C), and set the time to 15 minutes.
6. Repeat this process with the remaining ramekins.
7. Remove the ramekins from the grill and allow to cool on a wire rack for 10 minutes before serving

Brown Rice Fritters

Prep time: 10 minutes | Cook time: 8 to 10 minutes | Serves 4

1 (10-ounce / 284-g) bag frozen cooked brown rice, thawed
1 egg
3 tablespoons brown rice flour
$1/_3$ cup finely grated carrots
$1/_3$ cup minced red bell pepper
2 tablespoons minced fresh basil
3 tablespoons grated Parmesan cheese
2 teaspoons olive oil

1. In a small bowl, combine the thawed rice, egg, and flour and mix to blend.
2. Stir in the carrots, bell pepper, basil, and Parmesan cheese.
3. Form the mixture into 8 fritters and drizzle with the olive oil.
4. Put the fritters carefully into the crisper tray.
5. Place the crisper tray on the air fry position. Select Air Fry, set the temperature to 380°F (193°C), and set the time to 10 minutes.
6. Cook for 8 to 10 minutes, or until the fritters are golden brown and cooked through.
7. Serve immediately.

Beet Salad with Lemon Vinaigrette

Prep time: 10 minutes | Cook time: 12 to 15 minutes | Serves 4

6 medium red and golden beets, peeled and sliced
1 teaspoon olive oil
¼ teaspoon kosher
Vinaigrette:
2 teaspoons olive oil
2 tablespoons chopped
salt
½ cup crumbled feta cheese
8 cups mixed greens
Cooking spray

fresh chives
Juice of 1 lemon

1. In a large bowl, toss the beets, olive oil, and kosher salt.
2. Spray the crisper tray with cooking spray, then place the beets in the crisper tray.
3. Place the crisper tray on the air fry position. Select Air Fry, set the temperature to 360°F (182°C), and set the time to 15 minutes.
4. Cook for 12 to 15 minutes or until tender.
5. While the beets cook, make the vinaigrette in a large bowl by whisking together the olive oil, lemon juice, and chives.
6. Remove the beets from the grill, toss in the vinaigrette, and allow to cool for 5 minutes. Add the feta and serve on top of the mixed greens.

Scalloped Vegetable Bake

Prep time: 10 minutes | Cook time: 15 minutes | Serves 4

1 Yukon Gold potato, thinly sliced
1 small sweet potato, peeled and thinly sliced
1 medium carrot, thinly sliced
¼ cup minced onion
3 garlic cloves, minced
¾ cup 2 percent milk
2 tablespoons cornstarch
½ teaspoon dried thyme

1. In the baking pan, layer the Yukon Gold potato, sweet potato, carrot, onion, and garlic.
2. In a small bowl, whisk the milk, cornstarch, and thyme until blended. Pour the milk mixture evenly over the vegetables in the pan.
3. Place the baking pan on the bake position. Select Bake, set the temperature to 380°F (193°C), and set the time to 15 minutes.
4. Check the casserole—it should be golden brown on top, and the vegetables should be tender.
5. Serve immediately.

Mexican Street Corn

Prep time: 5 minutes | Cook time: 7 minutes | Serves 4

4 medium ears corn, husked
Cooking spray
2 tablespoons mayonnaise
1 tablespoon fresh lime juice
½ teaspoon ancho chile powder
¼ teaspoon kosher salt
2 ounces (57 g) crumbled Cotija or feta cheese
2 tablespoons chopped fresh cilantro

1. Spritz the corn with cooking spray. Working in batches, arrange the ears of corn in the crisper tray in a single layer.
2. Place the crisper tray on the air fry position. Select Air Fry, set the temperature to 375ºF (191ºC), and set the time to 7 minutes.
3. Cook for about 7 minutes, flipping halfway, until the kernels are tender when pierced with a paring knife. When cool enough to handle, cut the corn kernels off the cob.
4. In a large bowl, mix together mayonnaise, lime juice, ancho powder, and salt. Add the corn kernels and mix to combine. Transfer to a serving dish and top with the Cotija and cilantro. Serve immediately.

Crispy Brussels Sprouts

Prep time: 5 minutes | Cook time: 20 minutes | Serves 4

¼ teaspoon salt
⅛ teaspoon ground black pepper
1 tablespoon extra-virgin olive oil
1 pound (454 g) Brussels sprouts, trimmed and halved
Lemon wedges, for garnish

1. Combine the salt, black pepper, and olive oil in a large bowl. Stir to mix well.
2. Add the Brussels sprouts to the bowl of mixture and toss to coat well.
3. Arrange the Brussels sprouts in the crisper tray.
4. Place the crisper tray on the air fry position. Select Air Fry, set the temperature to 350ºF (177ºC), and set the time to 20 minutes.
5. Cook for 20 minutes or until lightly browned and wilted. Shake the crisper tray two times during the cooking.
6. Transfer the cooked Brussels sprouts to a large plate and squeeze the lemon wedges on top to serve.

Southwest Corn and Bell Peppers

Prep time: 10 minutes | Cook time: 10 minutes | Serves 4

For the Corn:
1½ cups thawed frozen corn kernels
1 cup mixed diced bell peppers
1 jalapeño, diced
1 cup diced yellow onion
½ teaspoon ancho chile powder
1 tablespoon fresh lemon juice
1 teaspoon ground cumin
½ teaspoon kosher salt
Cooking spray
For Serving:
¼ cup feta cheese
¼ cup chopped fresh cilantro
1 tablespoon fresh lemon juice

1. Spritz the crisper tray with cooking spray.
2. Combine the ingredients for the corn in a large bowl. Stir to mix well.
3. Pout the mixture into the crisper tray.
4. Place the crisper tray on the air fry position. Select Air Fry, set the temperature to 375ºF (191ºC), and set the time to 10 minutes.
5. Cook for 10 minutes or until the corn and bell peppers are soft. Shake the crisper tray halfway through the cooking time.
6. Transfer them onto a large plate, then spread with feta cheese and cilantro. Drizzle with lemon juice and serve.

Old Bay Shrimp

Prep time: 7 minutes | Cook time: 10 minutes | Makes 2 cups

½ teaspoon Old Bay Seasoning
1 teaspoon ground cayenne pepper
½ teaspoon paprika
1 tablespoon olive oil
⅛ teaspoon salt
½ pound (227 g) shrimps, peeled and deveined
Juice of half a lemon

1. Combine the Old Bay Seasoning, cayenne pepper, paprika, olive oil, and salt in a large bowl, then add the shrimps and toss to coat well.
2. Put the shrimps in the crisper tray.
3. Place the crisper tray on the air fry position. Select Air Fry, set the temperature to 390ºF (199ºC), and set the time to 10 minutes.
4. Cook for 10 minutes or until opaque. Flip the shrimps halfway through.
5. Serve the shrimps with lemon juice on top.

Hot Chicken Wings

Prep time: 5 minutes | Cook time: 30 minutes | Makes 16 wings

16 chicken wings
3 tablespoons hot
sauce
Cooking spray

1. Spritz the crisper tray with cooking spray.
2. Arrange the chicken wings in the crisper tray. You need to work in batches to avoid overcrowding.
3. Place the crisper tray on the air fry position. Select Air Fry, set the temperature to 360ºF (182ºC), and set the time to 15 minutes.
4. Cook for 15 minutes or until well browned. Shake the crisper tray at lease three times during the cooking.
5. Transfer the wings on a plate and serve with hot sauce.

Salmon and Carrot Croquettes

Prep time: 15 minutes | Cook time: 10 minutes | Serves 6

2 egg whites
1 cup almond flour
1 cup panko
breadcrumbs
1 pound (454 g)
chopped salmon fillet
2/3 cup grated carrots
2 tablespoons minced
garlic cloves
½ cup chopped onion
2 tablespoons chopped
chives
Cooking spray

1. Spritz the crisper tray with cooking spray.
2. Whisk the egg whites in a bowl. Put the flour in a second bowl. Pour the breadcrumbs in a third bowl. Set aside.
3. Combine the salmon, carrots, garlic, onion, and chives in a large bowl. Stir to mix well.
4. Form the mixture into balls with your hands. Dredge the balls into the flour, then egg, and then breadcrumbs to coat well.
5. Arrange the salmon balls in the crisper tray and spritz with cooking spray.
6. Place the crisper tray on the air fry position. Select Air Fry, set the temperature to 350ºF (177ºC), and set the time to 10 minutes.
7. Cook for 10 minutes or until crispy and browned. Shake the crisper tray halfway through.
8. Serve immediately.

Bacon-Wrapped Jalapeño Poppers

Prep time: 5 minutes | Cook time: 12 minutes | Serves 6

6 large jalapeños
4 ounces (113 g)
1/3-less-fat cream
cheese
¼ cup shredded
reduced-fat sharp
Cheddar cheese
2 scallions, green tops
only, sliced
6 slices center-cut
bacon, halved

1. Wearing rubber gloves, halve the jalapeños lengthwise to make 12 pieces. Scoop out the seeds and membranes and discard.
2. In a medium bowl, combine the cream cheese, Cheddar, and scallions. Using a small spoon or spatula, fill the jalapeños with the cream cheese filling. Wrap a bacon strip around each pepper and secure with a toothpick.
3. Working in batches, place the stuffed peppers in a single layer in the crisper tray.
4. Place the crisper tray on the bake position. Select Bake, set the temperature to 325ºF (163ºC), and set the time to 12 minutes.
5. Cook for 12 minutes, until the peppers are tender, the bacon is browned and crisp, and the cheese is melted.
6. Serve warm.

Roasted Veggies with Herbs

Prep time: 10 minutes | Cook time: 14 to 18 minutes | Serves 4

1 red bell pepper,
sliced
1 (8-ounce / 227-
g) package sliced
mushrooms
1 cup green beans,
cut into 2-inch pieces
1/3 cup diced red onion
3 garlic cloves, sliced
1 teaspoon olive oil
½ teaspoon dried basil
½ teaspoon dried
tarragon

1. In a medium bowl, mix the red bell pepper, mushrooms, green beans, red onion, and garlic. Drizzle with the olive oil. Toss to coat.
2. Add the herbs and toss again.
3. Place the vegetables in the crisper tray.
4. Place the crisper tray on the roast position. Select Roast, set the temperature to 350ºF (177ºC), and set the time to 18 minutes.
5. Cook for 14 to 18 minutes, or until tender. Serve immediately.

Parsnip Fries with Garlic-Yogurt Dip

Prep time: 10 minutes | Cook time: 10 minutes | Serves 4

3 medium parsnips, peeled, cut into sticks
¼ teaspoon kosher salt
Dip:
¼ cup plain Greek yogurt
⅛ teaspoon garlic powder
1 tablespoon sour

1 teaspoon olive oil
1 garlic clove, unpeeled
Cooking spray

cream
¼ teaspoon kosher salt
Freshly ground black pepper, to taste

1. Spritz the crisper tray with cooking spray.
2. Put the parsnip sticks in a large bowl, then sprinkle with salt and drizzle with olive oil.
3. Transfer the parsnip into the crisper tray and add the garlic.
4. Place the crisper tray on the air fry position. Select Air Fry, set the temperature to 360ºF (182ºC), and set the time to 10 minutes.
5. Cook for 5 minutes, then remove the garlic from the grill and shake the crisper tray. Cook for 5 more minutes or until the parsnip sticks are crisp.
6. Meanwhile, peel the garlic and crush it. Combine the crushed garlic with the ingredients for the dip. Stir to mix well.
7. When the frying is complete, remove the parsnip fries from the grill and serve with the dipping sauce.

Devils on Horseback

Prep time: 5 minutes | Cook time: 7 minutes | Serves 12

24 petite pitted prunes (4½ ounces / 128 g)
¼ cup crumbled blue cheese, divided

8 slices center-cut bacon, cut crosswise into thirds

1. Halve the prunes lengthwise, but don't cut them all the way through. Place ½ teaspoon of cheese in the center of each prune. Wrap a piece of bacon around each prune and secure the bacon with a toothpick.
2. Working in batches, arrange a single layer of the prunes in the crisper tray.
3. Place the crisper tray on the air fry position. Select Air Fry, set the temperature to 400ºF (204ºC), and set the time to 7 minutes.
4. Cook for about 7 minutes, flipping halfway, until the bacon is cooked through and crisp.
5. Let cool slightly and serve warm.

Lemon Pepper Green Beans

Prep time: 5 minutes | Cook time: 10 minutes | Makes 2 cups

½ teaspoon lemon pepper
2 teaspoons granulated garlic
½ teaspoon salt

1 tablespoon olive oil
2 cups fresh green beans, trimmed and snapped in half

1. Combine the lemon pepper, garlic, salt, and olive oil in a bowl. Stir to mix well.
2. Add the green beans to the bowl of mixture and toss to coat well.
3. Arrange the green beans in the crisper tray.
4. Place the crisper tray on the bake position. Select Bake, set the temperature to 370ºF (188ºC), and set the time to 10 minutes.
5. Cook for 10 minutes or until tender and crispy. Shake the crisper tray halfway through to make sure the green beans are cooked evenly.
6. Serve immediately.

Indian Sweet Potato Fries

Prep time: 5 minutes | Cook time: 8 minutes | Makes 20 fries

Seasoning Mixture:
¾ teaspoon ground coriander
½ teaspoon garam masala
½ teaspoon garlic
Fries:
2 large sweet potatoes, peeled
2 teaspoons olive oil

powder
½ teaspoon ground cumin
¼ teaspoon ground cayenne pepper

1. In a small bowl, combine the coriander, garam masala, garlic powder, cumin, and cayenne pepper.
2. Slice the sweet potatoes into ¼-inch-thick fries.
3. In a large bowl, toss the sliced sweet potatoes with the olive oil and the seasoning mixture.
4. Transfer the seasoned sweet potatoes to the crisper tray.
5. Place the crisper tray on the air fry position. Select Air Fry, set the temperature to 400ºF (204ºC), and set the time to 8 minutes.
6. Serve warm.

Baked Cherry Tomatoes

Prep time: 5 minutes | Cook time: 4 to 6 minutes | Serves 2

2 cups cherry tomatoes
1 clove garlic, thinly sliced
1 teaspoon olive oil
⅛ teaspoon kosher

salt
1 tablespoon freshly chopped basil, for topping
Cooking spray

1. Spritz the baking pan with cooking spray and set aside.
2. In a large bowl, toss together the cherry tomatoes, sliced garlic, olive oil, and kosher salt. Spread the mixture in an even layer in the prepared pan.
3. Place the baking pan on the bake position. Select Bake, set the temperature to 360°F (182°C), and set the time to 6 minutes.
4. Cook for 4 to 6 minutes, or until the tomatoes become soft and wilted.
5. Transfer to a bowl and rest for 5 minutes. Top with the chopped basil and serve warm.

Chile Toast

Prep time: 5 minutes | Cook time: 5 minutes | Serves 1

2 tablespoons grated Parmesan cheese
2 tablespoons grated Mozzarella cheese
2 teaspoons salted butter, at room temperature

10 to 15 thin slices serrano chile or jalapeño
2 slices sourdough bread
½ teaspoon black pepper

1. In a small bowl, stir together the Parmesan, Mozzarella, butter, and chiles.
2. Spread half the mixture onto one side of each slice of bread. Sprinkle with the pepper. Place the slices, cheese-side up, in the crisper tray.
3. Place the crisper tray on the bake position. Select Bake, set the temperature to 325°F (163°C), and set the time to 5 minutes.
4. Cook for 5 minutes, or until the cheese has melted and started to brown slightly.
5. Serve immediately.

Sweet and Sour Peanuts

Prep time: 5 minutes | Cook time: 5 minutes | Serves 9

3 cups shelled raw peanuts
1 tablespoon hot red

pepper sauce
3 tablespoons granulated white sugar

1. Put the peanuts in a large bowl, then drizzle with hot red pepper sauce and sprinkle with sugar. Toss to coat well.
2. Pour the peanuts in the crisper tray.
3. Place the crisper tray on the air fry position. Select Air Fry, set the temperature to 400°F (204°C), and set the time to 5 minutes.
4. Cook for 5 minutes or until the peanuts are crispy and browned. Shake the crisper tray halfway through.
5. Serve immediately.

Indian Masala Omelet

Prep time: 10 minutes | Cook time: 12 minutes | Serves 2

4 large eggs
½ cup diced onion
½ cup diced tomato
¼ cup chopped fresh cilantro
1 jalapeño, deseeded and finely chopped
½ teaspoon ground

turmeric
½ teaspoon kosher salt
½ teaspoon cayenne pepper
Olive oil, for greasing the pan

1. Generously grease a 3-cup Bundt pan.
2. In a large bowl, beat the eggs. Stir in the onion, tomato, cilantro, jalapeño, turmeric, salt, and cayenne.
3. Pour the egg mixture into the prepared pan.
4. Place the Bundt pan on the bake position. Select Bake, set the temperature to 250°F (121°C), and set the time to 12 minutes.
5. Cook for 12 minutes, or until the eggs are cooked through. Carefully unmold and cut the omelet into four pieces.
6. Serve immediately.

Baked Cheese Sandwich

Prep time: 5 minutes | Cook time: 8 minutes | Serves 2

2 tablespoons mayonnaise
4 thick slices sourdough bread

4 thick slices Brie cheese
8 slices hot capicola

1. Spread the mayonnaise on one side of each slice of bread. Place 2 slices of bread in the crisper tray, mayonnaise-side down.
2. Place the slices of Brie and capicola on the bread and cover with the remaining two slices of bread, mayonnaise-side up.
3. Place the crisper tray on the bake position. Select Bake, set the temperature to 350ºF (177ºC), and set the time to 8 minutes.
4. Cook for 8 minutes, or until the cheese has melted.
5. Serve immediately.

Garlic Asparagus

Prep time: 5 minutes | Cook time: 10 minutes | Makes 10 spears

10 spears asparagus (about ½ pound / 227 g in total), snap the ends off
1 tablespoon lemon juice

2 teaspoons minced garlic
½ teaspoon salt
¼ teaspoon ground black pepper
Cooking spray

1. Line the crisper tray with parchment paper.
2. Put the asparagus spears in a large bowl. Drizzle with lemon juice and sprinkle with minced garlic, salt, and ground black pepper. Toss to coat well.
3. Transfer the asparagus in the crisper tray and spritz with cooking spray.
4. Place the crisper tray on the air fry position. Select Air Fry, set the temperature to 400ºF (204ºC), and set the time to 10 minutes.
5. Cook for 10 minutes or until wilted and soft. Flip the asparagus halfway through.
6. Serve immediately.

South Carolina Shrimp and Corn Bake

Prep time: 10 minutes | Cook time: 18 minutes | Serves 2

1 ear corn, husk and silk removed, cut into 2-inch rounds
8 ounces (227 g) red potatoes, unpeeled, cut into 1-inch pieces
2 teaspoons Old Bay Seasoning, divided
2 teaspoons vegetable oil, divided
¼ teaspoon ground

black pepper
8 ounces (227 g) large shrimps (about 12 shrimps), deveined
6 ounces (170 g) andouille or chorizo sausage, cut into 1-inch pieces
2 garlic cloves, minced
1 tablespoon chopped fresh parsley

1. Put the corn rounds and potatoes in a large bowl. Sprinkle with 1 teaspoon of Old Bay seasoning and drizzle with vegetable oil. Toss to coat well.
2. Transfer the corn rounds and potatoes to the baking pan.
3. Place the baking pan on the bake position. Select Bake, set the temperature to 400ºF (204ºC), and set the time to 12 minutes.
4. Cook for 12 minutes or until soft and browned. Flip halfway through the cooking time.
5. Meanwhile, cut slits into the shrimps but be careful not to cut them through. Combine the shrimps, sausage, remaining Old Bay seasoning, and remaining vegetable oil in the large bowl. Toss to coat well.
6. When the baking of the potatoes and corn rounds is complete, add the shrimps and sausage and bake for 6 more minutes or until the shrimps are opaque. Flip halfway through the cooking time.
7. When the baking is finished, serve them on a plate and spread with parsley before serving.

Chapter 11 Pizza, Wraps, and Sandwiches

Turkey Hamburger

Prep time: 10 minutes | Cook time: 20 minutes | Serves 4

1 cup leftover turkey, cut into bite-sized chunks
1 leek, sliced
1 Serrano pepper, deveined and chopped
2 bell peppers, deveined and chopped
2 tablespoons Tabasco sauce
½ cup sour cream
1 heaping tablespoon fresh cilantro, chopped
1 teaspoon hot paprika
¾ teaspoon kosher salt
½ teaspoon ground black pepper
4 hamburger buns
Cooking spray

1. Spritz the baking pan with cooking spray.
2. Mix all the ingredients, except for the buns, in a large bowl. Toss to combine well.
3. Pour the mixture in the baking pan.
4. Place the baking pan on the bake position. Select Bake, set the temperature to 385°F (196°C), and set the time to 20 minutes.
5. Cook for 20 minutes, or until the turkey is well browned and the leek is tender.
6. Assemble the hamburger buns with the turkey mixture and serve immediately.

Bacon and Bell Pepper Sandwich

Prep time: 10 minutes | Cook time: 6 minutes | Serves 4

1/3 cup spicy barbecue sauce
2 tablespoons honey
8 slices cooked bacon, cut into thirds
1 red bell pepper, sliced
1 yellow bell pepper, sliced
3 pita pockets, cut in half
1¼ cups torn butter lettuce leaves
2 tomatoes, sliced

1. In a small bowl, combine the barbecue sauce and the honey. Brush this mixture lightly onto the bacon slices and the red and yellow pepper slices.
2. Put the peppers into the crisper tray.
3. Place the crisper tray on the roast position. Select Roast, set the temperature to 350°F (177°C), and set the time to 6 minutes.
4. Cook for 4 minutes. Then shake the crisper tray, add the bacon, and cook for 2 minutes or until the bacon is browned and the peppers are tender.
5. Fill the pita halves with the bacon, peppers, any remaining barbecue sauce, lettuce, and tomatoes, and serve immediately.

Mixed Greens Sandwich

Prep time: 15 minutes | Cook time: 10 to 13 minutes | Serves 4

1½ cups chopped mixed greens
2 garlic cloves, thinly sliced
2 teaspoons olive oil
2 slices low-sodium low-fat Swiss cheese
4 slices low-sodium whole-wheat bread
Cooking spray

1. In the baking pan, mix the greens, garlic, and olive oil.
2. Place the baking pan on the air fry position. Select Air Fry, set the temperature to 400°F (204°C), and set the time to 5 minutes.
3. Cook for 4 to 5 minutes, stirring once, until the vegetables are tender. Drain, if necessary.
4. Make 2 sandwiches, dividing half of the greens and 1 slice of Swiss cheese between 2 slices of bread. Lightly spray the outsides of the sandwiches with cooking spray. Transfer to the pan.
5. Bake for 6 to 8 minutes, turning with tongs halfway through, until the bread is toasted and the cheese melts.
6. Cut each sandwich in half and serve.

Cream Cheese Wontons

Prep time: 5 minutes | Cook time: 6 minutes | Serves 4

2 ounces (57 g) cream cheese, softened
1 tablespoon sugar
16 square wonton wrappers
Cooking spray

1. Spritz the crisper tray with cooking spray.
2. In a mixing bowl, stir together the cream cheese and sugar until well mixed. Prepare a small bowl of water alongside.
3. On a clean work surface, lay the wonton wrappers. Scoop ¼ teaspoon of cream cheese in the center of each wonton wrapper. Dab the water over the wrapper edges. Fold each wonton wrapper diagonally in half over the filling to form a triangle.
4. Arrange the wontons in the crisper tray. Spritz the wontons with cooking spray.
5. Place the crisper tray on the air fry position. Select Air Fry, set the temperature to 350°F (177°C), and set the time to 6 minutes.
6. Cook for 6 minutes, or until golden brown and crispy. Flip once halfway through to ensure even cooking.
7. Divide the wontons among four plates. Let rest for 5 minutes before serving.

Chicken Taquitos

Prep time: 15 minutes | Cook time: 12 minutes | Serves 4

1 cup cooked chicken, shredded
¼ cup Greek yogurt
¼ cup salsa
1 cup shredded

Mozzarella cheese
Salt and ground black pepper, to taste
4 flour tortillas
Cooking spray

1. Spritz the crisper tray with cooking spray.
2. Combine all the ingredients, except for the tortillas, in a large bowl. Stir to mix well.
3. Make the taquitos: Unfold the tortillas on a clean work surface, then scoop up 2 tablespoons of the chicken mixture in the middle of each tortilla. Roll the tortillas up to wrap the filling.
4. Arrange the taquitos in the crisper tray and spritz with cooking spray.
5. Place the crisper tray on the air fry position. Select Air Fry, set the temperature to 380ºF (193ºC), and set the time to 12 minutes.
6. Cook for 12 minutes or until golden brown and the cheese melts. Flip the taquitos halfway through.
7. Serve immediately.

BBQ Chicken Pizza

Prep time: 5 minutes | Cook time: 8 minutes | Serves 1

1 piece naan bread
¼ cup Barbecue sauce
¼ cup shredded Monterrey Jack cheese
¼ cup shredded Mozzarella cheese
½ chicken herby

sausage, sliced
2 tablespoons red onion, thinly sliced
Chopped cilantro or parsley, for garnish
Cooking spray

1. Spritz the bottom of naan bread with cooking spray, then transfer to the crisper tray.
2. Brush with the Barbecue sauce. Top with the cheeses, sausage, and finish with the red onion.
3. Place the crisper tray on the air fry position. Select Air Fry, set the temperature to 400ºF (204ºC), and set the time to 8 minutes.
4. Cook for 8 minutes until the cheese is melted.
5. Garnish with the chopped cilantro or parsley before slicing to serve.

Tuna English Muffin Sandwich

Prep time: 8 minutes | Cook time: 4 to 8 minutes | Serves 4

1 (6-ounce / 170-g) can chunk light tuna, drained
¼ cup mayonnaise
2 tablespoons mustard
1 tablespoon lemon juice
2 green onions,

minced
3 English muffins, split with a fork
3 tablespoons softened butter
6 thin slices Provolone or Muenster cheese

1. In a small bowl, combine the tuna, mayonnaise, mustard, lemon juice, and green onions. Set aside.
2. Butter the cut side of the English muffins. Place in the baking pan, butter-side up.
3. Place the baking pan on the bake position. Select Bake, set the temperature to 390ºF (199ºC), and set the time to 4 minutes.
4. Cook for 2 to 4 minutes, or until light golden brown. Remove the muffins from the grill.
5. Top each muffin with one slice of cheese and return to the grill. Bake for 2 to 4 minutes or until the cheese melts and starts to brown.
6. Remove the muffins from the grill, top with the tuna mixture, and serve.

Eggplant Hoagies

Prep time: 15 minutes | Cook time: 12 minutes | Makes 3 hoagies

6 peeled eggplant slices (about ½ inch thick and 3 inches in diameter)
¼ cup jarred pizza sauce

6 tablespoons grated Parmesan cheese
3 Italian sub rolls, split open lengthwise, warmed
Cooking spray

1. Spritz the crisper tray with cooking spray.
2. Arrange the eggplant slices in the crisper tray and spritz with cooking spray.
3. Place the crisper tray on the air fry position. Select Air Fry, set the temperature to 350ºF (177ºC), and set the time to 10 minutes.
4. Cook for 10 minutes or until lightly wilted and tender. Flip the slices halfway through.
5. Divide and spread the pizza sauce and cheese on top of the eggplant slice. Increase the temperature to 375ºF (191ºC). Air fry for 2 more minutes or until the cheese melts.
6. Assemble each sub roll with two slices of eggplant and serve immediately.

Shrimp Sandwich

Prep time: 10 minutes | Cook time: 5 to 7 minutes | Serves 4

1¼ cups shredded Colby, Cheddar, or Havarti cheese
1 (6-ounce / 170-g) can tiny shrimp, drained
3 tablespoons

mayonnaise
2 tablespoons minced green onion
4 slices whole grain or whole-wheat bread
2 tablespoons softened butter

1. In a medium bowl, combine the cheese, shrimp, mayonnaise, and green onion, and mix well.
2. Spread this mixture on two of the slices of bread. Top with the other slices of bread to make two sandwiches. Spread the sandwiches lightly with butter. Transfer to the crisper tray.
3. Place the crisper tray on the air fry position. Select Air Fry, set the temperature to 400°F (204°C), and set the time to 7 minutes.
4. Cook for 5 to 7 minutes, or until the bread is browned and crisp and the cheese is melted.
5. Cut in half and serve warm.

Mushroom-Prosciutto Pizza

Prep time: 10 minutes | Cook time: 5 minutes | Serves 3

3 portobello mushroom caps, cleaned and scooped
3 tablespoons olive oil
Pinch of salt
Pinch of dried Italian seasonings

3 tablespoons tomato sauce
3 tablespoons shredded Mozzarella cheese
12 slices prosciutto

1. Season both sides of the portobello mushrooms with a drizzle of olive oil, then sprinkle salt and the Italian seasonings on the insides.
2. With a knife, spread the tomato sauce evenly over the mushroom, before adding the Mozzarella on top.
3. Put the portobello in the crisper tray.
4. Place the crisper tray on the air fry position. Select Air Fry, set the temperature to 330°F (166°C), and set the time to 5 minutes.
5. Cook for 1 minute, before taking the crisper tray out of the grill and putting the prosciutto slices on top. Cook for another 4 minutes.
6. Serve warm.

Double-Cheese Clam Pizza

Prep time: 15 minutes | Cook time: 12 minutes | Serves 4

¼ cup extra-virgin olive oil, plus a little extra for forming the crust
2 large garlic cloves, chopped
¼ teaspoon red pepper flakes
1 pound (454 g) store-bought pizza dough
½ cup shredded Mozzarella cheese (4

ounces / 113 g)
2 (6.5-ounce / 184-g) cans chopped clams, drained
¼ cup grated Parmesan cheese
½ cup coarsely chopped fresh parsley
2 teaspoons chopped fresh oregano (optional)

1. In a small bowl, whisk together the olive oil with the garlic and red pepper flakes. Let it sit while you work on the dough.
2. Punch down the pizza dough to release as much air as possible. Place the dough in the baking pan and press it out toward the edges. The dough will likely spring back and shrink. Be patient and keep working at it, leaving it to relax for a few minutes from time to time. As it stretches, I find it helpful to coat my fingers with some olive oil and then poke the dough lightly with my fingertips to keep it from shrinking as much. Don't worry if you can't get it all the way to the edges of the pan.
3. Brush half of the garlic oil over the dough. Evenly distribute the Mozzarella cheese over the dough.
4. Place the pan on the roast position. Select Roast, set temperature to 425°F (218°C), and set time to 12 minutes.
5. After about 8 minutes, remove the pan from the grill. Scatter the clams over the pizza and sprinkle the Parmesan cheese on top. Return the pan to the grill and continue cooking for another 4 to 6 minutes. If you like a crisp crust, you can use a pizza peel or cake lifter (or even a very large spatula) to slide the pizza off the pan and directly onto the rack.
6. When cooking is complete, the cheese on top is lightly browned and bubbling and the crust is deep golden brown. Remove the pan from the grill (if you haven't already). Place the pizza on a wire rack to cool for a few minutes (a rack will keep the crust from getting soggy as it cools). Sprinkle the parsley and oregano (if using) over the pizza and drizzle with the remaining garlic oil. Slice and serve.

Strawberry Pizza

Prep time: 10 minutes | Cook time: 6 minutes | Serves 4

2 tablespoons all-purpose flour, plus more as needed	oil
½ store-bought pizza dough (about 8 ounces / 227 g)	1 cup sliced fresh strawberries
1 tablespoon canola	1 tablespoon sugar
	½ cup chocolate-hazelnut spread

1. Dust a clean work surface with the flour. Place the dough on the floured surface, and roll it out to a 9-inch round of even thickness. Dust your rolling pin and work surface with additional flour, as needed, to ensure the dough does not stick.
2. Brush the surface of the rolled-out dough evenly with half the oil. Flip the dough over, and brush with the remaining oil. Poke the dough with a fork 5 or 6 times across its surface to prevent air pockets from forming during cooking.
3. Place the dough on the grill plate.
4. Place the grill plate on the grill position. Select Grill, set the temperature to 450°F (232°C), and set the time to 6 minutes.
5. After 3 minutes, flip the dough. Continue grilling for the remaining 3 minutes.
6. Meanwhile, in a medium mixing bowl, combine the strawberries and sugar.
7. Transfer the pizza to a cutting board and let cool. Top with the chocolate-hazelnut spread and strawberries. Cut into pieces and serve.

Mozzarella Vegetable Pizza

Prep time: 10 minutes | Cook time: 10 minutes | Serves 2

2 tablespoons all-purpose flour, plus more as needed	1 cup shredded Mozzarella cheese
½ store-bought pizza dough (about 8 ounces / 227 g)	½ zucchini, thinly sliced
1 tablespoon canola oil, divided	½ red onion, sliced
½ cup pizza sauce	½ red bell pepper, seeded and thinly sliced

1. Dust a clean work surface with the flour.
2. Place the dough on the floured surface and roll it into a 9-inch round of even thickness. Dust your rolling pin and work surface with additional flour, as needed, to ensure the dough does not stick.

3. Evenly brush the surface of the rolled-out dough with ½ tablespoon of oil. Flip the dough over and brush the other side with the remaining ½ tablespoon of oil. Poke the dough with a fork 5 or 6 times across its surface to prevent air pockets from forming while it cooks.
4. Place the dough on the grill plate.
5. Place the grill plate on the grill position. Select Grill, set the temperature to 450°F (232°C), and set the time to 7 minutes.
6. After 4 minutes, flip the dough, then spread the pizza sauce evenly over it. Sprinkle with the cheese, and top with the zucchini, onion, and pepper.
7. Continue cooking for the remaining 2 to 3 minutes until the cheese is melted and the veggie slices begin to crisp.
8. When cooking is complete, let cool slightly before slicing.

Crab and Cream Cheese Wontons

Prep time: 10 minutes | Cook time: 10 minutes per batch | Serves 6 to 8

24 wonton wrappers, thawed if frozen	Cooking spray
For the Filling:	
5 ounces (142 g) lump crabmeat, drained and patted dry	1½ teaspoons toasted sesame oil
4 ounces (113 g) cream cheese, at room temperature	1 teaspoon Worcestershire sauce
2 scallions, sliced	Kosher salt and ground black pepper, to taste

1. Spritz the crisper tray with cooking spray.
2. In a medium-size bowl, place all the ingredients for the filling and stir until well mixed. Prepare a small bowl of water alongside.
3. On a clean work surface, lay the wonton wrappers. Scoop 1 teaspoon of the filling in the center of each wrapper. Wet the edges with a touch of water. Fold each wonton wrapper diagonally in half over the filling to form a triangle.
4. Arrange the wontons in the crisper tray. Spritz the wontons with cooking spray. Work in batches, 6 to 8 at a time.
5. Place the crisper tray on the air fry position. Select Air Fry, set the temperature to 350°F (177°C), and set the time to 10 minutes.
6. Cook for 10 minutes, or until crispy and golden brown. Flip once halfway through.
7. Serve immediately.

Veggie Pita Sandwich

Prep time: 10 minutes | Cook time: 9 to 12 minutes | Serves 4

1 baby eggplant, peeled and chopped
1 red bell pepper, sliced
½ cup diced red onion
½ cup shredded carrot
1 teaspoon olive oil
⅓ cup low-fat Greek yogurt
½ teaspoon dried tarragon
2 low-sodium whole-wheat pita breads, halved crosswise

1. In the baking pan, stir together the eggplant, red bell pepper, red onion, carrot, and olive oil.
2. Place the baking pan on the roast position. Select Roast, set the temperature to 390°F (199°C), and set the time to 9 minutes.
3. Cook for 7 to 9 minutes, stirring once, until the vegetables are tender. Drain if necessary.
4. In a small bowl, thoroughly mix the yogurt and tarragon until well combined.
5. Stir the yogurt mixture into the vegetables. Stuff one-fourth of this mixture into each pita pocket.
6. Place the sandwiches in the baking pan. Bake for 2 to 3 minutes, or until the bread is toasted.
7. Serve immediately.

Sweet Potato and Black Bean Burritos

Prep time: 15 minutes | Cook time: 1 hour | Makes 6 burritos

2 sweet potatoes, peeled and cut into a small dice
1 tablespoon vegetable oil
Kosher salt and ground black pepper, to taste
6 large flour tortillas
1 (16-ounce / 454-g) can refried black beans, divided
1½ cups baby spinach, divided
6 eggs, scrambled
¾ cup grated Cheddar cheese, divided
¼ cup salsa
¼ cup sour cream
Cooking spray

1. Put the sweet potatoes in a large bowl, then drizzle with vegetable oil and sprinkle with salt and black pepper. Toss to coat well.
2. Place the sweet potatoes in the crisper tray.
3. Place the crisper tray on the air fry position. Select Air Fry, set the temperature to 400°F (204°C), and set the time to 10 minutes.
4. Cook for 10 minutes or until lightly browned. Shake the crisper tray halfway through.
5. Unfold the tortillas on a clean work surface. Divide the black beans, spinach, sweet potatoes, scrambled eggs, and cheese on top of the tortillas.
6. Fold the long side of the tortillas over the filling, then fold in the shorter side to wrap the filling to make the burritos.
7. Work in batches, wrap the burritos in the aluminum foil and put in the crisper tray.
8. Adjust the temperature to 350°F (177°C). Air fry for 20 minutes. Flip the burritos halfway through.
9. Remove the burritos from the grill and put back to the grill. Spritz with cooking spray and air fry for 5 more minutes or until lightly browned. Repeat with remaining burritos.
10. Remove the burritos from the grill and spread with sour cream and salsa. Serve immediately.

Montreal Steak and Seeds Burgers

Prep time: 15 minutes | Cook time: 10 minutes | Serves 4

1 teaspoon cumin seeds
1 teaspoon mustard seeds
1 teaspoon coriander seeds
1 teaspoon dried minced garlic
1 teaspoon dried red pepper flakes
1 teaspoon kosher salt
2 teaspoons ground black pepper
1 pound (454 g) 85% lean ground beef
2 tablespoons Worcestershire sauce
4 hamburger buns
Mayonnaise, for serving
Cooking spray

1. Spritz the crisper tray with cooking spray.
2. Put the seeds, garlic, red pepper flakes, salt, and ground black pepper in a food processor. Pulse to coarsely ground the mixture.
3. Put the ground beef in a large bowl. Pour in the seed mixture and drizzle with Worcestershire sauce. Stir to mix well.
4. Divide the mixture into four parts and shape each part into a ball, then bash each ball into a patty.
5. Arrange the patties in the crisper tray.
6. Place the crisper tray on the air fry position. Select Air Fry, set the temperature to 350°F (177°C), and set the time to 10 minutes.
7. Cook for 10 minutes or until the patties are well browned. Flip the patties with tongs halfway through.
8. Assemble the buns with the patties, then drizzle the mayo over the patties to make the burgers. Serve immediately.

Turkey Sliders with Chive Mayo

Prep time: 10 minutes | Cook time: 15 minutes | Serves 6

12 burger buns	Cooking spray

For the Turkey Sliders:

¾ pound (340 g) turkey, minced	scallions
1 tablespoon oyster sauce	1 tablespoon chopped fresh cilantro
¼ cup pickled jalapeno, chopped	1 to 2 cloves garlic, minced
2 tablespoons chopped	Sea salt and ground black pepper, to taste

For the Chive Mayo:

1 tablespoon chives	Zest of 1 lime
1 cup mayonnaise	1 teaspoon salt

1. Spritz the crisper tray with cooking spray.
2. Combine the ingredients for the turkey sliders in a large bowl. Stir to mix well. Shape the mixture into 6 balls, then bash the balls into patties.
3. Arrange the patties in the crisper tray and spritz with cooking spray.
4. Place the crisper tray on the air fry position. Select Air Fry, set the temperature to 365ºF (185ºC), and set the time to 15 minutes.
5. Cook for 15 minutes or until well browned. Flip the patties halfway through.
6. Meanwhile, combine the ingredients for the chive mayo in a small bowl. Stir to mix well.
7. Smear the patties with chive mayo, then assemble the patties between two buns to make the sliders. Serve immediately.

Thai Pork Sliders

Prep time: 10 minutes | Cook time: 14 minutes | Makes 6 sliders

1 pound (454 g) ground pork	peeled fresh ginger
1 tablespoon Thai curry paste	1 tablespoon light brown sugar
1½ tablespoons fish sauce	1 teaspoon ground black pepper
¼ cup thinly sliced scallions, white and green parts	6 slider buns, split open lengthwise, warmed
2 tablespoons minced	Cooking spray

1. Spritz the crisper tray with cooking spray.
2. Combine all the ingredients, except for the buns in a large bowl. Stir to mix well.
3. Divide and shape the mixture into six balls, then bash the balls into six 3-inch-diameter patties.

4. Arrange the patties in the crisper tray and spritz with cooking spray.
5. Place the crisper tray on the air fry position. Select Air Fry, set the temperature to 375ºF (191ºC), and set the time to 14 minutes.
6. Cook for 14 minutes or until well browned. Flip the patties halfway through.
7. Assemble the buns with patties to make the sliders and serve immediately.

Cheesy Pepperoni Pizza Bites

Prep time: 12 minutes | Cook time: 16 minutes | Serves 8

½ cup (2 ounces / 57 g) pepperoni, finely chopped	variety
1 cup finely shredded Mozzarella cheese	1 (8-ounce / 227-g) can crescent roll dough
¼ cup Marinara Sauce or store-bought	All-purpose flour, for dusting

1. In a small bowl, toss together the pepperoni and cheese. Stir in the marinara sauce. (If you have one, this is a good time to use a food processor. Then you don't have to chop everything so fine; just dump everything in and pulse a few times to mix.)
2. Unroll the dough onto a lightly floured cutting board. Separate it into 4 rectangles. Firmly pinch the perforations together and pat or roll the dough pieces flat.
3. Divide the cheese mixture evenly between the rectangles and spread it out over the dough, leaving a ¼-inch border. Roll a rectangle up tightly, starting with the short end. Pinch the edge down to seal the roll. Repeat with the remaining rolls. If you have time, refrigerate or freeze the rolls for 5 to 10 minutes to firm up. This makes slicing easier.
4. Slice the rolls into 4 or 5 even slices. Place the slices in the baking pan, leaving a few inches between each.
5. Place the pan on the roast position. Select Roast, set temperature to 350ºF (177ºC), and set time to 12 minutes.
6. After 6 minutes, rotate the pan 180 degrees and continue cooking.
7. When cooking is complete, the rolls will be golden brown with crisp edges. Remove the pan from the grill. If you like, serve with additional marinara sauce for dipping.

Sloppy Joes

Prep time: 10 minutes | Cook time: 17 to 19 minutes | Makes 4 large sandwiches or 8 sliders

1 pound (454 g) very lean ground beef
1 teaspoon onion powder
1/3 cup ketchup
¼ cup water
½ teaspoon celery seed
1 tablespoon lemon juice
1½ teaspoons brown sugar
1¼ teaspoons low-sodium Worcestershire sauce
½ teaspoon salt (optional)
½ teaspoon vinegar
⅛ teaspoon dry mustard
Hamburger or slider buns, for serving
Cooking spray

1. Spray the crisper tray with cooking spray.
2. Break raw ground beef into small chunks and pile into the crisper tray.
3. Place the crisper tray on the roast position. Select Roast, set the temperature to 390ºF (199ºC), and set the time to 12 minutes.
4. Cook for 5 minutes. Stir to break apart and cook for 3 minutes. Stir and cook for 2 to 4 minutes longer, or until meat is well done.
5. Remove the meat from the grill, drain, and use a knife and fork to crumble into small pieces.
6. Give your crisper tray a quick rinse to remove any bits of meat.
7. Place all the remaining ingredients, except for the buns, in the baking pan and mix together. Add the meat and stir well.
8. Adjust the temperature to 330ºF (166ºC). Bake for 5 minutes. Stir and bake for 2 minutes.
9. Scoop into buns. Serve hot.

Pork and Cabbage Gyoza

Prep time: 10 minutes | Cook time: 10 minutes per batch | Makes 48 gyozas

1 pound (454 g) ground pork
1 small head Napa cabbage (about 1 pound / 454 g), sliced thinly and minced
½ cup minced scallions
1 teaspoon minced fresh chives
1 teaspoon soy sauce
1 teaspoon minced
fresh ginger
1 tablespoon minced garlic
1 teaspoon granulated sugar
2 teaspoons kosher salt
48 to 50 wonton or dumpling wrappers
Cooking spray

1. Make the filling: Combine all the ingredients, except for the wrappers in a large bowl. Stir to mix well.
2. Unfold a wrapper on a clean work surface, then dab the edges with a little water. Scoop up 2 teaspoons of the filling mixture in the center.
3. Make the gyoza: Fold the wrapper over to filling and press the edges to seal. Pleat the edges if desired. Repeat with remaining wrappers and fillings.
4. Spritz the crisper tray with cooking spray.
5. Arrange the gyozas in the crisper tray and spritz with cooking spray.
6. Place the crisper tray on the air fry position. Select Air Fry, set the temperature to 360ºF (182ºC), and set the time to 10 minutes.
7. Cook for 10 minutes or until golden brown. Flip the gyozas halfway through. Work in batches to avoid overcrowding.
8. Serve immediately.

Cheesy Potato Taquitos

Prep time: 5 minutes | Cook time: 6 minutes per batch | Makes 12 taquitos

2 cups mashed potatoes
½ cup shredded
Mexican cheese
12 corn tortillas
Cooking spray

1. Line the baking pan with parchment paper.
2. In a bowl, combine the potatoes and cheese until well mixed. Microwave the tortillas on high heat for 30 seconds, or until softened. Add some water to another bowl and set alongside.
3. On a clean work surface, lay the tortillas. Scoop 3 tablespoons of the potato mixture in the center of each tortilla. Roll up tightly and secure with toothpicks if necessary.
4. Arrange the filled tortillas, seam side down, in the prepared baking pan. Spritz the tortillas with cooking spray.
5. Place the baking pan on the air fry position. Select Air Fry, set the temperature to 400ºF (204ºC), and set the time to 6 minutes.
6. Cook for 6 minutes, or until crispy and golden brown, flipping once halfway through the cooking time. You may need to work in batches to avoid overcrowding.
7. Serve hot.

Pork Momos

Prep time: 20 minutes | Cook time: 10 minutes per batch | Serves 4

2 tablespoons olive oil
1 pound (454 g) ground pork
1 shredded carrot
1 onion, chopped
1 teaspoon soy sauce
16 wonton wrappers
Salt and ground black pepper, to taste

1. Heat the olive oil in a nonstick skillet over medium heat until shimmering.
2. Add the ground pork, carrot, onion, soy sauce, salt, and ground black pepper and sauté for 10 minutes or until the pork is well browned and carrots are tender.
3. Unfold the wrappers on a clean work surface, then divide the cooked pork and vegetables on the wrappers. Fold the edges around the filling to form momos. Nip the top to seal the momos.
4. Arrange the momos in the crisper tray and spritz with cooking spray.
5. Place the crisper tray on the air fry position. Select Air Fry, set the temperature to 320ºF (160ºC), and set the time to 10 minutes.
6. Cook for 10 minutes or until the wrappers are lightly browned. Work in batches to avoid overcrowding.
7. Serve immediately.

Lamb and Feta Hamburgers

Prep time: 15 minutes | Cook time: 16 minutes | Makes 4 burgers

1½ pounds (680 g) ground lamb
¼ cup crumbled feta
1½ teaspoons tomato paste
1½ teaspoons minced garlic
1 teaspoon ground dried ginger
1 teaspoon ground
coriander
¼ teaspoon salt
¼ teaspoon cayenne pepper
4 kaiser rolls or hamburger buns, split open lengthwise, warmed
Cooking spray

1. Spritz the crisper tray with cooking spray.
2. Combine all the ingredients, except for the buns, in a large bowl. Coarsely stir to mix well.
3. Shape the mixture into four balls, then pound the balls into four 5-inch diameter patties.
4. Arrange the patties in the crisper tray and spritz with cooking spray.
5. Place the crisper tray on the air fry position. Select Air Fry, set the temperature to 375ºF (191ºC), and set the time to 16 minutes.
6. Cook for 16 minutes or until well browned. Flip the patties halfway through.
7. Assemble the buns with patties to make the burgers and serve immediately.

Chicken Pita Sandwich

Prep time: 10 minutes | Cook time: 9 to 11 minutes | Serves 4

2 boneless, skinless chicken breasts, cut into 1-inch cubes
1 small red onion, sliced
1 red bell pepper, sliced
1/3 cup Italian salad
dressing, divided
½ teaspoon dried thyme
4 pita pockets, split
2 cups torn butter lettuce
1 cup chopped cherry tomatoes

1. Place the chicken, onion, and bell pepper in the crisper tray. Drizzle with 1 tablespoon of the Italian salad dressing, add the thyme, and toss.
2. Place the crisper tray on the bake position. Select Bake, set the temperature to 380ºF (193ºC), and set the time to 11 minutes.
3. Cook for 9 to 11 minutes, or until the chicken is 165ºF (74ºC) on a food thermometer, stirring once during cooking time.
4. Transfer the chicken and vegetables to a bowl and toss with the remaining salad dressing.
5. Assemble sandwiches with the pita pockets, butter lettuce, and cherry tomatoes. Serve immediately.

Margherita Pizza

Prep time: 15 minutes | Cook time: 12 minutes | Serves 4

1 pound (454 g) store-bought pizza dough
2 tablespoons extra-virgin olive oil, divided
½ cup Marinara Sauce or store-bought variety
6 ounces (170 g) shredded Mozzarella cheese
½ cup coarsely shredded Parmesan cheese (about 1½ ounces / 43 g)
2 large tomatoes, seeded and chopped (about 1½ cups)
¼ teaspoon kosher salt or ⅛ teaspoon fine salt
¼ cup chopped fresh basil
2 teaspoons wine vinegar

1. Punch down the pizza dough to release as much air as possible. Place the dough in the baking pan and press it out toward the edges. The dough will likely spring back and shrink. Be patient and keep working at it, leaving it alone to relax for a few minutes from time to time. As it stretches, I find it helpful to coat my fingers with 1 tablespoon of olive oil and then poke the dough lightly with my fingertips to keep it from shrinking as much. Don't worry if you can't get it all the way to the pan's edges.
2. Spread the marinara sauce over the dough. You'll be able to see the dough through the sauce in places; you don't want a thick coating. Evenly top the sauce with the Mozzarella cheese.
3. Place the pan on the roast position. Select Roast, set temperature to 425ºF (218ºC), and set time to 12 minutes.
4. After about 8 minutes, remove the pan from the grill. Sprinkle the Parmesan cheese over the pizza. Return the pan to the grill. Alternatively, if you like a crisp crust, use a pizza peel or cake lifter (or even a very large spatula) to slide the pizza off the pan and directly onto the grill rack. Continue cooking.
5. While the pizza cooks, place the tomatoes in a colander or fine-mesh strainer and sprinkle with the salt. Let them drain for a few minutes, then place in a small bowl. Mix in the remaining 1 tablespoon of olive oil, basil, and vinegar.
6. When cooking is complete, the cheese on top will be lightly browned and bubbling and the crust a deep golden brown. Remove the pizza from the baking pan, if you haven't already, and place it on a wire rack to cool for a few minutes (a rack will keep the crust from getting soggy as it cools). Distribute the tomato mixture evenly over the pizza, then transfer to a cutting board to slice and serve.

Egg and Arugula Pizza

Prep time: 10 minutes | Cook time: 8 minutes | Serves 2

2 tablespoons all-purpose flour, plus more as needed
½ store-bought pizza dough (about 8 ounces / 227 g)
1 tablespoon canola oil, divided
1 cup fresh ricotta cheese
4 large eggs
Sea salt, to taste
Freshly ground black pepper, to taste
4 cups arugula, torn
1 tablespoon extra-virgin olive oil
1 teaspoon freshly squeezed lemon juice
2 tablespoons grated Parmesan cheese

1. Dust a clean work surface with flour. Place the dough on the floured surface and roll it into a 9-inch round of even thickness. Dust your rolling pin and work surface with additional flour, as needed, to ensure the dough does not stick.
2. Brush the surface of the rolled-out dough evenly with ½ tablespoon of canola oil. Flip the dough over and brush with the remaining ½ tablespoon oil. Poke the dough with a fork 5 or 6 times across its surface to prevent air pockets from forming during cooking.
3. Place the dough on the grill plate.
4. Place the grill plate on the grill position. Select Grill, set the temperature to 450ºF (232ºC), and set the time to 7 minutes.
5. After 4 minutes, flip the dough, then spoon teaspoons of ricotta cheese across the surface of the dough, leaving a 1-inch border around the edges.
6. Crack one egg into a ramekin or small bowl. This way you can easily remove any shell that may break into the egg and keep the yolk intact. Imagine the dough is split into four quadrants. Pour one egg into each. Repeat with the remaining 3 eggs. Season the pizza with salt and pepper.
7. Continue cooking for the remaining 3 to 4 minutes until the egg whites are firm.
8. Meanwhile, in a medium bowl, toss together the arugula, oil, and lemon juice, and season with salt and pepper.
9. Transfer the pizza to a cutting board and let it cool. Top it with the arugula mixture, drizzle with olive oil, if desired, and sprinkle with Parmesan cheese. Cut into pieces and serve.

Chapter 12 Casseroles, Frittatas, and Quiches

Shrimp and Cauliflower Casserole

Prep time: 15 minutes | Cook time: 22 minutes | Serves 4

1 pound (454 g) shrimp, cleaned and deveined
2 cups cauliflower, cut into florets
2 green bell pepper, sliced
1 shallot, sliced
2 tablespoons sesame oil
1 cup tomato paste
Cooking spray

1. Spritz the baking pan with cooking spray.
2. Arrange the shrimp and vegetables in the baking pan. Then, drizzle the sesame oil over the vegetables. Pour the tomato paste over the vegetables.
3. Place the baking pan on the bake position. Select Bake, set the temperature to 360°F (182°C), and set the time to 22 minutes.
4. Cook for 10 minutes. Stir with a large spoon and cook for a further 12 minutes.
5. Serve warm.

Asparagus Frittata with Goat Cheese

Prep time: 5 minutes | Cook time: 25 minutes | Serves 2 to 4

1 cup asparagus spears, cut into 1-inch pieces
1 teaspoon vegetable oil
1 tablespoon milk
6 eggs, beaten
2 ounces (57 g) goat cheese, crumbled
1 tablespoon minced chives, optional
Kosher salt and pepper, to taste

1. Add the asparagus spears to a small bowl and drizzle with the vegetable oil. Toss until well coated and transfer to a cake pan.
2. Place the cake pan on the bake position. Select Bake, set the temperature to 400°F (204°C), and set the time to 5 minutes.
3. Cook for 5 minutes, or until the asparagus become tender and slightly wilted. Remove then pan from the grill.
4. Stir together the milk and eggs in a medium bowl. Pour the mixture over the asparagus in the pan. Sprinkle with the goat cheese and the chives (if using) over the eggs. Season with a pinch of salt and pepper.
5. Place the pan back to the grill and bake at 320°F (160°C) for 20 minutes or until the top is lightly golden and the eggs are set.
6. Transfer to a serving dish. Slice and serve.

Smoked Trout Frittata with Crème Fraiche

Prep time: 8 minutes | Cook time: 17 minutes | Serves 4

2 tablespoons olive oil
1 onion, sliced
1 egg, beaten
½ tablespoon horseradish sauce
6 tablespoons crème
fraiche
1 cup diced smoked trout
2 tablespoons chopped fresh dill
Cooking spray

1. Spritz the baking pan with cooking spray.
2. Heat the olive oil in a nonstick skillet over medium heat until shimmering.
3. Add the onion and sauté for 3 minutes or until translucent.
4. Combine the egg, horseradish sauce, and crème fraiche in a large bowl. Stir to mix well, then mix in the sautéed onion, smoked trout, and dill.
5. Pour the mixture in the prepared baking pan.
6. Place the baking pan on the bake position. Select Bake, set the temperature to 350°F (177°C), and set the time to 14 minutes.
7. Cook for 14 minutes or until the egg is set and the edges are lightly browned.
8. Serve immediately.

Greek Vegetable Frittata

Prep time: 7 minutes | Cook time: 8 minutes | Serves 2

1 cup chopped mushrooms
2 cups spinach, chopped
4 eggs, lightly beaten
3 ounces (85 g) feta cheese, crumbled
2 tablespoons heavy cream
A handful of fresh parsley, chopped
Salt and ground black pepper, to taste
Cooking spray

1. Spritz the baking pan with cooking spray.
2. Whisk together all the ingredients in a large bowl. Stir to mix well.
3. Pour the mixture in the prepared baking pan.
4. Place the baking pan on the bake position. Select Bake, set the temperature to 350°F (177°C), and set the time to 8 minutes.
5. Cook for 8 minutes or until the eggs are set.
6. Serve immediately.

Broccoli and Tomato Quiche

Prep time: 6 minutes | Cook time: 14 minutes | Serves 4

4 eggs
1 teaspoon dried thyme
1 cup whole milk
1 steamed carrots, diced
2 cups steamed broccoli florets
2 medium tomatoes, diced

¼ cup crumbled feta cheese
1 cup grated Cheddar cheese
1 teaspoon chopped parsley
Salt and ground black pepper, to taste
Cooking spray

1. Spritz the baking pan with cooking spray.
2. Whisk together the eggs, thyme, salt, and ground black pepper in a bowl and fold in the milk while mixing.
3. Put the carrots, broccoli, and tomatoes in the prepared baking pan, then spread with feta cheese and ½ cup Cheddar cheese. Pour the egg mixture over, then scatter with remaining Cheddar on top.
4. Place the baking pan on the bake position. Select Bake, set the temperature to 350ºF (177ºC), and set the time to 14 minutes.
5. Cook for 14 minutes or until the eggs are set and the quiche is puffed.
6. Remove the quiche from the grill and top with chopped parsley, then slice to serve.

Herbed Cheddar Frittata

Prep time: 10 minutes | Cook time: 20 minutes | Serves 4

½ cup shredded Cheddar cheese
½ cup half-and-half
4 large eggs
2 tablespoons chopped scallion greens
2 tablespoons chopped

fresh parsley
½ teaspoon kosher salt
½ teaspoon ground black pepper
Cooking spray

1. Spritz the baking pan with cooking spray.
2. Whisk together all the ingredients in a large bowl, then pour the mixture into the prepared baking pan.
3. Place the baking pan on the bake position. Select Bake, set the temperature to 300ºF (149ºC), and set the time to 20 minutes.
4. Cook for 20 minutes or until set.
5. Serve immediately.

Mac and Cheese

Prep time: 10 minutes | Cook time: 10 minutes | Serves 2

1 cup cooked macaroni
1 cup grated Cheddar cheese
½ cup warm milk

Salt and ground black pepper, to taste
1 tablespoon grated Parmesan cheese

1. In the baking pan, mix all the ingredients, except for Parmesan.
2. Place the baking pan on the bake position. Select Bake, set the temperature to 350ºF (177ºC), and set the time to 10 minutes.
3. Add the Parmesan cheese on top and serve.

Broccoli Chicken Divan

Prep time: 5 minutes | Cook time: 24 minutes | Serves 4

4 chicken breasts
Salt and ground black pepper, to taste
1 head broccoli, cut into florets
½ cup cream of

mushroom soup
1 cup shredded Cheddar cheese
½ cup croutons
Cooking spray

1. Spritz the crisper tray with cooking spray.
2. Put the chicken breasts in the crisper tray and sprinkle with salt and ground black pepper.
3. Place the crisper tray on the air fry position. Select Air Fry, set the temperature to 390ºF (199ºC), and set the time to 14 minutes.
4. Cook for 14 minutes or until well browned and tender. Flip the breasts halfway through the cooking time.
5. Remove the breasts from the grill and allow to cool for a few minutes on a plate, then cut the breasts into bite-size pieces.
6. Combine the chicken, broccoli, mushroom soup, and Cheddar cheese in a large bowl. Stir to mix well.
7. Spritz the baking pan with cooking spray. Pour the chicken mixture into the pan. Spread the croutons over the mixture.
8. Air fry for 10 minutes or until the croutons are lightly browned and the mixture is set.
9. Remove the baking pan from the grill and serve immediately.

Beef and Green Chile Casserole

Prep time: 10 minutes | Cook time: 15 minutes | Serves 4

1 pound (454 g) 85% lean ground beef	2 large eggs
1 tablespoon taco seasoning	1 cup shredded Mexican cheese blend
1 (7-ounce / 198-g) can diced mild green chiles	2 tablespoons all-purpose flour
½ cup milk	½ teaspoon kosher salt
	Cooking spray

1. Spritz the baking pan with cooking spray.
2. Toss the ground beef with taco seasoning in a large bowl to mix well. Pour the seasoned ground beef in the prepared baking pan.
3. Combing the remaining ingredients in a medium bowl. Whisk to mix well, then pour the mixture over the ground beef.
4. Place the baking pan on the bake position. Select Bake, set the temperature to 350ºF (177ºC), and set the time to 15 minutes.
5. Cook for 15 minutes or until a toothpick inserted in the center comes out clean.
6. Remove the casserole from the grill and allow to cool for 5 minutes, then slice to serve.

Chorizo and Corn Frittata

Prep time: 8 minutes | Cook time: 12 minutes | Serves 4

2 tablespoons olive oil	1 tablespoon chopped parsley
1 chorizo, sliced	½ cup feta cheese, crumbled
4 eggs	
½ cup corn	
1 large potato, boiled and cubed	Salt and ground black pepper, to taste

1. Heat the olive oil in a nonstick skillet over medium heat until shimmering.
2. Add the chorizo and cook for 4 minutes or until golden brown.
3. Whisk the eggs in a bowl, then sprinkle with salt and ground black pepper.
4. Mix the remaining ingredients in the egg mixture, then pour the chorizo and its fat into the baking pan. Pour in the egg mixture.
5. Place the baking pan on the bake position. Select Bake, set the temperature to 330ºF (166ºC), and set the time to 8 minutes.
6. Cook for 8 minutes or until the eggs are set.
7. Serve immediately.

Creamy Pork Gratin

Prep time: 15 minutes | Cook time: 21 minutes | Serves 4

2 tablespoons olive oil	1 teaspoon coarse sea salt
2 pounds (907 g) pork tenderloin, cut into serving-size pieces	½ teaspoon freshly ground black pepper
1 teaspoon dried marjoram	1 cup Ricotta cheese
¼ teaspoon chili powder	1½ cups chicken broth
	1 tablespoon mustard
	Cooking spray

1. Spritz the baking pan with cooking spray.
2. Heat the olive oil in a nonstick skillet over medium-high heat until shimmering.
3. Add the pork and sauté for 6 minutes or until lightly browned.
4. Transfer the pork to the prepared baking pan and sprinkle with marjoram, chili powder, salt, and ground black pepper.
5. Combine the remaining ingredients in a large bowl. Stir to mix well. Pour the mixture over the pork in the pan.
6. Place the baking pan on the bake position. Select Bake, set the temperature to 350ºF (177ºC), and set the time to 15 minutes.
7. Cook for 15 minutes or until frothy and the cheese melts. Stir the mixture halfway through.
8. Serve immediately.

Shrimp and Spinach Frittata

Prep time: 6 minutes | Cook time: 14 minutes | Serves 4

4 whole eggs	½ cup rice, cooked
1 teaspoon dried basil	½ cup Monterey Jack cheese, grated
½ cup shrimp, cooked and chopped	Salt, to taste
½ cup baby spinach	Cooking spray

1. Spritz the baking pan with cooking spray.
2. Whisk the eggs with basil and salt in a large bowl until bubbly, then mix in the shrimp, spinach, rice, and cheese.
3. Pour the mixture into the baking pan.
4. Place the baking pan on the bake position. Select Bake, set the temperature to 360ºF (182ºC), and set the time to 14 minutes.
5. Cook for 14 minutes or until the eggs are set and the frittata is golden brown.
6. Slice to serve.

Beef and Bean Casserole

Prep time: 15 minutes | Cook time: 31 minutes | Serves 4

1 tablespoon olive oil
½ cup finely chopped bell pepper
½ cup chopped celery
1 onion, chopped
2 garlic cloves, minced
1 pound (454 g) ground beef
1 can diced tomatoes
½ teaspoon parsley
½ tablespoon chili powder
1 teaspoon chopped cilantro
1½ cups vegetable broth
1 (8-ounce / 227-g) can cannellini beans
Salt and ground black pepper, to taste

1. Heat the olive oil in a nonstick skillet over medium heat until shimmering.
2. Add the bell pepper, celery, onion, and garlic to the skillet and sauté for 5 minutes or until the onion is translucent.
3. Add the ground beef and sauté for an additional 6 minutes or until lightly browned.
4. Mix in the tomatoes, parsley, chili powder, cilantro and vegetable broth, then cook for 10 more minutes. Stir constantly.
5. Pour them in the baking pan, then mix in the beans and sprinkle with salt and ground black pepper.
6. Place the baking pan on the bake position. Select Bake, set the temperature to 350°F (177°C), and set the time to 10 minutes.
7. Cook for 10 minutes or until the vegetables are tender and the beef is well browned.
8. Remove the baking pan from the grill and serve immediately.

Mini Quiche Cups

Prep time: 15 minutes | Cook time: 16 minutes | Makes 10 quiche cups

4 ounces (113 g) ground pork sausage
3 eggs
¾ cup milk
Cooking spray
4 ounces (113 g) sharp Cheddar cheese, grated

Special Equipment:
20 foil muffin cups

1. Spritz the crisper tray with cooking spray.
2. Divide sausage into 3 portions and shape each into a thin patty.
3. Put patties in the crisper tray.
4. Place the crisper tray on the air fry position. Select Air Fry, set the temperature to 390°F (199°C), and set the time to 6 minutes.

5. While sausage is cooking, prepare the egg mixture. Combine the eggs and milk in a large bowl and whisk until well blended. Set aside.
6. When sausage has cooked fully, remove patties from the crisper tray, drain well, and use a fork to crumble the meat into small pieces.
7. Double the foil cups into 10 sets. Remove paper liners from the top muffin cups and spray the foil cups lightly with cooking spray.
8. Divide crumbled sausage among the 10 muffin cup sets.
9. Top each with grated cheese, divided evenly among the cups.
10. Put 5 cups in the crisper tray.
11. Pour egg mixture into each cup, filling until each cup is at least ⅔ full.
12. Bake for 8 minutes. Check for doneness. A knife inserted into the center shouldn't have any raw egg on it when removed.
13. Repeat steps 8 through 11 for the remaining quiches.
14. Serve warm.

Lush Vegetable Frittata

Prep time: 15 minutes | Cook time: 21 minutes | Serves 2

4 eggs
¼ cup milk
Sea salt and ground black pepper, to taste
1 zucchini, sliced
½ bunch asparagus, sliced
½ cup mushrooms, sliced
½ cup spinach,
shredded
½ cup red onion, sliced
½ tablespoon olive oil
5 tablespoons feta cheese, crumbled
4 tablespoons Cheddar cheese, grated
¼ bunch chives, minced

1. In a bowl, mix the eggs, milk, salt and pepper.
2. Over a medium heat, sauté the vegetables for 6 minutes with the olive oil in a nonstick pan.
3. Put some parchment paper in the base of the baking pan. Pour in the vegetables, followed by the egg mixture. Top with the feta and grated Cheddar.
4. Place the baking pan on the bake position. Select Bake, set the temperature to 320°F (160°C), and set the time to 15 minutes.
5. Remove the frittata from the grill and leave to cool for 5 minutes.
6. Top with the minced chives and serve.

Western Prosciutto Casserole

Prep time: 5 minutes | Cook time: 10 minutes | Serves 2

1 cup day-old whole grain bread, cubed
3 large eggs, beaten
2 tablespoons water
⅛ teaspoon kosher salt
1 ounce (28 g) prosciutto, roughly chopped
1 ounce (28 g) Pepper Jack cheese, roughly chopped
1 tablespoon chopped fresh chives
Nonstick cooking spray

1. Spray the baking pan with nonstick cooking spray, then place the bread cubes in the pan.
2. In a medium bowl, stir together the beaten eggs and water, then stir in the kosher salt, prosciutto, cheese, and chives. Pour the egg mixture over the bread cubes.
3. Place the baking pan on the bake position. Select Bake, set the temperature to 360ºF (182ºC), and set the time to 10 minutes.
4. Cook for 10 minutes, or until the eggs are set and the top is golden brown.
5. Serve warm.

Sumptuous Vegetable Frittata

Prep time: 15 minutes | Cook time: 20 minutes | Serves 2

4 eggs
⅓ cup milk
2 teaspoons olive oil
1 large zucchini, sliced
2 asparagus, sliced thinly
⅓ cup sliced mushrooms
1 cup baby spinach
1 small red onion, sliced
⅓ cup crumbled feta cheese
⅓ cup grated Cheddar cheese
¼ cup chopped chives
Salt and ground black pepper, to taste

1. Line the baking pan with parchment paper.
2. Whisk together the eggs, milk, salt, and ground black pepper in a large bowl. Set aside.
3. Heat the olive oil in a nonstick skillet over medium heat until shimmering.
4. Add the zucchini, asparagus, mushrooms, spinach, and onion to the skillet and sauté for 5 minutes or until tender.

5. Pour the sautéed vegetables into the prepared baking pan, then spread the egg mixture over and scatter with cheeses.
6. Place the baking pan on the bake position. Select Bake, set the temperature to 380ºF (193ºC), and set the time to 15 minutes.
7. Cook for 15 minutes or until the eggs are set the edges are lightly browned.
8. Remove the frittata from the grill and sprinkle with chives before serving.

Mediterranean Quiche

Prep time: 10 minutes | Cook time: 30 minutes | Serves 4

4 eggs
¼ cup chopped Kalamata olives
½ cup chopped tomatoes
¼ cup chopped onion
½ cup milk
1 cup crumbled feta cheese
½ tablespoon chopped oregano
½ tablespoon chopped basil
Salt and ground black pepper, to taste
Cooking spray

1. Spritz the baking pan with cooking spray.
2. Whisk the eggs with remaining ingredients in a large bowl. Stir to mix well.
3. Pour the mixture into the prepared baking pan.
4. Place the baking pan on the bake position. Select Bake, set the temperature to 340ºF (171ºC), and set the time to 30 minutes.
5. Cook for 30 minutes or until the eggs are set and a toothpick inserted in the center comes out clean. Check the doneness of the quiche during the last 10 minutes of baking.
6. Serve immediately.

Chapter 13 Holiday Specials

Golden Nuggets

Prep time: 15 minutes | Cook time: 4 minutes per batch | Makes 20 nuggets

1 cup all-purpose flour, plus more for dusting
1 teaspoon baking powder
½ teaspoon butter, at room temperature, plus more for brushing
¼ teaspoon salt
¼ cup water
⅛ teaspoon onion powder
¼ teaspoon garlic powder
⅛ teaspoon seasoning salt
Cooking spray

1. Line the crisper tray with parchment paper.
2. Mix the flour, baking powder, butter, and salt in a large bowl. Stir to mix well. Gradually whisk in the water until a sanity dough forms.
3. Put the dough on a lightly floured work surface, then roll it out into a ½-inch thick rectangle with a rolling pin.
4. Cut the dough into about twenty 1- or 2-inch squares, then arrange the squares in a single layer in the crisper tray. Spritz with cooking spray. You need to work in batches to avoid overcrowding.
5. Combine onion powder, garlic powder, and seasoning salt in a small bowl. Stir to mix well, then sprinkle the squares with the powder mixture.
6. Place the crisper tray on the air fry position. Select Air Fry, set the temperature to 370°F (188°C), and set the time to 4 minutes.
7. Cook for 4 minutes or until golden brown. Flip the squares halfway through the cooking time.
8. Remove the golden nuggets from the grill and brush with more butter immediately. Serve warm.

Butter Cake

Prep time: 25 minutes | Cook time: 20 minutes | Serves 8

1 cup all-purpose flour
1¼ teaspoons baking powder
¼ teaspoon salt
½ cup plus 1½ tablespoons granulated white sugar
9½ tablespoons butter,
at room temperature
2 large eggs
1 large egg yolk
2½ tablespoons milk
1 teaspoon vanilla extract
Cooking spray

1. Spritz a cake pan with cooking spray.
2. Combine the flour, baking powder, and salt in a large bowl. Stir to mix well.
3. Whip the sugar and butter in a separate bowl with a hand mixer on medium speed for 3 minutes.
4. Whip the eggs, egg yolk, milk, and vanilla extract into the sugar and butter mix with a hand mixer.
5. Pour in the flour mixture and whip with hand mixer until sanity and smooth.
6. Scrape the batter into the cake pan and level the batter with a spatula.
7. Place the cake pan on the bake position. Select Bake, set the temperature to 325°F (163°C), and set the time to 20 minutes.
8. Cook for 20 minutes or until a toothpick inserted in the center comes out clean. Check the doneness during the last 5 minutes of the baking.
9. Invert the cake on a cooling rack and allow to cool for 15 minutes before slicing to serve.

Pão de Queijo

Prep time: 37 minutes | Cook time: 24 minutes | Makes 12 balls

2 tablespoons butter, plus more for greasing
½ cup milk
1½ cups tapioca flour
½ teaspoon salt
1 large egg
²/₃ cup finely grated aged Asiago cheese

1. Put the butter in a saucepan and pour in the milk, heat over medium heat until the liquid boils. Keep stirring.
2. Turn off the heat and mix in the tapioca flour and salt to form a soft dough. Transfer the dough in a large bowl, then wrap the bowl in plastic and let sit for 15 minutes.
3. Break the egg in the bowl of dough and whisk with a hand mixer for 2 minutes or until a sanity dough forms. Fold the cheese in the dough. Cover the bowl in plastic again and let sit for 10 more minutes.
4. Grease the cake pan with butter.
5. Scoop 2 tablespoons of the dough into the cake pan. Repeat with the remaining dough to make dough 12 balls. Keep a little distance between each two balls. You may need to work in batches to avoid overcrowding.
6. Place the cake pan on the bake position. Select Bake, set the temperature to 375°F (191°C), and set the time to 12 minutes.
7. Cook for 12 minutes or until the balls are golden brown and fluffy. Flip the balls halfway through the cooking time.
8. Remove the balls from the grill and allow to cool for 5 minutes before serving.

Jewish Cheese Blintzes

Prep time: 5 minutes | Cook time: 10 minutes | Makes 8 blintzes

2 (7½-ounce / 213-g) packages farmer cheese, mashed
¼ cup cream cheese
¼ teaspoon vanilla extract
¼ cup granulated white sugar
8 egg roll wrappers
4 tablespoons butter, melted

1. Combine the farmer cheese, cream cheese, vanilla extract, and sugar in a bowl. Stir to mix well.
2. Unfold the egg roll wrappers on a clean work surface, spread ¼ cup of the filling at the edge of each wrapper and leave a ½-inch edge uncovering.
3. Wet the edges of the wrappers with water and fold the uncovered edge over the filling. Fold the left and right sides in the center, then tuck the edge under the filling and fold to wrap the filling.
4. Brush the wrappers with melted butter, then arrange the wrappers in a single layer in the crisper tray, seam side down. Leave a little space between each two wrappers. Work in batches to avoid overcrowding.
5. Place the crisper tray on the air fry position. Select Air Fry, set the temperature to 375ºF (191ºC), and set the time to 10 minutes.
6. Cook for 10 minutes or until golden brown.
7. Serve immediately.

Hasselback Potatoes

Prep time: 5 minutes | Cook time: 50 minutes | Serves 4

4 russet potatoes, peeled
Salt and freshly ground black pepper,
to taste
¼ cup grated Parmesan cheese
Cooking spray

1. Spray the crisper tray lightly with cooking spray.
2. Make thin parallel cuts into each potato, ⅛-inch to ¼-inch apart, stopping at about ½ of the way through. The potato needs to stay intact along the bottom.
3. Spray the potatoes with cooking spray and use the hands or a silicone brush to completely coat the potatoes lightly in oil.
4. Put the potatoes, sliced side up, in the crisper tray in a single layer. Leave a little room between each potato. Sprinkle the potatoes lightly with salt and black pepper.
5. Place the crisper tray on the air fry position. Select Air Fry, set the temperature to 400ºF (204ºC), and set the time to 50 minutes.
6. Cook for 20 minutes. Reposition the potatoes and spritz lightly with cooking spray again. Cook until the potatoes are fork-tender and crispy and browned, for another 20 to 30 minutes.
7. Sprinkle the potatoes with Parmesan cheese and serve.

Kale Salad Sushi Rolls

Prep time: 10 minutes | Cook time: 10 minutes | Serves 12

Kale Salad:
1½ cups chopped kale
1 tablespoon sesame seeds
¾ teaspoon soy sauce
¾ teaspoon toasted sesame oil
½ teaspoon rice vinegar
¼ teaspoon ginger
⅛ teaspoon garlic powder

Sushi Rolls:
3 sheets sushi nori
1 batch cauliflower
rice
½ avocado, sliced

Sriracha Mayonnaise:
¼ cup Sriracha sauce
¼ cup vegan
mayonnaise

Coating:
½ cup panko breadcrumbs

1. In a medium bowl, toss all the ingredients for the salad together until well coated and set aside.
2. Place a sheet of nori on a clean work surface and spread the cauliflower rice in an even layer on the nori. Scoop 2 to 3 tablespoon of kale salad on the rice and spread over. Place 1 or 2 avocado slices on top. Roll up the sushi, pressing gently to get a nice, tight roll. Repeat to make the remaining 2 rolls.
3. In a bowl, stir together the Sriracha sauce and mayonnaise until smooth. Add breadcrumbs to a separate bowl.
4. Dredge the sushi rolls in Sriracha Mayonnaise, then roll in breadcrumbs till well coated.
5. Place the coated sushi rolls in the crisper tray.
6. Place the crisper tray on the air fry position. Select Air Fry, set the temperature to 390ºF (199ºC), and set the time to 10 minutes.
7. Cook for 10 minutes, or until golden brown and crispy. Flip the sushi rolls gently halfway through to ensure even cooking..
8. Transfer to a platter and rest for 5 minutes before slicing each roll into 8 pieces. Serve warm.

Bourbon Monkey Bread

Prep time: 15 minutes | Cook time: 25 minutes | Serves 6 to 8

1 (16.3-ounce / 462-g) can store-bought refrigerated biscuit dough
¼ cup packed light brown sugar
1 teaspoon ground cinnamon
½ teaspoon freshly grated nutmeg
½ teaspoon ground ginger
½ teaspoon kosher salt
¼ teaspoon ground allspice
⅛ teaspoon ground cloves
4 tablespoons (½ stick) unsalted butter, melted
½ cup powdered sugar
2 teaspoons bourbon
2 tablespoons chopped candied cherries
2 tablespoons chopped pecans

1. Open the can and separate the biscuits, then cut each into quarters. Toss the biscuit quarters in a large bowl with the brown sugar, cinnamon, nutmeg, ginger, salt, allspice, and cloves until evenly coated.
2. Transfer the dough pieces and any sugar left in the bowl to the cake pan and drizzle evenly with the melted butter.
3. Place the cake pan on the bake position. Select Bake, set the temperature to 310°F (154°C), and set the time to 25 minutes.
4. Cook for 25 minutes until the monkey bread is golden brown and cooked through in the middle. Transfer the pan to a wire rack and let cool completely. Unmold from the pan.
5. In a small bowl, whisk the powdered sugar and the bourbon into a smooth glaze. Drizzle the glaze over the cooled monkey bread and, while the glaze is still wet, sprinkle with the cherries and pecans to serve.

Spicy Sriracha Shrimp

Prep time: 15 minutes | Cook time: 10 minutes per batch | Serves 4

1 tablespoon Sriracha sauce
1 teaspoon Worcestershire sauce
2 tablespoons sweet chili sauce
¾ cup mayonnaise
1 egg, beaten
1 cup panko
breadcrumbs
1 pound (454 g) raw shrimp, shelled and deveined, rinsed and drained
Lime wedges, for serving
Cooking spray

1. Spritz the crisper tray with cooking spray.
2. Combine the Sriracha sauce, Worcestershire sauce, chili sauce, and mayo in a bowl. Stir to mix well. Reserve ⅓ cup of the mixture as the dipping sauce.
3. Combine the remaining sauce mixture with the beaten egg. Stir to mix well. Put the panko in a separate bowl.
4. Dredge the shrimp in the sauce mixture first, then into the panko. Roll the shrimp to coat well. Shake the excess off.
5. Place the shrimp in the crisper tray, then spritz with cooking spray. You may need to work in batches to avoid overcrowding.
6. Place the crisper tray on the air fry position. Select Air Fry, set the temperature to 360°F (182°C), and set the time to 10 minutes.
7. Cook for 10 minutes or until opaque. Flip the shrimp halfway through the cooking time.
8. Remove the shrimp from the grill and serve with reserve sauce mixture and squeeze the lime wedges over.

Spicy Black Olives

Prep time: 10 minutes | Cook time: 5 minutes | Serves 4

12 ounces (340 g) pitted black extra-large olives
¼ cup all-purpose flour
1 cup panko bread crumbs
2 teaspoons dried thyme
1 teaspoon red pepper flakes
1 teaspoon smoked paprika
1 egg beaten with 1 tablespoon water
Vegetable oil for spraying

1. Drain the olives and place them on a paper towel-lined plate to dry.
2. Put the flour on a plate. Combine the panko, thyme, red pepper flakes, and paprika on a separate plate. Dip an olive in the flour, shaking off any excess, then coat with egg mixture. Dredge the olive in the panko mixture, pressing to make the crumbs adhere, and place the breaded olive on a platter. Repeat with the remaining olives.
3. Spray the olives with oil and place them in a single layer in the crisper tray. Work in batches if necessary so as not to overcrowd the crisper tray.
4. Place the crisper tray on the air fry position. Select Air Fry, set the temperature to 400°F (204°C), and set the time to 5 minutes.
5. Cook for 5 minutes until the breading is browned and crispy. Serve warm

Pigs in a Blanket

Prep time: 10 minutes | Cook time: 8 minutes per batch | Makes 16 rolls

1 can refrigerated crescent roll dough
1 small package mini smoked sausages, patted dry
2 tablespoons melted
butter
2 teaspoons sesame seeds
1 teaspoon onion powder

1. Place the crescent roll dough on a clean work surface and separate into 8 pieces. Cut each piece in half and you will have 16 triangles.
2. Make the pigs in the blanket: Arrange each sausage on each dough triangle, then roll the sausages up.
3. Brush the pigs with melted butter and place half of the pigs in the blanket in the baking pan. Sprinkle with sesame seeds and onion powder.
4. Place the baking pan on the bake position. Select Bake, set the temperature to 330°F (166°C), and set the time to 8 minutes.
5. Cook for 8 minutes or until the pigs are fluffy and golden brown. Flip the pigs halfway through.
6. Serve immediately.

Teriyaki Shrimp Skewers

Prep time: 10 minutes | Cook time: 6 minutes | Makes 12 skewered shrimp

1½ tablespoons mirin
1½ teaspoons ginger juice
1½ tablespoons soy sauce
12 large shrimp (about 20 shrimps per
pound), peeled and deveined
1 large egg
¾ cup panko breadcrumbs
Cooking spray

1. Combine the mirin, ginger juice, and soy sauce in a large bowl. Stir to mix well.
2. Dunk the shrimp in the bowl of mirin mixture, then wrap the bowl in plastic and refrigerate for 1 hour to marinate.
3. Spritz the crisper tray with cooking spray.
4. Run twelve 4-inch skewers through each shrimp.
5. Whisk the egg in the bowl of marinade to combine well. Pour the breadcrumbs on a plate.
6. Dredge the shrimp skewers in the egg mixture, then shake the excess off and roll over the breadcrumbs to coat well.

7. Arrange the shrimp skewers in the crisper tray and spritz with cooking spray. You need to work in batches to avoid overcrowding.
8. Place the crisper tray on the air fry position. Select Air Fry, set the temperature to 400°F (204°C), and set the time to 6 minutes.
9. Cook for 6 minutes or until the shrimp are opaque and firm. Flip the shrimp skewers halfway through.
10. Serve immediately.

Garlic Olive Stromboli

Prep time: 25 minutes | Cook time: 25 minutes | Serves 8

4 large cloves garlic, unpeeled
3 tablespoons grated Parmesan cheese
½ cup packed fresh basil leaves
½ cup marinated, pitted green and black olives
¼ teaspoon crushed
red pepper
½ pound (227 g) pizza dough, at room temperature
4 ounces (113 g) sliced provolone cheese (about 8 slices)
Cooking spray

1. Spritz the crisper tray with cooking spray.
2. Put the unpeeled garlic in the crisper tray.
3. Place the crisper tray on the air fry position. Select Air Fry, set the temperature to 370°F (188°C), and set the time to 10 minutes.
4. Cook for 10 minutes or until the garlic is softened completely. Remove them from the grill and allow to cool until you can handle.
5. Peel the garlic and place into a food processor with 2 tablespoons of Parmesan, basil, olives, and crushed red pepper. Pulse to mix well. Set aside.
6. Arrange the pizza dough on a clean work surface, then roll it out with a rolling pin into a rectangle. Cut the rectangle in half.
7. Sprinkle half of the garlic mixture over each rectangle half, and leave ½-inch edges uncover. Top them with the provolone cheese.
8. Brush one long side of each rectangle half with water, then roll them up. Spritz the crisper tray with cooking spray. Transfer the rolls to the crisper tray. Spritz with cooking spray and scatter with remaining Parmesan.
9. Air fry for 15 minutes or until golden brown. Flip the rolls halfway through.
10. Remove the rolls from the grill and allow to cool for a few minutes before serving.

Honey Yeast Rolls

Prep time: 10 minutes | Cook time: 20 minutes | Makes 8 rolls

¼ cup whole milk, heated to 115ºF (46ºC) in the microwave
½ teaspoon active dry yeast
1 tablespoon honey
²/₃ cup all-purpose flour, plus more for

dusting
½ teaspoon kosher salt
2 tablespoons unsalted butter, at room temperature, plus more for greasing
Flaky sea salt, to taste

1. In a large bowl, whisk together the milk, yeast, and honey and let stand until foamy, about 10 minutes.
2. Stir in the flour and salt until just combined. Stir in the butter until absorbed. Scrape the dough onto a lightly floured work surface and knead until smooth, about 6 minutes. Transfer the dough to a lightly greased bowl, cover loosely with a sheet of plastic wrap or a kitchen towel, and let sit until nearly doubled in size, about 1 hour.
3. Uncover the dough, lightly press it down to expel the bubbles, then portion it into 8 equal pieces. Prep the work surface by wiping it clean with a damp paper towel (if there is flour on the work surface, it will prevent the dough from sticking lightly to the surface, which helps it form a ball). Roll each piece into a ball by cupping the palm of the hand around the dough against the work surface and moving the heel of the hand in a circular motion while using the thumb to contain the dough and tighten it into a perfectly round ball. Once all the balls are formed, nestle them side by side in the crisper tray.
4. Cover the rolls loosely with a kitchen towel or a sheet of plastic wrap and let sit until lightly risen and puffed, 20 to 30 minutes.
5. Place the crisper tray on the air fry position. Select Air Fry, set the temperature to 270ºF (132ºC), and set the time to 12 minutes.
6. Uncover the rolls and gently brush with more butter, being careful not to press the rolls too hard. Cook for 12 minutes until the rolls are light golden brown and fluffy.
7. Remove the rolls from the grill and brush liberally with more butter, if you like, and sprinkle each roll with a pinch of sea salt. Serve warm.

Pecan Tart

Prep time: 25 minutes | Cook time: 30 minutes | Serves 8

Tart Crust:
¼ cup firmly packed brown sugar
¹/₃ cup butter, softened
Filling:
¼ cup whole milk
4 tablespoons butter, diced
½ cup packed brown sugar
¼ cup pure maple

1 cup all-purpose flour
¼ teaspoon kosher salt

syrup
1½ cups finely chopped pecans
¼ teaspoon pure vanilla extract
¼ teaspoon sea salt

1. Line the baking pan with aluminum foil, then spritz the pan with cooking spray.
2. Stir the brown sugar and butter in a bowl with a hand mixer until puffed, then add the flour and salt and stir until crumbled.
3. Pour the mixture in the prepared baking pan and tilt the pan to coat the bottom evenly.
4. Place the baking pan on the bake position. Select Bake, set the temperature to 350ºF (177ºC), and set the time to 13 minutes.
5. Cook for 13 minutes or until the crust is golden brown.
6. Meanwhile, pour the milk, butter, sugar, and maple syrup in a saucepan. Stir to mix well. Bring to a simmer, then cook for 1 more minute. Stir constantly.
7. Turn off the heat and mix the pecans and vanilla into the filling mixture.
8. Pour the filling mixture over the golden crust and spread with a spatula to coat the crust evenly.
9. Bake for an additional 12 minutes or until the filling mixture is set and frothy.
10. Remove the baking pan from the grill and sprinkle with salt. Allow to sit for 10 minutes or until cooled.
11. Transfer the pan to the refrigerator to chill for at least 2 hours, then remove the aluminum foil and slice to serve.

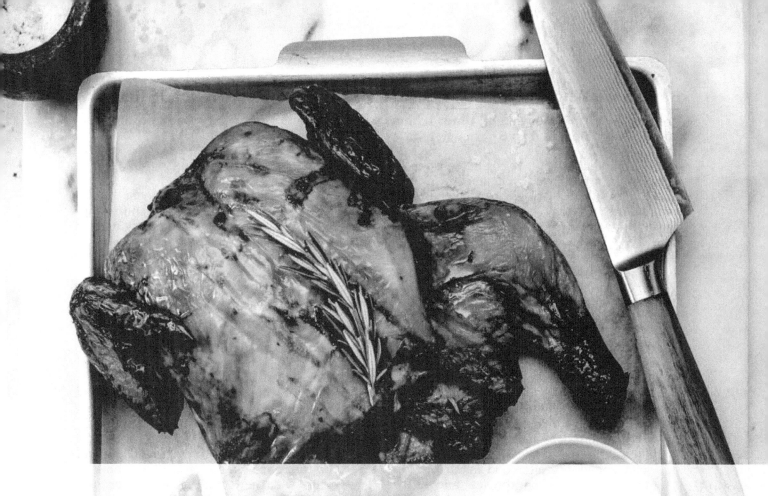

Chapter 14 Rotisserie

Barbecued Whole Chicken

Prep time: 15 minutes | Cook time: 1 hour 10 minutes | Serves 4 to 6

1 whole chicken, 3 to 4 pounds (1.4 to 1.8 kg)
1 medium-size onion, peeled but whole (for cavity)
Barbecue Sauce:
¾ cup ketchup
⅔ cup cherry cola
Rub:
2 teaspoons salt
2 teaspoons onion powder
1 teaspoon mustard powder

¼ cup apple cider vinegar
2 tablespoons packed brown sugar
1 tablespoon molasses
¼ teaspoon salt
¼ teaspoon freshly ground black pepper

½ teaspoon freshly ground black pepper
½ teaspoon garlic powder

1. To make the barbecue sauce: Combine all the ingredients in a medium-size saucepan over medium heat and simmer for 5 to 6 minutes, until the mixture is smooth and well blended. Stir often and watch for burning. Remove from the heat and let the sauce cool at least 10 minutes before using.
2. To make the rub: Combine all the rub ingredients in a small bowl.
3. Pat the chicken dry inside and out with paper towels. Apply the rub all over the bird, under the breast skin, and inside the body cavity.
4. Truss the chicken with kitchen twine. Run the rotisserie spit through the onion and insert it into the chicken cavity. Use a paring knife to cut a pilot hole in the onion to make this easier. Continue to run the spit through the chicken and secure with the rotisserie forks.
5. Select Grill, set the temperature to 400ºF (205ºC), and set the time to 70 minutes.
6. Place the chicken in the grill and set a drip tray underneath. Cook until the meat in the thighs and legs reaches 175ºF (79ºC). The breasts should be 165ºF (74ºC). Baste the chicken with the barbecue sauce during the last half of the cooking time. Do so every 7 to 10 minutes, until the bird is nearly done and well coated with the sauce.
7. Remove from the heat, carefully remove the rotisserie forks and slide the spit out, and then set the chicken on a large cutting board. Tent the chicken with aluminum foil and let it rest for 10 to 15 minutes before cutting off the twine and carving.

Tri-Tip Roast with Ketchup Sauce

Prep time: 15 minutes | Cook time: 1 hour 30 minutes | Serves 8

2 tri-tip roasts, 2
Sauce:
¾ cup ketchup
¾ cup Dr Pepper
¼ cup packed brown sugar
2 teaspoons apple
Rub:
1 tablespoon kosher salt
1½ teaspoons freshly ground black pepper
1½ teaspoons paprika

pounds (907 g) each

cider vinegar
¼ teaspoon freshly ground black pepper
⅛ teaspoon salt

1½ teaspoons mild chili powder
½ teaspoon garlic powder

1. Place one tri-tip on top of the other with the small ends on opposite sides. Fold in these ends and tie the roasts with kitchen twine, creating one single, uniform roast. Run a long sword skewer through the center of the roast lengthwise to create a pilot hole. Run the rotisserie spit through the hole and secure with the forks. Balance as necessary.
2. To make the sauce: Combine the sauce ingredients in a small saucepan and simmer over medium heat for 5 to 6 minutes, stirring often. Watch for burning and lower the heat if necessary. Remove from the heat and let sit for 15 to 30 minutes before using.
3. To make the rub: Combine the rub ingredients in a small bowl and evenly apply all over the roast.
4. Select Grill, set the temperature to 400ºF (205ºC), and set the time to 85 minutes.
5. Place the roast in the grill and set a drip tray underneath. During the last 30 minutes of cooking time, begin basting with the sauce. Do this 6 to 8 times, until the roast is well coated with the barbecue sauce and the internal temperature reaches 140ºF (60ºC). The roast will shrink during the cooking process, so adjust the forks when appropriate.
6. Remove the roast from the grill, carefully remove the rotisserie forks and slide the spit out, and then place the roast on a large cutting board. Cover the meat with aluminum foil and let rest for 12 to 15 minutes. Cut off the twine. Separate the roasts, slice against the grain, and serve.

Sirloin Roast with Porcini Baste

Prep time: 20 minutes | Cook time: 2 hours | Serves 8

1 top sirloin roast, 4 to 4½ pounds (1.8 to 2.0 kg)

Wet Rub:

½ cup dried porcini mushrooms
¼ cup olive oil
4 teaspoons salt
1 tablespoon chopped fresh thyme
2 cloves garlic, minced

1 teaspoon onion powder
1 teaspoon chili powder
1 teaspoon coarsely ground black pepper

Baste:

½ cup dried porcini mushrooms
1 or 2 cups boiling water
½ cup red wine (Cabernet Sauvignon

recommended)
1 tablespoon wet rub mixture
1 teaspoon Worcestershire sauce

1. For the wet rub: Chop the mushrooms into small pieces. Place in a clean spice or coffee grinder and grind to a fine powder. Transfer to a bowl and add the remaining rub ingredients. Remove 1 tablespoon (6 g) of the mixture and set aside.
2. If the sirloin roast is loose or uneven, tie it with kitchen twine to hold it to a consistent and even shape. Run a long sword skewer through the center of the roast lengthwise to create a pilot hole. Run the rotisserie spit through the hole and secure with the forks. Balance as necessary. Apply the wet rub evenly to the meat.
3. Select Grill, set the temperature to 400ºF (205ºC), and set the time to 2 hours.
4. Place the roast in the grill and set a drip tray underneath. Cook until it reaches the desired doneness: 125ºF (52ºC) for rare, 135ºF (57ºC) for medium rare, 145ºF (63ºC) for medium, 155ºF (68ºC) for medium well, or 165ºF (74ºC) for well done. Adjust the forks when appropriate.
5. While the roast cooks, make the baste: Add the dried porcini mushrooms to 1 cup boiling water, or 2 cups boiling water if you would like to use the porcini broth for the gravy. Steep the mushrooms for 30 minutes, covered. Strain the broth and reserve the porcinis (for the gravy) and broth separately. Divide the broth into two equal portions, one for the baste and one for the gravy. Combine 1 cup broth with remaining baste ingredients. Let sit for 15 to 30 minutes to come to room temperature

before using. Begin basting the roast during the last half of the cooking time and repeat every 10 to 12 minutes until the roast is ready.
6. Carefully remove the rotisserie forks and slide the spit out. Tent the roast with aluminum foil and let the meat rest for 20 minutes. Cut into ¼-inch slices and serve.

Prime Rib Roast with Garlic Rub

Prep time: 5 minutes | Cook time: 2 hours | Serves 8 to 10

1 4-bone prime rib roast (8 to 10 pounds / 3.6 to 4.5 kg)

Rub:

3½ tablespoons kosher salt

3 or 4 cloves garlic, minced
1½ tablespoons olive oil
1 tablespoon coarsely ground black pepper

1. Trim off any straggling pieces of meat or fat from the roast. If the fat cap is too thick, cut it down to between ¼ to ½ inch in thickness depending on how you like your prime rib. Run a long sword skewer through the center of the roast lengthwise to create a pilot hole. Run the rotisserie spit through the hole and secure with the forks. Balance as necessary. This is a large roast and it is important that it be well balanced.
2. To make the rub: Combine the rub ingredients in a small bowl and apply evenly to the roast. Concentrate the rub on the rounded end and not the cut sides, though it should still get some. The rub will then be on the edges of the slices once the roast has been carved.
3. Select Grill, set the temperature to 400ºF (205ºC), and set the time to 2 hours.
4. Place the roast in the grill and set a drip tray underneath. Cook until it is near the desired doneness: 125ºF (52ºC) for rare, 135ºF (57ºC) for medium rare, 145ºF (63ºC) for medium, 155ºF (68ºC) for medium well, or 165ºF (74ºC) for well done. The roast will shrink during cooking, so adjust the forks when appropriate.
5. Carefully remove the rotisserie forks and slide the spit out, and then place the roast on a large cutting board. Tent the roast with aluminum foil and let the meat rest for 15 to 20 minutes. The roast temperature will continue to rise an additional 5ºF during the rest phase. Cut away the bones first by passing a knife against the bones and cutting through (save the bones for later). Cut the meat into slices ¹/₃ to ½ inch thick.

Tri-Tip with Chimichurri Sauce

Prep time: 20 minutes | Cook time: 1 hour 20 minutes | Serves 10 to 12

2 tri-tip roasts, 4 to 5 pounds (1.8 to 2.3 kg) each	1 small shallot, chopped
Chimichurri Sauce:	2 tablespoons white vinegar
½ cup packed fresh flat-leaf parsley, chopped	¼ teaspoon salt
	¼ teaspoon freshly ground black pepper
⅓ cup packed fresh cilantro leaves, chopped	¼ teaspoon red pepper flakes (optional)
3 or 4 cloves garlic	½ cup olive oil
Rub:	
1½ tablespoons kosher salt	1 teaspoon onion powder
2 teaspoons freshly ground black pepper	½ teaspoon cayenne

1. To make the chimichurri sauce: Prepare the sauce 1 to 2 hours before the meat will be finished cooking. Place all the sauce ingredients, except the oil, into a food processor. Pulse a few times. Slowly pour in the oil while pulsing 10 or so more times. You do not want to purée the chimichurri, but all the ingredients should be finely chopped and well combined with the oil. Remove the sauce from the food processor, transfer to a bowl, and set aside until ready to eat.
2. Place one tri-tip on top of the other with the small ends on opposite sides. Fold in these ends and tie the roasts with kitchen twine, creating one single, uniform roast. Run a long sword skewer through the center of the roast lengthwise to create a pilot hole. Run the rotisserie spit through the hole and secure with the forks. Balance as necessary.
3. To make the rub: Combine the rub ingredients in a small bowl and apply evenly all over the meat.
4. Select Grill, set the temperature to 400ºF (205ºC), and set the time to 80 minutes.
5. Place the roast in the grill and set a drip tray underneath. Cook until near the desired doneness. The roast will shrink during the cooking process, so adjust the forks when appropriate.
6. Carefully remove the rotisserie forks and slide the spit out, and then place the roast on a large cutting board. Cover the meat with aluminum foil and let rest for 15 minutes. Cut off the twine. Separate the roasts, slice against the grain ⅓ to ½ inch thick and serve with the chimichurri sauce.

Rosemary Prime Rib Roast in Red Wine

Prep time: 10 minutes | Cook time: 2 hours | Serves 8 to 10

1 boneless prime rib roast, 4 to 5 pounds	(1.8 to 2.3 kg)
Rub:	
3 to 3½ tablespoons kosher salt	2 or 3 cloves garlic, minced
1 tablespoon finely chopped fresh rosemary	2 teaspoons freshly ground black pepper
Baste:	
1 cup Cabernet Sauvignon	1½ teaspoons soy sauce
½ cup low-sodium beef broth	1½ teaspoons Worcestershire sauce

1. To make the rub: Combine the rub ingredients in a small bowl and mix well. Use the salt to grind the garlic and rosemary together.
2. Run a long sword skewer through the center of the roast lengthwise to create a pilot hole. Run the rotisserie spit through the hole and secure with the forks. Balance as necessary.
3. Apply the rub to the roast. Cover with plastic wrap and set in a safe place at room temperature for 30 minutes (rotisserie spit and all).
4. To make the baste: Combine the baste ingredients in a small bowl and store in the refrigerator until ready to use. It will separate, so stir occasionally. Warm the baste for 30 seconds to 1 minute in the microwave before applying to the roast.
5. Select Grill, set the temperature to 400ºF (205ºC), and set the time to 2 hours.
6. Place the roast in the grill and set a drip tray underneath. Baste intermittently during the last half of the cooking time, until it reaches the desired doneness: 125ºF (52ºC) for rare, 135ºF (57ºC) for medium rare, 145ºF (63ºC) for medium, 155ºF (68ºC) for medium well, or 165ºF (74ºC) for well done. The roast will shrink during cooking, so adjust the forks when appropriate.
7. Carefully remove the rotisserie forks and slide the spit out, and then set the roast on a large cutting board. Tent the roast with aluminum foil and let the meat rest for 15 to 20 minutes. Slice and serve.

Spareribs with Ketchup-Garlic Sauce

Prep time: 15 minutes | Cook time: 3½ hours | Serves 4 to 6

2 racks spareribs
Sauce:

1 tablespoon olive oil	sugar
2 cloves garlic, minced	1 tablespoon paprika
1 cup ketchup	2 teaspoons mild chili
¾ cup water	powder
⅓ cup packed brown	¼ teaspoon cayenne

Rub:

⅓ cup packed brown sugar	1 teaspoon onion powder
2 tablespoons paprika	½ teaspoon garlic
2 teaspoons salt	powder
2 teaspoons mild chili powder	¼ teaspoon cayenne

1. To make the sauce: Heat the oil in a medium-size saucepan over medium heat and sauté the garlic for 15 seconds, until aromatic. Add the remaining sauce ingredients and simmer for 5 minutes, stirring often. Remove from the heat and let cool to room temperature before using.
2. To make the rub: Combine the rub ingredients in a small bowl and set aside.
3. Place the ribs on a cutting board and pat dry with paper towels. Cut away any excess fat from the ribs. Remove the membrane from the back of the ribs by using a blunt knife to work the membrane away from the bone in one corner. Grab hold of the membrane with a paper towel for a good grip and gently peel away. With a little practice, this becomes an easy process.
4. Lay the rib racks meat-side down. Apply a small portion of the rub, just enough to season, to the bone side of the racks. Lay one rack on top of the other, bone side to bone side, to form an even shape. Tie the two racks together with kitchen twine between every other bone. The ribs should be held tightly together. Run the rotisserie spit between the racks and secure with the forks. The fork tines should run through the meat as best as possible. The ribs will move a little as the rotisserie turns. They should not flop around, however. Secure to prevent this. Apply the remaining rub evenly over the outer surface of the ribs. A general rule with rubs is that what sticks is the amount needed.
5. Select Grill, set the temperature to 375ºF (190ºC), and set the time to 3½ hours.

6. Place the ribs in the grill and set a drip tray underneath. Cook until the ribs reach an internal temperature of 185ºF (85ºC). Test the temperature in several locations. Baste the ribs several times with the sauce during the last hour of cooking to build up a sticky surface.
7. Remove from the heat, carefully remove the rotisserie forks and slide the spit out, and then set the ribs on a large cutting board. Tent the ribs with aluminum foil and let the meat rest for 5 to 10 minutes. Cut away the twine and cut the racks into individual ribs. Serve.

Pork Loin Roast with Spice Rub

Prep time: 10 minutes | Cook time: 45 minutes | Serves 4

1 (4-pound / 1.8-kg)	bone-in pork loin roast

Brine:

3 quarts water	garlic press
½ cup table salt (or 1 cup kosher salt)	1 teaspoon minced rosemary
¼ cup brown sugar	1 teaspoon fresh
Spice Rub:	ground black pepper
4 cloves garlic, minced or pressed through a	½ teaspoon hot red pepper flakes

1. Combine the brine ingredients in a large container and stir until the salt and sugar dissolve. Submerge the pork in the brine. Store in the refrigerator for four to eight hours.
2. One hour before cooking, remove the pork from the brine and pat dry with paper towels. Mix the rub ingredients in a small bowl, then rub over the pork shoulder, working the rub into any natural seams in the meat. Truss the pork roast, skewer it on the rotisserie spit, and secure it with the rotisserie forks. Let the pork rest at room temperature.
3. Select Grill, set the temperature to 450ºF (235ºC), and set the time to 45 minutes. Set a drip tray in the middle of the grill.
4. Put the spit in the grill and make sure the drip tray is centered beneath the pork roast. Cook the pork until it reaches 135ºF (57ºC) in its thickest part.
5. Remove the pork from the rotisserie spit and remove the twine trussing the roast. Be careful - the spit and forks are blazing hot. Let the pork rest for 15 minutes, then slice and serve.

Ham with Honey-Orange Glaze

Prep time: 10 minutes | Cook time: 45 minutes | Serves 12 to 14

1 ham, bone in and unsliced, 7 to 8 pounds (3.2 to 3.6 kg)

Glaze:

1½ cups orange juice
½ cup honey
2 tablespoons packed brown sugar
¼ teaspoon ground cinnamon
⅛ teaspoon ground nutmeg
⅛ teaspoon ground allspice
⅛ teaspoon ground cloves
⅛ teaspoon white pepper
2 tablespoons unsalted butter

1 cup packed brown sugar

1. To make the glaze: Combine the orange juice, honey, brown sugar, and spices in a saucepan and bring almost to a boil over medium-high heat. Decrease the heat to medium and simmer for 10 minutes, stirring often. The mixture should be a little runnier than real maple syrup. Remove from the heat and add the butter, stirring until melted. Let the mixture cool.
2. Run a long sword skewer through the center of the ham lengthwise to create a pilot hole. There is a bone in the middle of this ham, but generally it is just to one side. The skewer should easily go through, but feel for the bone before you start so you will know how to navigate around it. Run the rotisserie spit through the hole and secure with the forks. Balance the ham on the spit as well as possible.
3. Select Grill, set the temperature to 375ºF (190ºC), and set the time to 45 minutes.
4. Place the ham in the grill and set a drip tray underneath, if there is room. The ham should not take too long to heat up. Look for an internal temperature around 130ºF (54ºC). The surface should be hot.
5. Baste the ham with the glaze after 20 minutes in the grill. Repeat the process every 5 minutes and about 3 more times.
6. During the last 5 to 10 minutes of cooking time, the ham should be hot as well as sticky from the glaze. Increase the temperature to 400ºF (205ºC) and sprinkle the brown sugar evenly on the surface of the ham in small amounts until it is completely coated. Continue to cook until the sugar starts to bubble. Move quickly, as sugar tends to burn.

7. Once the sugar is bubbling rapidly, remove the ham from the heat and place on a large cutting board. Remove the rotisserie forks and slide the spit out, loosely cover the ham with aluminum foil, and let it rest for 5 minutes. Carve into thin slices and serve warm.

Pulled Pork with Paprika

Prep time: 10 minutes | Cook time: 6 hours | Serves 10

1 pork butt, 5 to 6 pounds (2.3 to 2.7 kg)

Rub:

2 tablespoons paprika
2 tablespoons packed brown sugar
1 tablespoon kosher salt
1 tablespoon mild chili powder
1 teaspoon freshly ground black pepper
1 teaspoon celery salt
½ teaspoon cayenne
½ teaspoon garlic powder

1. Run a long sword skewer through the center of the roast lengthwise to create a pilot hole. Run the rotisserie spit through the hole and secure with the forks. Balance as necessary.
2. To make the rub: Combine the rub ingredients in a small bowl and apply evenly all over the roast. Let sit at room temperature for 15 minutes.
3. Select Grill, set the temperature to 350ºF (180ºC), and set the time to 6 hours.
4. Place the roast in the grill with a drip tray underneath. Cook until the internal temperature reaches 185ºF (85ºC). The roast will shrink during cooking, so adjust the forks when appropriate.
5. Remove from the heat, carefully remove the rotisserie forks and slide the spit out, and then set the pork on a large cutting board. Tent the roast with aluminum foil and let the meat rest for 20 minutes. Remove the foil and let stand for an additional 10 minutes.
6. Using two forks, check to see how easily the meat shreds. Some parts will do this more easily than others. Be sure to use heat-resistant gloves to break the roast apart. Begin shredding each large chunk one at a time. Add pieces to a large bowl and either add the barbecue sauce directly to the shredded meat or serve on the side. Keep the bowl covered as you're working on each section. This will help keep the meat warm. Serve by itself or with your favorite sides or in sandwiches.

Port-Marinated Chuck Roast

Prep time: 15 minutes | Cook time: 1 hour | Serves 8

1 chuck roast, 4 to 4½ pounds (1.8 to 2.0 kg)	½ teaspoon freshly ground black pepper
1¼ teaspoons salt	
Marinade:	
1 tablespoon olive oil	balsamic vinegar
1 shallot, finely chopped	1 teaspoon Worcestershire sauce
2 or 3 cloves garlic, minced	1 teaspoon chopped fresh thyme
1½ cups tawny port	¼ teaspoon salt
¼ cup beef broth	¼ teaspoon freshly
1½ tablespoons	ground black pepper

1. To make the marinade: Heat the olive oil in a saucepan over medium-low heat and cook the shallot for 3 minutes until translucent. Add the garlic and cook for 30 seconds. Increase the heat to medium-high and add the port. Stir thoroughly and cook for 1 minute. Add the remaining ingredients and simmer the sauce for 5 minutes, stirring occasionally. Remove from the heat and let cool for 10 to 15 minutes. Divide the mixture into two even portions, reserving one half for the baste and one for the marinade. Store in the refrigerator until ready to cook, then bring to room temperature before using.
2. Trim away excess fat from the outer edges of the chuck roast. Place the roast in a resealable plastic bag. Add half of the port mixture to the bag, making sure that all of the meat is well covered. Seal the bag and place in the refrigerator for 6 to 8 hours.
3. Remove the roast from the bag, discarding the marinade, and place on a large cutting board or platter. With kitchen twine, tie the roast into a round and uniform shape, pulling tightly. Start in the center and work toward the ends until it is tied into a solid round roast. This will take four or five ties. Run a long sword skewer through the center of the roast lengthwise to create a pilot hole. Run the rotisserie spit through the hole and secure with the forks. Balance as necessary. Season the roast with the salt and pepper.
4. Select Grill, set the temperature to 400ºF (205ºC), and set the time to 1 hour.
5. Place the roast in the grill and set a drip tray underneath. Cook until it reaches the desired doneness: 125ºF (52ºC) for rare, 135ºF (57ºC) for medium rare, 145ºF (63ºC)

for medium, 155ºF (68ºC) for medium well, or 165ºF (74ºC) for well done. Baste halfway through the cooking time, and repeat the process at least 3 times until the roast is done.
6. Remove from the heat, carefully remove the rotisserie forks and slide the spit out, and then set the roast on a large cutting board. Tent the roast with aluminum foil and let the meat rest for 15 to 20 minutes. Cut off the twine. Slice into ¼-inch slices and serve.

Chicken with Teriyaki Sauce

Prep time: 5 minutes | Cook time: 1 hour 10 minutes | Serves 4

1 (4-pound / 1.8-kg) chicken	1 tablespoon kosher salt
Teriyaki Sauce:	
¼ cup soy sauce	sugar)
¼ cup mirin (Japanese sweet rice wine)	¼ inch slice of ginger, smashed
¼ cup honey (or	

1. Season the chicken with the salt, inside and out. Gently work your fingers under the skin on the breast, then rub some of the salt directly onto the breast meat. Fold the wingtips under the wings and truss the chicken. Skewer the chicken on the rotisserie spit, securing it with the rotisserie forks. Let the chicken rest at room temperature.
2. Select Grill, set the temperature to 450ºF (235ºC), and set the time to 1 hour. Set a drip tray in the middle of the grill.
3. Combine the soy sauce, mirin, honey, and ginger in a saucepan. Bring to a boil over medium-high heat, stirring often, then decrease the heat to low and simmer for 10 minutes, until the liquid is reduced by half.
4. Put the spit in the grill and make sure the drip tray is centered beneath the chicken. Cook until the chicken reaches 160ºF (70ºC) in the thickest part of the breast. During the last 15 minutes of cooking, brush the chicken with the teriyaki sauce every five minutes.
5. Remove the chicken from the rotisserie spit and transfer to a platter. Be careful - the spit and forks are blazing hot. Remove the trussing twine, then brush the chicken one last time with the teriyaki sauce. Let the chicken rest for 15 minutes, then carve and serve, passing any remaining teriyaki sauce at the table.

Prime Rib Roast with Whiskey Baste

Prep time: 10 minutes | Cook time: 2 hours | Serves 8 to 10

1 4-bone prime rib roast (8 to 10 pounds / 3.6 to 4.5 kg)

Rub:
¼ cup coarse salt
1 small shallot, finely chopped
2 cloves garlic, minced
2 tablespoons olive oil
1 tablespoon coarsely ground black pepper
Zest of 1 large lemon
1 teaspoon paprika
1 teaspoon sugar

Baste:
1/3 cup whiskey
¼ cup water
Juice of 1 lemon
1/8 teaspoon salt

1. Trim off any straggling pieces of meat or fat from the roast. If the fat cap is too thick, cut it down to between ¼ to ½ inch in thickness depending on how you like your prime rib.
2. Run a long sword skewer through the center of the roast lengthwise to create a pilot hole. Run the rotisserie spit through the hole and secure with the forks. Balance as necessary.
3. To make the rub: Combine the rub ingredients in a small bowl to form an even paste. Use additional olive oil if necessary to get it to a thick but workable consistency. Apply evenly to the roast, focusing on the outer shell of the roast.
4. To make the baste: Combine the baste ingredients in a small bowl and set aside for 15 to 30 minutes to come to room temperature.
5. Select Grill, set the temperature to 400ºF (205ºC), and set the time to 2 hours.
6. Place the roast in the grill and set a drip tray underneath.
7. During the last hour of cooking time, begin basting. Apply the baste gently so as not to wash away the seasonings on the outside of the roast. Do this 6 to 8 times, until the roast is well coated with the baste. Cook until it is near the desired doneness: 125ºF (52ºC) for rare, 135ºF (57ºC) for medium rare, 145ºF (63ºC) for medium, 155ºF (68ºC) for medium well, or 165ºF (74ºC) for well done. The roast will shrink during cooking, so adjust the forks when appropriate.
8. Carefully remove the rotisserie forks and slide the spit out, and then set the roast on a large cutting board. Tent the roast with aluminum foil and let the meat rest for 15 to 20 minutes. Cut away the bones first by passing a knife against the bones and cutting through (save the bones for later). Cut the meat into thin slices.

Chipotle Chuck Roast with Garlic

Prep time: 10 minutes | Cook time: 2½ hours | Serves 6 to 8

1 chuck roast, 3½ to 4 pounds (1.5 to 1.8 kg)

Marinade:
1 (7-ounce / 198-g) can chipotle peppers in adobo
1 cup diced onion
½ cup beef or vegetable broth
3 cloves garlic, cut into fourths
1 tablespoon ground cumin
2 tablespoons water
1 tablespoon white vinegar
1 tablespoon salt
2 teaspoons dried oregano

1. To make the marinade: Place the marinade ingredients in a food processor and pulse 8 to 10 times. Everything should be very finely chopped and combined. Reserve 1 cup of the mixture to use as a baste and refrigerate until ready to cook, then bring to room temperature before using.
2. Trim away any loose or excess pieces of fat from the roast. Place in a large glass dish or large resealable plastic bag. Pour the marinade over the meat, making sure all sides are well covered. Seal the bag or cover the dish with plastic wrap and place in the refrigerator for 12 to 24 hours.
3. Remove the roast from the bag, discarding the marinade. Lay the roast out on a large cutting board. With kitchen twine, tie the roast into a round and uniform shape, pulling tightly. Start in the center and work toward the ends until it is tied into a solid round roast. This will take four or five ties. Run a long sword skewer through the center of the roast lengthwise to create a pilot hole. Run the rotisserie spit through the hole and secure with the forks. Balance as necessary.
4. Select Grill, set the temperature to 400ºF (205ºC), and set the time to 2½ hours.
5. Place the roast in the grill and set a drip tray underneath. Cook until the meat reaches an internal temperature of about 160ºF (70ºC). Baste with the reserved marinade during the last 30 to 40 minutes of cooking. This roast is intentionally overcooked so that it can be shredded easily. It will be tender and juicy.
6. Remove from the heat, carefully remove the rotisserie forks and slide the spit out, and then set the roast on a large cutting board. Tent the roast with aluminum foil and let the meat rest for 20 minutes. Cut off the twine. Shred into small pieces or carve into thin slices and serve with warmed tortillas, Spanish rice, beans, and fresh salsa.

Baby Back Ribs with Ketchup Sauce

Prep time: 15 minutes | Cook time: 2½ hours | Serves 4 to 6

2 racks baby back ribs
Sauce:

1 tablespoon vegetable oil	vinegar
1 cup finely chopped sweet onion	¼ cup packed brown sugar
2 cloves garlic, minced	2 tablespoons yellow mustard
1½ cups ketchup	⅛ teaspoon salt
¼ cup red wine	

Rub:

1 tablespoon paprika	ground black pepper
2 teaspoons salt	½ teaspoon cayenne
2 teaspoons freshly	

1. To make the sauce: Heat the oil in a medium-size saucepan over medium heat. Add the onions and sauté for 5 minutes. Add the garlic and sauté for 15 seconds. Add the remaining sauce ingredients and simmer for 4 to 5 minutes, stirring often. Remove from the heat and let cool for 15 to 30 minutes before using.
2. To make the rub: Combine the rub ingredients in a small bowl and set aside.
3. Place the ribs on a cutting board and pat dry with paper towels. Cut away any excess fat from the ribs. Remove the membrane from the back of the ribs by using a blunt knife to work the membrane away from the bone in one corner. Grab hold of the membrane with a paper towel for a good grip and gently peel away. With a little practice, this becomes an easy process. Apply the rub all over the ribs' surface, focusing more on the meat side than the bone side.
4. Place one rack of ribs bone-side up on a large cutting board. Place the other rack of ribs bone-side down on top. Position to match up the racks of ribs as evenly as possible. With kitchen twine, tie the racks together between ever other bone, end to end. The whole bundle should be secure and tight. Run the rotisserie spit between the racks and secure tightly with the rotisserie forks. There will be a little movement in the middle, which is fine. As the ribs cook it may be necessary to tighten the forks to keep them secure. Make sure the forks pass through the meat of each rack on each end.
5. Select Grill, set the temperature to 375ºF (190ºC), and set the time to 2½ hours.
6. Place the racks in the grill and set a drip tray underneath. Cook until the internal temperature reaches 185ºF (85ºC). Test the temperature in several locations. Baste the ribs evenly with barbecue sauce during the last 45 minutes of cooking time.
7. Remove from the heat, carefully remove the rotisserie forks and slide the spit out, and then set the ribs on a large cutting board. Tent the ribs with aluminum foil and let the meat rest for 5 to 10 minutes.
8. Cut away the twine and cut the racks into individual ribs. Serve.

Bacon-Wrapped Sirloin Roast

Prep time: 5 minutes | Cook time: 45 minutes | Serves 4

1 (4-pound / 1.8-kg) sirloin roast	salt
1 tablespoon kosher	4 slices bacon

1. Season the roast with the salt, then refrigerate for at least two hours, preferably overnight.
2. One hour before cooking, remove the roast from the refrigerator. Cut the butcher's twine and lay the strings on a platter, spaced where you want to tie the roast. Put two slices of bacon on top of the string, with a gap between them. Put the sirloin on top of the bacon, then lay the last two pieces of bacon on top of the roast. Tie the twine to truss the roast and the bacon. Trim off any loose ends of bacon so they don't burn in the grill. Skewer the roast on the rotisserie spit, securing it with the rotisserie forks. Let the beef rest at room temperature until the grill is ready.
3. Select Grill, set the temperature to 450ºF (235ºC), and set the time to 45 minutes. Set a drip tray in the middle of the grill.
4. Put the spit in the grill and make sure the drip tray is centered beneath the sirloin roast. Cook the beef until it reaches 120ºF (49ºC) in its thickest part for medium-rare. (Cook to 115ºF (46ºC) for rare, 130ºF (54ºC) for medium.)
5. Remove the sirloin roast from the rotisserie spit and remove the twine trussing the roast, leaving as much bacon behind as possible. Be careful - the spit and forks are blazing hot. Let the beef rest for 15 minutes, then carve into thin slices and serve.

Pork Loin with Apple Cider Brine

Prep time: 10 minutes | Cook time: 50 minutes | Serves 4

2 (2-pound / 907-g) boneless pork loin	roasts

Apple Cider Brine:

2 quarts apple cider	apricots, cranberries and raisins)
1 quart water	
½ cup table salt	1 teaspoon fresh ground black pepper
Dried Fruit Stuffing:	
2 cups mixed dried fruit, chopped (apples,	½ teaspoon dried ginger

1. Combine the brine ingredients in a large container and stir until the salt and sugar dissolve. Roll cut the pork roasts to open them up like a book. Set a roast with the fat cap facing down. Make a cut the length of the roast, one third of the way from the bottom, which goes almost all the way to the other side of the roast but not through. Open the roast up like a book along that cut, then make another cut halfway up the opened part of the roast, almost all the way to the other side, and open up the roast again. Submerge the pork roasts in the brine. Store in the refrigerator for one to four hours.
2. One hour before cooking, remove the pork from the brine and pat dry with paper towels. Open up the pork with the cut side facing up, and sprinkle evenly with the chopped fruit, ginger, and pepper. Carefully roll the pork back into a cylinder, then truss each roast at the edges to hold the cylinder shape. Truss the roasts together with the fat caps facing out, then skewer on the rotisserie spit, running the spit between the roasts and securing them with the rotisserie forks. Let the pork rest at room temperature.
3. Select Grill, set the temperature to 450ºF (235ºC), and set the time to 50 minutes. Set a drip tray in the middle of the grill.
4. Put the spit in the grill and make sure the drip tray is centered beneath the pork roast. Cook the pork until it reaches 135ºF (57ºC) in its thickest part.
5. Remove the pork from the rotisserie spit and remove the twine trussing the roast. Be careful - the spit and forks are blazing hot. Let the pork rest for 15 minutes, then slice into ½ inch thick rounds and serve.

Lamb Leg with Tapenade Stuffing

Prep time: 10 minutes | Cook time: 45 minutes | Serves 3

1 (2½-pound / 1.1-kg) boneless leg of lamb	1 tablespoon kosher salt

Tapenade:

1 clove garlic, peeled	ground black pepper
2 basil leaves	1 anchovy fillet, rinsed (optional)
1 cup pitted Kalamata olives, rinsed	
1 teaspoon capers	2 tablespoons grapeseed oil or vegetable oil
Juice of ½ lemon	
½ teaspoon fresh	

1. Season the leg of lamb with the salt, then refrigerate for at least two hours, preferably overnight.
2. Drop the garlic clove into a running food processor and process until completely minced. Turn the processor off, add the basil, and process with one second pulses until finely minced. Add the olives, capers, lemon juice, pepper, and anchovy. Process with one second pulses until finely minced, scraping down the sides of the bowl if necessary. Turn the processor on and slowly pour the oil through the feed tube into the running processor. Once all the oil is added the tapenade should be a thick paste. Use immediately, or store in the refrigerator for up to a week.
3. One hour before cooking, remove the lamb from the refrigerator. Right before heating the grill, spread the tapenade over the cut side of the lamb, fold the roast back into its original shape, and truss it. (You're going to lose a little of the tapenade as you truss the roast; that's OK.) Skewer the lamb on the rotisserie spit, securing it with the rotisserie forks. Let the lamb rest at room temperature until the grill is ready.
4. Select Grill, set the temperature to 450ºF (235ºC), and set the time to 45 minutes. Set a drip tray in the middle of the grill.
5. Put the spit in the grill and make sure the drip tray is centered beneath the lamb. Cook the lamb until it reaches 130ºF (54ºC) in its thickest part for medium. (Cook to 115ºF (46ºC) for rare, 120ºF (49ºC) for medium-rare.)
6. Remove the lamb from the rotisserie spit and remove the twine trussing the roast. Be careful - the spit and forks are blazing hot. Let the lamb rest for 15 minutes, then carve and serve.

Prime Rib Roast with Grainy Mustard

Prep time: 10 minutes | Cook time: 2 hours | Serves 8 to 10

1 4-bone prime rib roast (8 to 10 pounds	/ 3.6 to 4.5 kg)

Rub:

½ cup grainy mustard	chopped fresh marjoram
¼ cup olive oil	1 tablespoon chopped fresh thyme
1 large shallot, finely chopped	
3 tablespoons kosher salt	1 tablespoon coarsely ground black pepper
1½ tablespoons	

1. Trim off any straggling pieces of meat or fat from the roast. If the fat cap is too thick, cut it down to between ¼ to ½ inch in thickness depending on how you like your prime rib.
2. To make the rub: Combine the rub ingredients in a small bowl and coat the roast thoroughly with it. Loosely cover with plastic wrap and let the roast sit at room temperature for 30 minutes.
3. Run a long sword skewer through the center of the roast lengthwise to create a pilot hole. Run the rotisserie spit through the hole and secure with the forks. Balance as necessary.
4. Select Grill, set the temperature to 400ºF (205ºC), and set the time to 2 hours.
5. Place the roast in the grill and set a drip tray underneath. Cook until it is near the desired doneness: 125ºF (52ºC) for rare, 135ºF (57ºC) for medium rare, 145ºF (63ºC) for medium, 155ºF (68ºC) for medium well, or 165ºF (74ºC) for well done. The roast will shrink during cooking, so adjust the forks when appropriate. Remove the roast when it is 5ºF to 10ºF below the desired doneness. It will continue to cook during the resting phase.
6. Carefully remove the rotisserie forks and slide the spit out, and then place the roast on a large cutting board. Tent the roast with aluminum foil and a kitchen towel and let the meat rest for 15 to 20 minutes. Cut away the bones first by passing a knife against the bones and cutting through (save the bones for later). Cut the meat into thin slices.

Porchetta with Fennel-Sage Rub

Prep time: 15 minutes | Cook time: 3½ hours | Serves 6

1 slab pork belly, skin on, 5 to 6 pounds (2.3 to 2.7 kg)	1 boneless pork loin roast, about 3 pounds (1.4 kg)

Rub:

2 tablespoons fennel seeds	ground black pepper
1 tablespoon finely chopped fresh sage	1 teaspoon chopped fresh rosemary
Zest of 1 lemon	1 teaspoon red pepper flakes
4 or 5 cloves garlic	1½ teaspoons coarse salt
2 teaspoons coarse salt	1 teaspoon freshly ground black pepper
2 teaspoons freshly	

1. Lay the pork belly, skin-side down, on a large cutting board. Place the pork loin on top and roll the pork belly together so that the ends meet. Trim any excess pork belly and loin so that it is a uniform cylinder. Do not tie yet.
2. To make the rub: Using a mortar and pestle or spice grinder, crush the fennel seeds to a medium grind. Combine with the remaining rub ingredients in a small bowl and apply all over the pork loin.
3. Roll the pork loin inside the pork belly and tie with kitchen twine every inch into a secure, round bundle. Season the outside of the pork belly with the coarse salt and pepper. Set onto a baking sheet and place in the refrigerator, uncovered, for 24 hours.
4. Run a long sword skewer through the center of the roast lengthwise to create a pilot hole. Run the rotisserie spit through the hole and secure with the forks. Balance as necessary.
5. Select Grill, set the temperature to 400ºF (205ºC), and set the time to 3½ hours.
6. Place the porchetta in the grill with a drip tray underneath. Watch for burning or excessive browning and adjust the heat as necessary. Once the porchetta has reached an internal temperature of 145ºF (63ºC), the roast is done. If the skin is not a deep brown and crispy in texture, increase the temperature to 450ºF (235ºC) and roast for an additional 10 minutes.
7. Remove from the heat, carefully remove the rotisserie forks and slide the spit out, and then set the meat on a large cutting board. Tent the roast with aluminum foil and let the meat rest for 15 minutes. Slice the meat ½ inch thick and serve.

Bourbon Ham with Apple Butter

Prep time: 5 minutes | Cook time: 50 minutes | Serves 10 to 12

1 ham, unsliced, 5 to 6 pounds (2.3 to 2.7	kg)

Baste:

⅓ cup apple butter	mustard
¼ cup packed brown sugar	¼ teaspoon ground ginger
2 tablespoons bourbon	¼ teaspoon white pepper
1½ teaspoons Dijon	

1. Run a long sword skewer through the center of the ham lengthwise to create a pilot hole. Run the rotisserie spit through the hole and secure with the forks. Balance as necessary and secure tightly. Place the ham in the grill and cook for 50 to 60 minutes. If there is room, set a drip tray underneath.
2. To make the baste: Combine all the baste ingredients in a small saucepan and simmer over medium heat for 2 minutes, stirring often. Remove from the heat and let sit for 5 to 10 minutes before using.
3. Select Grill, set the temperature to 400ºF (205ºC), and set the time to 45 minutes.
4. Place the ham in the grill and set a drip tray underneath, if there is room. During the last 20 minutes of the cooking time, begin basting the ham with the apple butter-bourbon mixture. Make at least 4 or 5 passes with the baste to coat evenly. Focus the coating on the outside of the ham and not on the cut side. The ham should not take too long to heat up. Look for an internal temperature around 130ºF (54ºC). The surface should be hot.
5. Remove from the heat, carefully remove the rotisserie forks and slide the spit out, and then set the ham on a large cutting board. Tent the ham with aluminum foil and let the meat rest for 10 minutes. Carve and serve immediately.

Mutton Roast with Barbecue Dip

Prep time: 15 minutes | Cook time: 4½ hours | Serves 8 to 10

1 mutton roast (shoulder or leg), 5	pounds (2.3 kg)

Barbecue Dip:

1 cup water	1 tablespoon packed brown sugar
¼ cup Worcestershire sauce	1 tablespoon freshly squeezed lemon juice
¼ cup apple cider vinegar	1 tablespoon salt
1 tablespoon freshly ground black pepper	½ teaspoon ground allspice

Baste:

1 cup apple cider vinegar	squeezed lemon juice
½ cup Worcestershire sauce	2 tablespoons freshly ground black pepper
¼ cup freshly	1 tablespoon salt

1. To make the barbecue dip: Combine the dip ingredients in a jar. Cover with a lid and refrigerate, shaking periodically. Warm the dip in the microwave just before serving.
2. To make the baste: Combine the baste ingredients in a small bowl and set aside.
3. Using kitchen twine, tie the mutton roast into a uniform shape. Run a long sword skewer through the center of the roast lengthwise to create a pilot hole. Run the rotisserie spit through the hole and secure with the forks. Balance as necessary.
4. Select Grill, set the temperature to 375ºF (190ºC), and set the time to 4½ hours.
5. Place the roast in the grill and set a drip tray underneath. Apply the baste mixture every 30 minutes, until the roast reaches an internal temperature of 185ºF (85ºC). The roast will shrink during cooking, so adjust the forks when appropriate.
6. Remove from the heat, carefully remove the rotisserie forks and slide the spit out, and then set the roast on a large cutting board. Tent the roast with aluminum foil and let the meat rest for 20 minutes.
7. Shred or carve the mutton into small pieces. Serve with the warmed barbecue dip on the side.

Dijon Chicken with Herbes De Provence

Prep time: 5 minutes | Cook time: 1 hour | Serves 4

1 (4-pound / 1.8-kg)	chicken

Mustard Paste:

¼ cup Dijon mustard	de Provence
1 tablespoon kosher salt	1 teaspoon freshly ground black pepper
1 tablespoon Herbes	

1. Mix the mustard paste ingredients in a small bowl. Rub the chicken with the mustard paste, inside and out. Gently work your fingers under the skin on the breast, then rub some of the paste directly onto the breast meat. Refrigerate for at least two hours, preferably overnight.
2. One hour before cooking, remove the chicken from the refrigerator. Fold the wingtips under the wings and truss the chicken. Skewer the chicken on the rotisserie spit, securing it with the rotisserie forks. Let the chicken rest at room temperature.
3. Select Grill, set the temperature to 450ºF (235ºC), and set the time to 1 hour. Set a drip tray in the middle of the grill.
4. Put the spit in the grill and make sure the drip tray is centered beneath the chicken. Cook until the chicken reaches 160ºF (70ºC) in the thickest part of the breast.
5. Remove the chicken from the rotisserie spit and remove the twine trussing the chicken. Be careful - the spit and forks are blazing hot. Let the chicken rest for 15 minutes, then carve and serve.

Chicken with Brown Sugar Brine

Prep time: 5 minutes | Cook time: 1 hour | Serves 4

1 (4-pound / 1.8-kg)	chicken

Brine:

2 quarts cold water	crushed
½ cup table salt (or 1 cup kosher salt)	3 bay leaves, crumbled
¼ cup brown sugar	1 tablespoon
½ head of garlic (6 to 8 cloves), skin on,	peppercorns, crushed or coarsely ground

1. Combine the brine ingredients in large container, and stir until the salt and sugar dissolve. Submerge the chicken in the brine. Store in the refrigerator for at least one hour, preferably four hours, no longer than eight hours.

2. Remove the chicken from the brine and pat dry with paper towels, picking off any pieces of bay leaves or garlic that stick to the chicken. Fold the wingtips underneath the wings, then truss the chicken. Skewer the chicken on the rotisserie spit, securing it with the rotisserie forks. Let the chicken rest at room temperature.
3. Select Grill, set the temperature to 450ºF (235ºC), and set the time to 1 hour. Set a drip tray in the middle of the grill.
4. Put the spit in the grill and make sure the drip tray is centered beneath the chicken. Cook until the chicken reaches 160ºF (70ºC) in the thickest part of the breast.
5. Remove the chicken from the rotisserie spit and remove the twine trussing the chicken. Be careful - the spit and forks are blazing hot. Let the chicken rest for 15 minutes, then carve and serve.

Lamb Shoulder with Mustard Herb Paste

Prep time: 5 minutes | Cook time: 2 hours | Serves 4

1 (4-pound / 1.8-kg) boneless lamb	shoulder roast

Mustard Herb Paste:

¼ cup whole grain mustard	1 teaspoon minced fresh oregano
1 tablespoon kosher salt	1 teaspoon minced fresh rosemary
1 tablespoon minced fresh thyme	1 teaspoon fresh ground black pepper

1. Mix the paste ingredients in a small bowl. Open up the lamb like a book, then rub all over with the paste, working it into any natural seams in the meat. Refrigerate for at least two hours, preferably overnight.
2. One hour before cooking, remove the lamb from the refrigerator. Fold the lamb into its original shape, truss the lamb, and skewer it on the rotisserie spit, securing it with the rotisserie forks. Let the lamb rest at room temperature until the grill is ready.
3. Select Grill, set the temperature to 375ºF (190ºC), and set the time to 2 hours. Set a drip tray in the middle of the grill.
4. Put the spit in the grill and make sure the drip tray is centered beneath the lamb shoulder. Cook the lamb until it reaches 190ºF (88ºC) in its thickest part.
5. Remove the lamb shoulder from the rotisserie spit and remove the twine trussing the roast. Be careful - the spit and forks are blazing hot. Let the lamb rest for 15 minutes, then carve and serve.

Lamb Leg with Brown Sugar Rub

Prep time: 10 minutes | Cook time: 1 hour 20 minutes | Serves 6 to 8

1 boneless leg of lamb (partial bone-in is fine), 4 to 5 pounds (1.8 to 2.3 kg)
Rub:
¼ cup packed brown sugar
1 tablespoon coarse salt
2 teaspoons smoked paprika
1½ to 2 teaspoons spicy chili powder or cayenne
2 teaspoons onion powder
1 teaspoon garlic powder
1 teaspoon freshly ground black pepper
½ teaspoon ground cloves
⅛ teaspoon ground cinnamon

1. Trim off the excess fat and any loose hanging pieces from the lamb. With kitchen twine, tie the roast into a uniform and solid roast. It will take four to five ties to hold it together properly. Run a long sword skewer through the center of the roast lengthwise to create a pilot hole. Run the rotisserie spit through the hole and secure with the forks. Balance as necessary.
2. To make the rub: Combine the rub ingredients in a small bowl and apply evenly to the lamb. Make sure you get as much of the rub on the meat as possible.
3. Select Grill, set the temperature to 375ºF (190ºC), and set the time to 80 minutes.
4. Place the lamb in the grill and set a drip tray underneath. Cook until the lamb reaches an internal temperature of 140ºF (60ºC) for medium or 150ºF (66ºC) for medium well. The lamb will shrink during cooking, so adjust the forks when appropriate.
5. Remove from the heat, carefully remove the rotisserie forks and slide the spit out, and then set the lamb on a large cutting board. Tent the roast with aluminum foil and let the meat rest for 10 to 12 minutes. Cut off the twine and carve. Serve.

Lamb Leg with Feta Stuffing

Prep time: 5 minutes | Cook time: 45 minutes | Serves 3

1 (2½-pound / 1.1-kg) boneless leg of lamb roast
Feta Stuffing:
2 ounces crumbled feta cheese
1 teaspoon minced fresh rosemary
2 teaspoons kosher salt
1 teaspoon minced fresh thyme
Zest of ½ lemon

1. Season the leg of lamb with the salt, then refrigerate for at least two hours, preferably overnight.
2. One hour before cooking, remove the lamb from the refrigerator. Just before heating the grill, mix the stuffing ingredients. Open up the lamb like a book, then spread the stuffing over the cut side of the lamb. Fold the roast back into its original shape. Truss the lamb, then skewer it on the rotisserie spit, securing it with the rotisserie forks. (You're going to lose a little of the stuffing when you tie down the trussing twine; that's OK.) Let the lamb rest at room temperature until the grill is ready.
3. Select Grill, set the temperature to 450ºF (235ºC), and set the time to 45 minutes. Set a drip tray in the middle of the grill.
4. Put the spit in the grill and make sure the drip tray is centered beneath the lamb. Cook the lamb until it reaches 130ºF (54ºC) in its thickest part for medium. (Cook to 115ºF (46ºC) for rare, 120ºF (49ºC) for medium-rare.)
5. Remove the lamb from the rotisserie spit and remove the twine trussing the roast. Be careful - the spit and forks are blazing hot. Let the lamb rest for 15 minutes, then carve and serve.

Chapter 15 Staples

Homemade Marinara Sauce

Prep time: 15 minutes | Cook time: 30 minutes | Makes 3 cups

¼ cup extra-virgin olive oil
1 small onion, chopped (about ½ cup)
3 garlic cloves, minced
2 tablespoons minced or puréed sun-dried tomatoes (optional)
1 (28-ounce / 794-g)

can crushed tomatoes
½ teaspoon dried oregano
½ teaspoon dried basil
¼ teaspoon red pepper flakes
1 teaspoon kosher salt or ½ teaspoon fine salt

1. Place the oil into a medium saucepan over medium heat. When the oil shimmers, add the onion and garlic. Cook, stirring frequently, for 2 to 3 minutes, or until the onion has started to soften. Add the sun-dried tomatoes (if using) and cook for 1 minute, or until fragrant. Add the crushed tomatoes and stir to combine, scraping the bottom of the pot if there is anything stuck. Stir in the oregano, basil, red pepper flakes, and salt.
2. Bring to a simmer and cover the saucepan. Cook, stirring occasionally, for about 30 minutes.
3. Turn off the heat and let the sauce cool for about 10 minutes. Taste and adjust the seasoning, adding more salt if necessary. Refrigerate in an airtight container for up to a week or freeze for 4 to 6 weeks if not using right away.

Mixed Berry Vinaigrette

Prep time: 15 minutes | Cook time: 0 minutes | Makes about 1½ cups

1 cup mixed berries, thawed if frozen
½ cup balsamic vinegar
⅓ cup extra-virgin olive oil
2 tablespoons freshly squeezed lemon or lime juice

1 tablespoon lemon or lime zest
1 tablespoon Dijon mustard
1 tablespoon raw honey or maple syrup
1 teaspoon salt
½ teaspoon freshly ground black pepper

1. Place all the ingredients in a blender and purée until thoroughly mixed and smooth.
2. You can serve it over a bed of greens, grilled meat, or fresh fruit salad.

Coconut-Lime Dressing

Prep time: 5 minutes | Cook time: 0 minutes | Makes about 1 cup

8 ounces (227 g) plain coconut yogurt
2 tablespoons chopped fresh parsley
2 tablespoons freshly squeezed lemon juice

1 tablespoon snipped fresh chives
½ teaspoon salt
Pinch freshly ground black pepper

1. Stir together the coconut yogurt, parsley, lemon juice, chives, salt, and pepper in a medium bowl until completely mixed.
2. Transfer to an airtight container and refrigerate until ready to use.
3. This dressing perfectly pairs with spring mix greens, grilled chicken, or even your favorite salad.

Cashew Ranch Dressing

Prep time: 15 minutes | Cook time: 0 minutes | Serves 12

1 cup cashews, soaked in warm water for at least 1 hour
½ cup water
2 tablespoons freshly squeezed lemon juice

1 tablespoon vinegar
1 teaspoon garlic powder
1 teaspoon onion powder
2 teaspoons dried dill

1. In a food processor, combine the cashews, water, lemon juice, vinegar, garlic powder, and onion powder. Blend until creamy and smooth. Add the dill and pulse a few times until combined.

Tahini Lime Dressing

Prep time: 5 minutes | Cook time: 0 minutes | Makes about ¾ cup

⅓ cup tahini
3 tablespoons filtered water
2 tablespoons freshly squeezed lime juice
1 tablespoon apple cider vinegar

1 teaspoon lime zest
1½ teaspoons raw honey
¼ teaspoon garlic powder
¼ teaspoon salt

1. Whisk together the tahini, water, vinegar, lime juice, lime zest, honey, salt, and garlic powder in a small bowl until well emulsified.
2. Serve immediately, or refrigerate in an airtight container for to 1 week.

Sweet Ginger Sauce

Prep time: 5 minutes | Cook time: 5 minutes | Makes ²/₃ cup

3 tablespoons ketchup
2 tablespoons water
2 tablespoons maple syrup
1 tablespoon rice vinegar
2 teaspoons peeled

minced fresh ginger root
2 teaspoons soy sauce (or tamari, which is a gluten-free option)
1 teaspoon cornstarch

1. In a small saucepan over medium heat, combine all the ingredients and stir continuously for 5 minutes, or until slightly thickened. Enjoy warm or cold.

Asian Sauce

Prep time: 15 minutes | Cook time: 0 minutes | Makes 1 cup

¼ cup low-sodium chicken or vegetable stock
¼ cup rice vinegar
¼ cup hoisin sauce
3 tablespoons soy sauce

1 teaspoon chili-garlic sauce or sriracha (or more to taste)
1 tablespoon minced or pressed garlic
1 tablespoon minced or grated ginger

1. In a small bowl, whisk together all the ingredients or place in a jar with a tight-fitting lid and shake to combine.

Kale Almond Pesto

Prep time: 15 minutes | Cook time: 0 minutes | Makes about 1 cup

2 cups chopped kale leaves, rinsed well and stemmed
½ cup toasted almonds
2 garlic cloves
3 tablespoons extra-virgin olive oil
3 tablespoons freshly

squeezed lemon juice
2 teaspoons lemon zest
1 teaspoon salt
½ teaspoon freshly ground black pepper
¼ teaspoon red pepper flakes

1. Place all the ingredients in a food processor and pulse until smoothly puréed.
2. It tastes great with the eggs, salads, soup, pasta, cracker, and sandwiches.

Creamy Ranch Dressing

Prep time: 5 minutes | Cook time: 0 minutes | Serves 8

1 cup plain Greek yogurt
¼ cup chopped fresh dill
2 tablespoons chopped fresh chives

Zest of 1 lemon
1 garlic clove, minced
½ teaspoon sea salt
⅛ teaspoon freshly cracked black pepper

1. Mix together the yogurt, dill, chives, lemon zest, garlic, sea salt, and pepper in a small bowl and whisk to combine.
2. Serve chilled.

Enchilada Sauce

Prep time: 15 minutes | Cook time: 0 minutes | Makes 2 cups

3 large ancho chiles, stems and seeds removed, torn into pieces
1½ cups very hot water
2 garlic cloves, peeled and lightly smashed
2 teaspoons kosher

salt or 1 teaspoon fine salt
½ teaspoon dried oregano
½ teaspoon ground cumin
1½ teaspoons sugar
2 tablespoons wine vinegar

1. Place the chile pieces in the hot water and let sit for 10 to 15 minutes.
2. Pour the chiles and water into a blender jar and add the garlic, salt, oregano, cumin, sugar, and vinegar. Blend until smooth.

Pico de Gallo

Prep time: 5 minutes | Cook time: 0 minutes | Serves 2

3 large tomatoes, chopped
½ small red onion, diced
⅛ cup chopped fresh cilantro
3 garlic cloves, chopped

2 tablespoons chopped pickled jalapeño pepper
1 tablespoon lime juice
¼ teaspoon pink Himalayan salt (optional)

1. In a medium bowl, combine all the ingredients and mix with a wooden spoon.

Lemon Garlic Dijon Vinaigrette

Prep time: 5 minutes | Cook time: 0 minutes | Makes about 6 tablespoons

¼ cup extra-virgin olive oil
1 garlic clove, minced
2 tablespoons freshly squeezed lemon juice

1 teaspoon Dijon mustard
½ teaspoon raw honey
¼ teaspoon salt
¼ teaspoon dried basil

1. Place all the ingredients in a mason jar. Cover and shake vigorously until thoroughly mixed and well emulsified.
2. Serve chilled.

Cashew Pesto with Basil

Prep time: 10 minutes | Cook time: 0 minutes | Makes 1 cup

¼ cup raw cashews
Juice of 1 lemon
2 garlic cloves
1/3 red onion (about 2 ounces / 56 g in total)
1 tablespoon olive oil

4 cups basil leaves, packed
1 cup wheatgrass
¼ cup water
¼ teaspoon salt

1. Put the cashews in a heatproof bowl and add boiling water to cover. Soak for 5 minutes and then drain.
2. Put all ingredients in a blender and blend for 2 to 3 minutes or until fully combined.

Peanut Lime Dressing

Prep time: 5 minutes | Cook time: 0 minutes | Serves 8

1 cup lite coconut milk
¼ cup freshly squeezed lime juice
¼ cup creamy peanut butter
2 tablespoons low-

sodium soy sauce or tamari
3 garlic cloves, minced
1 tablespoon grated fresh ginger

1. Place all the ingredients in a food processor or blender and process until completely mixed and smooth.
2. It's delicious served over grilled chicken or tossed with noodles and green onions.

Easy Hummus

Prep time: 5 minutes | Cook time: 0 minutes | Serves 2

1 (19-ounce / 539-g) can chickpeas, drained and rinsed
¼ cup tahini
3 tablespoons cold water
2 tablespoons freshly squeezed lemon juice

1 garlic clove
½ teaspoon turmeric powder
⅛ teaspoon black pepper
Pinch of pink Himalayan salt

1. Combine all the ingredients in a food processor and blend until smooth.

Polenta (Grits)

Prep time: 3 minutes | Cook time: 65 minutes | Makes 4 cups

1 cup polenta or grits (not instant or quick cook)
2 cups milk
2 cups chicken or vegetable stock

1 teaspoon kosher salt or ½ teaspoon fine salt
2 tablespoons unsalted butter, cut into 4 pieces

1. Place the grits in a baking pan. Add the milk, stock, salt, and butter and stir gently.
2. Place the pan on the bake position. Select Bake, set temperature to 325°F (163°C), and set time to 1 hour, 5 minutes.
3. After 15 minutes, remove the pan from the grill and stir the polenta. Return the pan to the grill and continue cooking.
4. After 30 minutes, remove the pan again and stir the polenta. Return the pan to the grill and continue cooking. After another 15 minutes (1 hour total), remove the pan from the grill. The polenta should be soft and creamy, with all the liquid absorbed. If necessary, continue cooking for 5 to 10 minutes more.
5. When cooking is complete, remove the pan from the grill. Serve, or let cool to room temperature, then cover and refrigerate for up to 3 days.

Caesar Dressing

Prep time: 5 minutes | Cook time: 0 minutes | Serves ⅔ cup

1 teaspoon anchovy paste
¼ teaspoon minced or pressed garlic
¼ teaspoon kosher salt or ⅛ teaspoon

fine salt
1 egg
2 tablespoons freshly squeezed lemon juice
½ cup extra-virgin olive oil

1. Place all the ingredients in the order listed in a tall narrow container. Place the blade of the immersion blender in the bottom of the container. Turn the blender on and slowly bring it up to the top of the ingredients, repeating if necessary to thoroughly emulsify the dressing.

Basic Rice

Prep time: 3 minutes | Cook time: 35 minutes | Makes 4 cups

1 cup long-grain white rice
1 tablespoon unsalted butter, melted, or 1 tablespoon extra-

virgin olive oil
2 cups water
1 teaspoon kosher salt or ½ teaspoon fine salt

1. Rinse the rice well under cold water and let drain.
2. Place the butter in a baking pan and add the rice. Stir it to coat with the fat, then pour in the water and add the salt. Stir to dissolve the salt.
3. Place the pan on the bake position. Select Bake, set temperature to 325ºF (163ºC), and set time to 35 minutes.
4. After 20 minutes, remove the pan from the grill and stir the rice. Return the pan to the grill and continue cooking. After 10 more minutes, check the rice again. It should be mostly cooked through, and the water should be absorbed. If not, continue cooking for a few more minutes.
5. When cooking is complete, remove the pan from the grill and cover with aluminum foil. Let sit for 10 minutes, then gently fluff the rice with a fork. Serve immediately, or let cool for 20 minutes, then refrigerate in an airtight container.

Southwestern Seasoning

Prep time: 5 minutes | Cook time: 0 minutes | Makes ¾ cup

3 tablespoons paprika
3 tablespoons ancho chile powder
2 teaspoons cayenne
2 tablespoons freshly ground black pepper
2 teaspoons cumin

1 tablespoon granulated garlic
1 tablespoon granulated onion
2 tablespoons dried oregano

1. Place all the ingredients in a small bowl and whisk to combine. Store in an airtight container in the pantry.

Roasted Mushrooms

Prep time: 8 minutes | Cook time: 30 minutes | Makes 1½ cups

1 pound (454 g) button or cremini mushrooms, washed, stems trimmed
¼ cup water
1 teaspoon kosher salt

or ½ teaspoon fine salt
3 tablespoons unsalted butter, cut into pieces, or extra-virgin olive oil

1. Place a large piece of aluminum foil in the baking pan. Cut the mushrooms into quarters or thick slices and place them in the middle of the foil. Spread them out into a single layer as much as possible. Pour the water over them, then sprinkle with the salt and add the butter. Seal the foil, fully enclosing the mushrooms.
2. Place the pan on the roast position. Select Roast, set temperature to 325ºF (163ºC), and set time to 15 minutes.
3. After 15 minutes, remove the pan from the grill. Carefully place the foil packet on a cutting board and open it up. Pour the mushrooms and liquid from the foil into the baking pan.
4. Place the pan on the roast position. Select Roast, set temperature to 350ºF (177ºC), and set time to 15 minutes.
5. After about 10 minutes, remove the pan from the grill and stir the mushrooms. The liquid should be evaporating. Return the pan to the grill and continue cooking.
6. When cooking is complete, the liquid will be mostly gone and the mushrooms will have begun to brown, anywhere from 5 to 15 more minutes. Use immediately or refrigerate in an airtight container up to 5 days.

Teriyaki Sauce

Prep time: 5 minutes | Cook time: 0 minutes | Makes ¾ cup

½ cup soy sauce
3 tablespoons honey
1 tablespoon rice vinegar
1 tablespoon rice wine
or dry sherry
2 teaspoons minced fresh ginger
2 garlic cloves, smashed

1. In a small bowl, whisk together all the ingredients.

Chimichurri

Prep time: 15 minutes | Cook time: 0 minutes | Makes 2 cups

1 cup minced fresh parsley
½ cup minced fresh cilantro
¼ cup minced fresh mint leaves
¼ cup minced garlic (about 6 cloves)
2 tablespoons minced
fresh oregano leaves
1 teaspoon fine Himalayan salt
1 cup olive oil or avocado oil
½ cup red wine vinegar
Juice of 1 lemon

1. Thoroughly mix the parsley, cilantro, mint leaves, garlic, oregano leaves, and salt in a medium bowl. Add the olive oil, vinegar, and lemon juice and whisk to combine.
2. Store in an airtight container in the refrigerator and shake before using.
3. You can serve the chimichurri over vegetables, poultry, meats, and fish. It also can be used as a marinade, dipping sauce, or condiment.

Shawarma Seasoning

Prep time: 5 minutes | Cook time: 0 minutes | Makes 1 tablespoon

1 teaspoon cumin
1 teaspoon smoked paprika
¼ teaspoon kosher salt or ⅛ teaspoon fine salt
¼ teaspoon turmeric
¼ teaspoon allspice
¼ teaspoon cinnamon
¼ teaspoon freshly ground black pepper
¼ teaspoon red pepper flakes

1. In a small bowl, combine all the ingredients. Store in an airtight container in the pantry.

Dijon Balsamic Dressing

Prep time: 5 minutes | Cook time: 0 minutes | Makes 1 cup

2 tablespoons Dijon mustard
¼ cup balsamic
vinegar
¾ cup olive oil

1. Put all ingredients in a jar with a tight-fitting lid. Put on the lid and shake vigorously until thoroughly combined. Refrigerate until ready to use and shake well before serving.

Appendix 1 Measurement Conversion Chart

VOLUME EQUIVALENTS(DRY)

US STANDARD	METRIC (APPROXIMATE)
1/8 teaspoon	0.5 mL
1/4 teaspoon	1 mL
1/2 teaspoon	2 mL
3/4 teaspoon	4 mL
1 teaspoon	5 mL
1 tablespoon	15 mL
1/4 cup	59 mL
1/2 cup	118 mL
3/4 cup	177 mL
1 cup	235 mL
2 cups	475 mL
3 cups	700 mL
4 cups	1 L

VOLUME EQUIVALENTS(LIQUID)

US STANDARD	US STANDARD (OUNCES)	METRIC (APPROXIMATE)
2 tablespoons	1 fl.oz.	30 mL
1/4 cup	2 fl.oz.	60 mL
1/2 cup	4 fl.oz.	120 mL
1 cup	8 fl.oz.	240 mL
1 1/2 cup	12 fl.oz.	355 mL
2 cups or 1 pint	16 fl.oz.	475 mL
4 cups or 1 quart	32 fl.oz.	1 L
1 gallon	128 fl.oz.	4 L

TEMPERATURES EQUIVALENTS

FAHRENHEIT(F)	CELSIUS(C) (APPROXIMATE)
225 °F	107 °C
250 °F	120 °C
275 °F	135 °C
300 °F	150 °C
325 °F	160 °C
350 °F	180 °C
375 °F	190 °C
400 °F	205 °C
425 °F	220 °C
450 °F	235 °C
475 °F	245 °C
500 °F	260 °C

WEIGHT EQUIVALENTS

US STANDARD	METRIC (APPROXIMATE)
1 ounce	28 g
2 ounces	57 g
5 ounces	142 g
10 ounces	284 g
15 ounces	425 g
16 ounces (1 pound)	455 g
1.5 pounds	680 g
2 pounds	907 g

Appendix 2 Air Fryer Cooking Chart

Beef					
Item	Temp (°F)	Time (mins)	**Item**	Temp (°F)	Time (mins)
Beef Eye Round Roast (4 lbs.)	400 °F	45 to 55	Meatballs (1-inch)	370 °F	7
Burger Patty (4 oz.)	370 °F	16 to 20	Meatballs (3-inch)	380 °F	10
Filet Mignon (8 oz.)	400 °F	18	Ribeye, bone-in (1-inch, 8 oz)	400 °F	10 to 15
Flank Steak (1.5 lbs.)	400 °F	12	Sirloin steaks (1-inch, 12 oz)	400 °F	9 to 14
Flank Steak (2 lbs.)	400 °F	20 to 28			

Chicken					
Item	Temp (°F)	Time (mins)	**Item**	Temp (°F)	Time (mins)
Breasts, bone in (1 ¼ lb.)	370 °F	25	Legs, bone-in (1 ¾ lb.)	380 °F	30
Breasts, boneless (4 oz)	380 °F	12	Thighs, boneless (1 ½ lb.)	380 °F	18 to 20
Drumsticks (2 ½ lb.)	370 °F	20	Wings (2 lb.)	400 °F	12
Game Hen (halved 2 lb.)	390 °F	20	Whole Chicken	360 °F	75
Thighs, bone-in (2 lb.)	380 °F	22	Tenders	360 °F	8 to 10

Pork & Lamb					
Item	Temp (°F)	Time (mins)	**Item**	Temp (°F)	Time (mins)
Bacon (regular)	400 °F	5 to 7	Pork Tenderloin	370 °F	15
Bacon (thick cut)	400 °F	6 to 10	Sausages	380 °F	15
Pork Loin (2 lb.)	360 °F	55	Lamb Loin Chops (1-inch thick)	400 °F	8 to 12
Pork Chops, bone in (1-inch, 6.5 oz)	400 °F	12	Rack of Lamb (1.5 – 2 lb.)	380 °F	22

Fish & Seafood					
Item	Temp (°F)	Time (mins)	**Item**	Temp (°F)	Time (mins)
Calamari (8 oz)	400 °F	4	Tuna Steak	400 °F	7 to 10
Fish Fillet (1-inch, 8 oz)	400 °F	10	Scallops	400 °F	5 to 7
Salmon, fillet (6 oz)	380 °F	12	Shrimp	400 °F	5
Swordfish steak	400 °F	10			

Vegetables

INGREDIENT	AMOUNT	PREPARATION	OIL	TEMP	COOK TIME
Asparagus	2 bunches	Cut in half, trim stems	2 Tbsp	420°F	12-15 mins
Beets	1½ lbs	Peel, cut in ½-inch cubes	1Tbsp	390°F	28-30 mins
Bell peppers (for roasting)	4 peppers	Cut in quarters, remove seeds	1Tbsp	400°F	15-20 mins
Broccoli	1 large head	Cut in 1-2-inch florets	1Tbsp	400°F	15-20 mins
Brussels sprouts	1lb	Cut in half, remove stems	1Tbsp	425°F	15-20 mins
Carrots	1lb	Peel, cut in ¼-inch rounds	1 Tbsp	425°F	10-15 mins
Cauliflower	1 head	Cut in 1-2-inch florets	2 Tbsp	400°F	20-22 mins
Corn on the cob	7 ears	Whole ears, remove husks	1 Tbps	400°F	14-17 mins
Green beans	1 bag (12 oz)	Trim	1 Tbps	420°F	18-20 mins
Kale (for chips)	4 oz	Tear into pieces,remove stems	None	325°F	5-8 mins
Mushrooms	16 oz	Rinse, slice thinly	1 Tbps	390°F	25-30 mins
Potatoes, russet	1½ lbs	Cut in 1-inch wedges	1 Tbps	390°F	25-30 mins
Potatoes, russet	1lb	Hand-cut fries, soak 30 mins in cold water, then pat dry	½ -3 Tbps	400°F	25-28 mins
Potatoes, sweet	1lb	Hand-cut fries, soak 30 mins in cold water, then pat dry	1 Tbps	400°F	25-28 mins
Zucchini	1lb	Cut in eighths lengthwise, then cut in half	1 Tbps	400°F	15-20 mins

Appendix 3 Recipe Index